John H.A. Bomberger

Reformed, Not Ritualistic

Apostolic, not patristic. A reply to Dr. Nevin's Vindication.

John H.A. Bomberger

Reformed, Not Ritualistic
Apostolic, not patristic. A reply to Dr. Nevin's Vindication.

ISBN/EAN: 9783337295837

Printed in Europe, USA, Canada, Australia, Japan

Cover: Foto ©Lupo / pixelio.de

More available books at **www.hansebooks.com**

REFORMED,

NOT RITUALISTIC.

APOSTOLIC, NOT PATRISTIC.

A REPLY

TO

Dr. NEVIN'S "VINDICATION," &c.

BY

J. H. A. BOMBERGER, D.D.

PHILADELPHIA:
JAS. B. RODGERS, PRINTER, 52 & 54 NORTH SIXTH STREET.
1867.

CORRESPONDENCE.

Rev. J. H. A. Bomberger, D.D.

Dear Brother:—As your tract, entitled "The Revised Liturgy: A History and Criticism of the Ritualistic movement in the Reformed Church," has been violently assailed in a reply by the Rev. J. W. Nevin, D.D., entitled "Vindication of the Revised Liturgy," in which the author not only indulges in gross personal abuse of yourself and many of your brethren, but makes statements which we believe to be utterly groundless; advocates views which are believed to be at variance with historical facts, the doctrinal standard of the German Reformed Church and the Holy Scriptures, most earnestly labors to introduce a Liturgy which is not German Reformed; and to the introduction of which into our Church we most decidedly object: the undersigned Elders of said Church would respectfully request you to furnish for publication such a defence of your former tract as you may deem proper to write, and especially such an exhibition of the Liturgical principles and of the doctrines of our Church upon the points involved, as may serve to fortify us and the members of the Church generally, against what are regarded as dangerous errors.

Permit us to request, however, that whatever plainness of speech and pointedness of proof you may think proper to employ, you will not allow yourself to be tempted by the unfortunate style used by the author of the "Vindication" to imitate his example in this respect. It is with pain and sorrow that we refer to the uncalled for unkindness and bitterness manifested by Rev. Dr. Nevin.

We trust, therefore, that you will not write one word in your defence, that you would wish had been omitted when you close your career here below, and that will not aid in maintaining the truth as taught by the fathers of our Church, and advance the cause of our Redeemer's kingdom. With kind regards,

Very truly yours,

John Wiest,	Abraham Kline,
W. E. Schmertz,	Dr. Thos. Ingram,
Geo. Besore,	C. C. Reepheim,
R. F. Kelker,	W. H. Schall,
Col. Daniel Follmer,	Chas. Wannemacher,
Charles Newhard,	Abraham Bausmann,
W. H. Frymire,	Abraham Peters,
Levi Balliet,	J. L. Hoffmeier,
Peter Sheffer,	Sam'l Yost,
Jacob M. Follmer,	Christian Gast,
Jacob Yeisly,	Jos. K. Milnor,

David M'Williams.

Philadelphia, May 9, 1867.

To the Elders George Besore, Wm. E. Schmertz, John Wiest and others:

My Dear Brethren:—In the following pages you will find, it is hoped, a satisfactory answer to your request:

But why have you asked for a continuance of this controversy? And why should I comply with your request? A tract abounding in such bitter personal abuse, indulging in a tone so insultingly imperious, assuming airs so lofty and dictatorial, and yet relying, in its sense of real weakness, upon fierce denials for rebutting proofs, and upon bold dogmatic assertions and evasive sophistries for facts and honest arguments, might seem beneath criticism and wholly unworthy of notice. No mere personal consideration, certainly, could have induced me to give it any attention. And you are perfectly right, brethren, in deprecating the thought that the style and logic of Dr. Nevin's "last words," should be retaliated either in manner or in kind. At the same time I accede to your opinion, that the unhappy tract referred to demands some reply. Dr. Nevin has been long regarded as an almost unerring oracle in our Church. We have been accustomed to pay well-nigh unquestioning deference to his opinions. It is one of our ecclesiastical virtues to cherish and manifest sentiments of profound respect for those who occupy posts of responsibility, or who may seem to be endowed with superior gifts. But it is easy to see how all this may be perverted and abused. The oracle may err. Opinions once received as the synonyms of truth, may involve the very quintessence of false doctrine. Reverence for dignitaries may degenerate into blind servility, and become a snare. More than one illustration in point is furnished by ecclesiastical history.

And yet a generous and confiding people will commonly be slow to believe that their very confidence is placing in jeopardy their dearest and holiest interests. This is especially apt to be the case when those by whose influence and measures the peril is occasioned, seem to be sincere, when, indeed, no one may dispute that they are acting in full accordance with deep convictions. The teachers whose lessons we have been long accustomed to receive with meek docility, must go very far and openly astray, before we can consent to doubt their doctrines, or even to scrutinize their theories and schemes. To abandon or condemn those who have for many years been trustingly followed as safe and certain guides, involves humiliation and exposes to reproach. We naturally shrink not only from such humiliation, but from a course which impliedly condemns those guides.

All this gives to errors and subversive measures a dangerous power. While hesitating to believe them such, they secure overwhelming ascendancy, accomplish their schemes, and involve the Church in ruin. Hence the necessity for a prompt and decided exposure of what are believed to be pernicious errors and menacing evils. Hence also the full justification of such exposures. That this does not imply what Dr. Nevin has labored so unjustly to make out, an accusation of conspiracy, has, I think, been fully shown on pp. 16–24 of the present tract. But Dr. Nevin's attempt to distort this point, must not be allowed to conceal what it does involve. And when we are plainly told that the purpose of the ritualistic movement is to revolutionize our Church, it is time to be aroused to a sense of the great peril which threatens us. To sound the alarm in such an emergency is not to be troublers in Israel. They are the troublers who seek to subvert Israel's faith and worship, and to lead both into bondage. To point out the evils of such a scheme may provoke angry maledictions. But what is there in the malediction thundered from a source like this to frighten loyal hearts from the discharge of a solemn duty.

None could find less pleasure in controversy, than those who have felt constrained to oppose the extreme turn taken by the present ritualistic movement. None could more earnestly desire than they, that there had been no occasion for such opposition. But their Church, in her true historical character, is more to them than the peculiar theology or ritualistic scheme of Dr. Nevin and those who embrace and advocate his views. And the movement has been forced to a point at which the choice lay between firm opposition to its further progress, or the abandonment of the Church to the subversive tendency of the ritualistic "new measures."

If any ask why this resistance was not made long ago, I reply: 1. That it is not long since the Liturgical movement has assumed openly the extreme ritualistic character which it now avows. 2. That we were too slow to believe that so radical a revolution in our cultus would ever be seriously attempted or pressed; and 3. That it seemed proper to wait for the full development of the scheme, as now made in the Revised Liturgy. But although for these reasons, the force of which all generous minds will appreciate, the opposition has been delayed so long, why should it be too late to arrest the further progress, or defeat the purposes of this extreme ritualistic movement? Only let the Church realize what the points at issue are, and duly consider them. Our greatest danger lies in a prevailing reluctance to believe that Dr. Nevin and those who favor his scheme, really mean what they avow. If the Church can once be persuaded that the new "Order of Worship" means a fundamental and radical revolution mainly of our Church practice, and incidentally of some essential articles of our faith, her decision will not be doubtful. I do not believe, notwithstanding all the influence with which this movement is pressed, that one member in twenty of our Church, would vote for the adoption of this new system of worship, knowing what such adoption would involve.

In the following reply to Dr. Nevin's "Vindication," it has been my desire and endeavor to shun the bad example of his tract, in regard to spirit and style. And yet as I was brought so closely in contact with it, my pen may occasionally have caught the contagion.

Of course I did not limit myself for proofs to the "Vindication." The discussion fair involves all that has been written or said on that side, by responsible parties. Especially does the tract of 1862, "The Liturgical Question," belong here. Indeed it is the proper key to the true design of the ritualistic scheme; and no one can rightly estimate the present posture of the case, without studying that memorable tract.

Committing the whole matter to Him who is the Head of the Church Militant as well as the Church Triumphant, in the full confidence that He will deliver our Zion from its present dangers, I remain sincerely
Your Brother,
J. H. A. BOMBERGER

PRELIMINARIES.

One of the most painful positions in which it is possible for a man to be placed, is to find himself arrayed in open and decided antagonism against those in whose fellowship he once found sincere pleasure, and with whose real or supposed views he once thought himself in happy agreement. To differ positively from intimate friends, or from those for whom sentiments of fraternal regard may be cherished, even on matters of lesser importance, is undesirable. But when the points of diversity affect, or are honestly believed to affect, the substance and the form of evangelical faith and practice, as avowed and maintained by the Church to which the parties owe spiritual fealty, the duties imposed by such antagonism become, most literally, a cross. It must be a cold heart which can bend to that cross, without reluctance. It must be an easy, indifferent friendship, which can render unhesitating, eager compliance with the demands of those duties.

And yet, in such exigencies, the clear dictates of duty must prevail over all mere personal considerations. If professed reverence and regard for long established Church doctrines and customs, founded upon Apostolic authority and primitive practice, have not prevented an attempt, "materially and essentially," to change those customs and doctrines, why should sentiments of inferior value deter us from earnestly resisting such an attempt? Opposition to innovating schemes, subversive of the historical life and traditional character of the Church, may indeed, expose those who make it, to bitter denunciation. By impugning their motives, by vituperative misrepresentations of their views and aims, the entire enginery of party power and partizan animosity may be turned upon them, if possible to crush them, and with them the opposition made to the bold new measures. The very influence with which they have helped to invest some of the advocates of those measures, may be used to injure them. Nevertheless, the established faith and practice of the Church should be defended, no matter by whom assailed, or to what denunciations those who engage in the defence may be exposed. And this defence, whilst it should be made in a manner consistent with the requirements of decency and of charity, should be also unequivocal and decided. Error is naturally artful and insidious. In its first approaches, it may wear a harmless aspect, and seem wholly inoffensive. Its advocates may not be arrogant, presumptuous, or dictatorial. Gentle of speech, unassuming, meek, they may timidly ask only for a hearing, for toleration, for the opportunity of a harmless experiment, under a pledge or promise at once to desist, if objection should be made to their further advancement. But no sooner have they thus gained a foothold, and acquired some strength under the fostering influence of such unsuspicious toleration, than they make bold to speak in quite a different tone, confidently assume a more commanding posture, and, instead of asking for favors, dictate their dogmas and measures in terms of lordly authority. Now, they defiantly challenge contradiction; and if any attempt is made, in the interest of the old faith, or through honest zeal for the maintenance of ecclesiastical integrity, to resist and arrest their progress, they strive not only to defeat the attempt, but to overwhelm all who make it with a torrent of ridicule and defamation. No scene exactly like that at Ephesus, in St. Paul's day, or at the same Ephesus, in A. D. 449, may be re-enacted in form. But the same furious and bitter spirit betrays itself; a spirit of angry determination to carry by violence, what might not be won by more decorous means.

Shall error and revolutionary innovations, grown into such magnitude, and arrogating such defiant manners, be therefore allowed to have their way? Shall the hallowed heritage of centuries be timidly abandoned to the inroads of bold adventurousness and wild presumptuous speculations, because they may carry the Creed as their standard, and shout, as their battle-cry: The Church, the Church! By no means. Come what may, they must be opposed and withstood, if the hallowed faith and traditions of our fathers shall not be forfeited and lost. Those fathers were the honored instruments in the hands of God, in producing or perfecting that "Reformation which was *the resurrection of the Truth*, once more, in its genuine, original life." (See Dr. Nevin's "Anxious Bench," 2d ed., p. 51.) Their Creed, their Cultus, founded upon that revived Truth, and framed in accordance with the simplicity of Apostolic and Primitive usage, are the most precious legacies bequeathed to us by the consecrated past. The Church of the present holds them as a solemn trust. They are talents which are not, indeed, to be buried in the ground, and left unimproved, but talents which are to be improved according to their kind, and not to be tampered with as a medium of mercenary traffic in all sorts of theological and ecclesiastical commodities, and to be bartered back again for the conceits and measures of that false "philosophy by which the Church of Rome, *from the fourth century downward*, was actuated in all her innovations." (See "Anxious Bench," 2d ed., p. 53.)

To the past, as well as to the future, therefore, the Church of the present is under solemn obligations to preserve her inherited faith and practice inviolate, and to defend it, with firm, undaunted courage against all "material improvements," however plausible, and against all "innovation upon her old system," however specious. Indeed, this obligation is formally confessed in the Constitution of our Church. Her Professors of theology are not left at liberty to invent doctrinal and liturgical systems of their own, and then to use the influence of their position in endeavoring to secure the adoption those systems. They are required to affirm as by an oath, and in the presence of God, that they believe "the doctrine contained in the Heidelberg Catechism is the doctrine of the Holy Scriptures" (even including the 44th, 47th, 48th, 49th, 54th, 56th and 80th questions), that they will make it "the basis of all their instructions, and *faithfully maintain and defend* the same, in their preaching and writing, as well as in their instructions." (See Constit., Art. 19.) All her ministers are bound by a similar pledge (Art. 4.) This, then, is a statute imposed alike upon all. There is no exemption. The Church avows her debt of fealty to the past, by laying those entrusted with the official custody of her spiritual treasures, under the most solemn oath of fidelity to the trust. They must swear, not merely that they will not themselves exchange these treasures for any which may seem more valuable, but that they will, zealously defend them against every attempt which others may make to purloin them. Though they may sometimes deceive themselves, or be deceived, by the specious pleas and forms under which such attempts may be commenced, and let themselves be deluded into the belief that they contemplate nothing more than the burnishing of what, in time, had become dim, or repairing what may have been marred or broken; yet, when they find reason to believe that the effort involves "materially" more than such mere renovation, and contemplates essential substitutions, they cannot regard the process with indifference, without violating their sacred obligations.

And in such emergencies, they have not only a right, but it is their solemn duty, to speak and to claim a calm, dispassionate hearing. Those who may seem to be implicated in attempts to effect such "material changes" in the established faith and practice of the Church, or who may openly advocate views which involve "a scheme of religious belief materially at variance with preconceived opinions," may take offence at being even impliedly blamed with such attempts. They may raise a clamorous outcry against all who utter a word of warning, or charge their theory and measures with tendencies of a subversive and revolutionary character. By violent vituperations, by representing themselves as vilified and slandered, by appealing to prejudices and inflaming bitter partizan passions, they may endeavor to excite a very hurricane of indignation against those whom they decry as false accusers, and so try to pervert their testimony and to drown their voice. All this has often been done in like cases, and may be constantly repeated. There is no doubt, also, that the apprehension of such a storm being raised, combines frequently with considerations of personal regard, in long deterring many who may see reason for alarm, from uttering their fears, and publicly directing attention to the threatening peril. But when, at length, they feel constrained to speak, and do so in plain and earnest, but decorous and moderate terms, should they be smitten on the cheek, or rudely cast down and trampled under foot? May it not rather be expected, that as they would most certainly not have spoken at all, but from a firm persuasion of danger, and a strong conviction of duty, so now, that they have, perhaps after too long delay, made bold to express their anxieties and give their reasons for those anxieties, they will at least be calmly and fairly heard?

But whether heard, or discarded, they must be true to their solemn oath. The dictates of duty must be obeyed, and consequences be left with Him who is able to control them. Even though denounced as false witnesses, if their testimony of warning is true, time will vindicate it. Conscious of integrity of purpose, and convinced of the reality of the evils they expose, they can afford patiently to bide their time.

It was with such sentiments, and after a struggle which continued through the several months immediately preceding the Synod of York, in October last, that I felt myself compelled at length to make the written statement submitted to that Synod, adverse to the results reached by the other members of the Liturgical Committee. And it was with such convictions, that I subsequently acceded to the request of a number of Brethren, to prepare and publish a History and brief Criticism of the Revised Liturgy. The facts of the history were gathered fairly and faithfully from official documentary sources. Its purpose was to show by official evidence, that if the Provisional Liturgy was, what some members of the Committee declared it to be, a unit, and as such a true Liturgy in their sense of the term; and that if the Revised Liturgy, or "Order of Worship" reported to the Synod, was in true essential harmony with the Provisional Liturgy, that then both were not in accordance with instructions given from time to time, by successive Synods, to the Committee, for their government in the preparation of the work. This point will be more fully examined in a subsequent section of the present tract. For my purpose now, it is sufficient to state it. After giving, in my former tract, the historical proofs of this position, I showed, in a necessarily brief criticism, in what respects the Revised Liturgy, both as to its ritualistic and doctrinal peculiarities, differed "materially" from the established worship and standard doctrines of the German Reformed Church, and, indeed, was "essentially" contrary to them. "Essential" diversities in regard to the mode of worship, were admitted to be proposed by the Committee; even important diversity at least in the manner of presenting some doctrines, was not denied.

It was delicate ground to go over. There were items in the history of the movement, which could not be otherwise than most offensive to any one cherishing, not bigoted and prejudiced, but only proper and natural affection, for our ecclesiastical traditions. More than once had the Committee treated with disdain the cultus handed down to us by our fathers. Not merely were certain extravagances of extemporaneous prayer ridiculed, but the whole system was stigmatized. Without reserve, it was affirmed that its "natural character was to be jejune, confused, prosy, not sapid, not satisfying nor nourishing for the soul. * * * The misery of the extemporaneous system is * * that it proves the liberty of being weak, and of doing in a weak way, what there is no power of doing in a way that is strong." (Liturgy, Question, p. 21.) This wholesale condemnation, let it be remembered, was passed upon the mode of worship prevailingly practiced by our Church for at least two centuries, and authorized even from the first. This, moreover, was not condemning and stigmatizing *the system* only, but all who, during those centuries, had practiced it. To Dr. Nevin, and those who joined him in endorsing his sentiments on this point, it may seem pleasant pastime to indulge in such sarcastic criticisms upon the customs of those who cannot answer them from the silence of the grave. There are others, however, to whom such sarcastic reproaches are insufferable. This is not all. Such "pulpit handbooks" as the Old Palatinate Liturgy, met with no better treatment at the hands of this ritualistic surgery. They are set down as "no true liturgies;" as "a sort of unbound-book service;" as a "mummery of ritualistic forms;" as a kind of worship which "*ceases to be distinctively Christian, and becomes necessarily more or less Gnostically spiritualistic only, ending at last, indeed, in mere humanitarian deism.*" (Liturgy. Q. pp. 18—27, 28.)

Let the above quotations suffice as a few specimens of the indignity put upon the labors and legacies of our Church when this "new flood" broke in upon her. Let them suffice, also, to show how much occasion was thus given for severe animadversion upon the temper evinced, and the language employed by the advocates of the innovations (the difference between which and the Old Palatinate order of worship, is affirmed "*to be wider altogether than their common difference from worship in the free form.*" Liturgy. Q. p. 5.)

But with all the provocation thus given, it was my steady aim and effort, in preparing the tract published last November, to avoid all harshness of style, all ribald epithets, all obnoxious personalities. As a history, facts had to be taken and given, as they were furnished by the record; they could not be altered or modified, for they were a part of the unchangeable past. They had to be given, also, in their true connection and their historical import. But though the recital of them, as any reflecting mind can see, furnished frequent and tempting occasion for the sharpest criticisms (Sartor resartus), scarcely any such were indulged in, beyond what may be involved in obvious and necessary inferences. This characteristic of the tract has been appreciated, also, by others. And when Dr. Nevin affirms (p. 5), that its criticisms "*turn for the most part on the use of invidious terms of reproach*, and appeals to popular prejudice," he says what he does not attempt to prove, what he cannot prove, and what every reader of that tract knows to be untrue.

And yet that tract, in gross violation of parliamentary order, was dragged into the public debate, and seized upon by the Rev. Dr. Nevin (as the leader of the ultra ritualistic party in the German Reformed Church, at the General Synod in Dayton, and made the occasion of a personal attack upon me, which may be mildly characterized as vulgar and vituperative to an extreme degree. And to prove the strength and depth of the malevolent purpose which inspired that assault, it is now repeated, with a large addition and intensification of virulence, in his recent pamphlet, entitled "Vindication, &c."

If this published assault, and the pretended exhibition and defence of the peculiarities of the Revised Liturgy, were issued upon the responsibility of the author alone, and depended for their influence and effects upon their own merits, nothing, assuredly, would be hazarded by me personally, or for the interest of the true faith and practice of the Church, in letting it drop, unnoticed, into its own natural element. It appears, however, in a form which *seems* to make lay Brethren for whom I cherish sincere private regard, and whom I hold no way answerable for Dr. Nevin's language and sentiments, endorse the bitter denunciations of his pamphlet, and so, possibly, secure for them a consideration which they could not otherwise command. Ardent zeal, also, for the cause so unworthily defended, may gather warmly around this "Vindication," and labor to secure currency for it by concealing or extenuating its faults, and by lauding its sophistries and assumptions, meant for arguments.

It is thought proper, therefore, that the "Vindication" should be answered; that its true character should be exposed; that its misrepresentations of facts should be corrected; and that the superior excellence of the liturgical and doctrinal inheritance of the Reformed Church should be exhibited in contrast with the ritualistic "new measures" and Christo-centric conceits, which are now striving to usurp the claims and place of that inheritance.

With these preliminary explanations, therefore, I proceed to the task of replying, so far as it may deserve an answer, to Dr. Nevin's so-called "Vindication of the Revised Liturgy," and of considering the important questions involved in this controversy, *Historical, Ritualistic,* and *Theological:*

The "Vindication" calls, *first of all*, for some

GENERAL CRITICISM.

Wholly apart from any arguments, or assertions meant for arguments, which Dr. Nevin's tract contains, it is pervaded by a spirit, and characterized by a style of rhetoric, which must have excited feelings of profound regret in the heart of every impartial reader. On every page of the historical section, including the introduction, the writer betrays a passionate determination to give the fullest license to the promptings of ridicule, sarcasm and invective. And to show the depth and strength of that determination, and the inexhaustible violence of those promptings of embittered passion, the fifty pages devoted to what is miscalled "The Historical Vindication," are found insufficient to contain the overflowing of the turbid torrent. They mar large portions even of that "Theological" *Christo-centric* section, which, by the very sacredness and solemnity of the subjects treated, should have forewarned the champion to leave at its threshhold the sandals soiled with the grime and gore of the field he had just so furiously traversed. Language is employed which should have no currency among Christians. Epithets are heaped upon the objects of his anger, which should find no place in a noble-minded theologian's vocabulary. Contempt, disdain, ribald contumely, fierce vituperation, constitute the staple of a large part of the tract. The unhappy author appears to have set out with the fell purpose of trying to do his worst; and surely his success is not more manifest than, for his own sake, it is deplorable.

All this, too, without any real, justifying occasion. Nothing had been said or done by those who so materially differ in their views from Dr. Nevin and his more zealous disciples to merit or to provoke such treatment at his hands. That my former tract did not, has been admitted by more than one unbiassed reader. And how little occasion for any thing of the sort was given by what was said in opposition to the Revised Liturgy innovations, at Dayton, must be evident even from the imperfect sketches published in our Church papers. No one denies, of course, that some things, both in my tract and in the speeches at Synod, might be distorted and exaggerated into shapes and proportions which would make them hideous and abominable. Nor will any one familiar with some of the phases of the movement now agitating our Church, question the facility with which such distortions can be practiced, whether in the way of ridicule or misrepresentation, by some advocates of ultra ritualism. But those to whose possible disadvantage, for the time, this may be done, are not responsible for perversions of their words or acts. And candid, intelligent observers of what is said and done on both sides, will not be easily deluded or misled by any malpractice of this kind. The world is too old, and the discernment of good common sense is too penetrating, to allow the use of such devices to escape detection. As far back as the days of Ahab, the artifice of putting an odious construction upon the words of one whom it was designed to brand with infamy and blast in reputation, and of attributing to him sentiments never uttered, was familiar. Occasionally it has been successful for a season. Ultimately, however, it falls headlong into its own pit.

A writer of Dr. Nevin's experience, would of course not use this method of controversy without design. The vindictive ebullitions which so overrun the pages of his tract, are not the involuntary outbursts of a holy indignation, at a real or imaginary wrong done him or the party he represents. They indeed reveal intense excitement, often even furious animosity. But amidst all the violence of the storm, the rocking, creaking vessel of his anger is, as by a strong, unbending will, kept steadily on one course. Whither? Towards a desired port or haven, where it may be safely anchored, and find rest? By no means. It is guided by quite a different purpose. In the same waters in which it is tossed, there are other vessels, "*small, contemptible craft,*" which dare to cross the track of the leviathan, nay, which even have the audacity to dispute its progress. And now, like another Atlanta, he turns his prow upon them, as if determined to run them down, and sink them to the bottom of the sea. That he missed his aim, or failed in the execution of his strategy, proves, not the absence of the purpose, but only its fury and its folly.

It must be a cause of deep regret to many of Dr. Nevin's more considerate admirers, even, that he has so often displayed this spirit of bitter, overbearing intolerance towards those who may differ from him, or become obnoxious to his displeasure; and that he is so ready to indulge in low ridicule and disparaging sarcasm, even when dealing with things in themselves sacred, and therefore entitled to serious consideration and at least decorous treatment, though they may not be quite according to his mind. This spirit and manner are unworthy of a Christian, and must always damage the cause they profess to serve. Without convicting those against whom they are directed of error or wrong (for ridicule is no test of truth, and although sarcasm may wound, it can never heal), they offend and pain others by a superfluity of irony which can never compensate for a lack of logic. Who does not know that madly to tear in pieces a lawyer's brief, does not destroy his argument? And yet, both at Dayton and in this "Vindication," Dr. Nevin has acted recklessly upon the contrary hypothesis. Under whatever spell, he has assumed that nothing is necessary in dealing with those who differ from him, and oppose his "new measures," than to hold them up to be laughed or hissed at by those who may be ready to respond to his appeal. Poor Burns' address to his "Young Friend" contains a stanza which might have taught a better lesson. All this is done, moreover, without any excuse. Those whom he allows himself so unrestrainedly to asperse, and to treat with such supercilious disdain, are in every sense his peers. He possesses no qualities, natural or acquired, which entitle him to the imperious manner he arrogates; or give him a right to speak to his equals as though they were his serfs. And notwithstanding all the flattery bestowed, the Church has never conferred upon him prerogatives beyond those enjoyed by all her ministers. From the prevailing tone and style, however, of his speech at Dayton, and still more of this latest effusion of his pen, it is painfully evident that he holds very different views.

For myself, I may be allowed to say, that whilst amazed and indignant at the perverse exaggeration and misrepresentation of some portions of my former tract, (of which more anon) Dr. Nevin's violent and abusive personal assault upon me has filled me with far more sorrow and shame for the assailant than with concern for myself. It is most sad and humiliating to see a man of his years, position, and opportunities, stoop to means so unworthy, and to words so low. And yet what else might have been expected from the author of the "Liturgical Question," of 1862, not to name other effusions which betray, to a mournful degree, the same infirmity? That tract is history, though not "a God-send." It should never have been written. Nay more; the thoughts and feelings to which it gives the most unrestrained utterance, should never have been conceived or cherished in a Christian mind or heart. But they were cherished. It was written. And until the author recants, it bears its painful testimony against him. Part of that testimony declares, that personal vituperation from one who could cast such indecorous ridicule upon *free prayer*, though such prayer was sanctioned by the Church for centuries, rests upon Apostolic precedent and Primitive usage, and was uniformly practiced by our fathers, is of small account; that to be derided and denounced, however unsparingly, by one whose professed veneration for the past, did not deter him from pouring contempt and reproach upon pulpit hand-books like the old Palatinate Liturgy, should not be taken much to heart. The hand that had no compassion on the tree, could not be expected to deal tenderly with one of its branches. Let me not be censured, therefore, for regarding with profound indifference, so far as I am personally concerned, the persistent attempts of Dr. Nevin, to cover me with reproach. His calumnies, however, badly meant, tell a far worse tale for the fountain whence they issue, than for the objects they seek to asperse. Partizan zealotry may, of course, refuse to admit this. Its interests require both that I and my former tract, should be exhibited in the most odious light, and that Dr. Nevin's "Vindication" should be shielded against censure. But the case will be adjudicated before a more equitable tribunal than partizan partiality.

The unhappy author of that "Vindication" is not content, however, with hurling the missiles of his ridicule, sarcasm, and denunciation at me alone. His vast displeasure cannot be appeased with the attempted annihilation of a single mark. It must take in a wider range. The Professors in Tiffin, and other Brethren of the Western Church, of the same mind, in regard to the ritualistic innovations, not excepting the Rev. David Winters, one of the Vice Presidents of the General Synod, whose years and long continued faithful services in the Church, if nothing else, should have shielded him from such abuse, and the Delegates from the Classis of North Carolina, are massed into one common herd, with the "miserable faction" from the East, (including men whose money Mercersburg was glad enough to accept in times past, and to solicit even since the tornado at Dayton,) and assailed with equal fury, and the same deadly weapons. The Liturgical Committee of the Western Synod is ridiculed, and its labors are derided as having resulted in an abortion, and come to an "inglorious end." The title of their specimen *Manual* is ridiculed. The "Western Missionary" is ridiculed for having displayed some zeal in the case. The brethren from North Carolina are ridiculed as mere "cyphers." All indiscriminately are branded as Gnostics, Phrygian Montanists, Rationalists, Socinians, Pelagians, Muggletonians, and, worst of all, as pietistic Puritans. And why pierce them with all these dreadful epithetic javelins? Because they dared to lift up their hand and voice or record only their vote (many, including the North Carolina delegates, did no more than merely vote) against Dr. Nevin's Mercersburg "new measures," and "new theology." They had withstood the edict of the king, and refused to do homage at his shrine. Were they not worthy of the consuming flames?

Such is the general spirit unfortunately displayed by Dr. Nevin, and especially in his recent tract, towards all who adversely cross his path. And whilst many of those who in the main, perhaps, share his sentiments, wholly disapprove of his manner of dealing with opponents, it is to be lamented that a few of his more devoted pupils evince only too great a willingness to imbibe the same spirit, and deplorable aptitude in imitating its supercilious, vindictive manners. For him, and those thus following in his footsteps, it is quite allowable to write and speak in defamatory terms not only of good and learned men in other Churches, but, impliedly at least, of the founders and fathers of our own Church in this country, decrying all as nothing better, on the whole, than bold and shallow rationalists, and as abettors of a style of worship "not distinctively Christian, but more or less Gnostically spiritualistic, ending at last in mere humanitarian deism." But let any one venture to demur at his theological discoveries or revolutionary ecclesiastical schemes, and although the demurrer may be couched in respectful terms, and be pressed in a courteous manner—as I may boldly affirm was done, both at York and Dayton—and at once they are assailed with the most caustic indignation. On the floor of the Synod at York, Dr. Harbaugh, among other vulgar jests, held up to public ridicule the Old Palatinate form of comforting penitents, by making it appear, as he and some others seemed to think, absurdly stupid. Dr. Nevin could join in the profane merriment thus excited, and cheer the speaker with an approving smile. But if some one, unable to appreciate the witticism indulged in dishonor to the Church, should dare to denounce the system which in this way seeks to magnify itself by casting reproach upon the memory of our fathers, and to win applause for its pretended excellencies by detracting from their reputation, he must at once be run down and crushed. It must be made a fatal, unpardonable offence to rebuke such raillery, or even to intimate that it involves ecclesiastical disloyalty. All who may differ from the theory, and feel unfavorable to the measures of this school, must see how terrible is the doom of those who may have the audacity to challenge its leader, or attempt to thwart the consummation of his schemes. Love for the Church, zeal for the maintenance of her denominational integrity, all go for nothing, unless that love and zeal defer to his fancies, and surrender themselves as subservient instruments in the furtherance of his schemes. Not under the irritation of some momentary offence at Synod, but for weeks and months, this spirit of detraction, denunciation and bitter hatred is harbored in the depths of this Mercersburg heart. And lest its implacable virulence should be doubted, it gives proof of its unrelenting animosity, by filling a tract of ninety-three pages, *not* "hastily written," with its double-distilled wormwood and gall.

Next to these general remarks, demanded by the ruling spirit and prevailing style of Dr. Nevin's controversial discussions, oral and written, and emphatically of this last production of his pen, his mode of warfare requires the notice in detail of some

SPECIAL POINTS.

These are raised very much at random, and are, indeed, for the most part wholly irrelevant to the subject avowedly under consideration. Inwardly as disconnected from each other, as they are severally foreign to the questions at issue, they can be taken up one by one in any order, without disturbing their sense, or affecting the real bearing of the various sentences or paragraphs in which they occur, whether in the speech at Dayton or in this "Vindication." It will have been noticed by those to whose attention they have come, that they are mostly side issues, in the way of personal thrusts. Their obvious aim is threefold: 1, To inflict a severe chastisement upon offending parties, by holding them up to mockery, scorn and condemnation: 2, To bring, in this way, the cause espoused by those offenders, under derision and contempt: 3, To divert calm and earnest attention from the true merits of that cause, and to occasion a general confusion of thought and judgment by the excitement and agitation thus produced. Perhaps they might be allowed to pass unnoticed, without much disadvantage either to the parties assailed, or the interests they represent. But such disregard of them would again be liable to perverse interpretations. And past experience in our dealings with a few of the advocates of the "new measures," has taught us some significant lessons on this point. For however irrelevant the points thus introduced are, they are largely substituted for argument, and adroitly made to wear the semblance of triumphant answers to the objections urged, and the proofs presented against the proposed innovations. And as the responsibility of their introduction, and of the consequent necessity of noticing them, rests upon others rather than upon ourselves, it will not be thought an abuse of patience to devote some space to their consideration. They spring, furthermore, wholly from the misapprehensions and errors of those who raise them, and may, therefore, be treated as so many *grave mistakes* of Dr. Nevin and his associates in this work.

The *first mistake* made, consists in asserting that my tract of last November charges the Liturgical Committee with *a conspiracy to perpetrate a fraud* upon the Church. This grave accusation was started in York, industriously propagated in private, reiterated, with divers variations, during a full hour of the time occupied by Dr. Nevin in his speech at Dayton, and is now again repeated in more permanent form in the so-called "Vindication." The terms in which the accusation is variously expressed, need not be quoted here; it is enough that they have been selected by their author as the medium of giving vent to his displeasure. And they shall most certainly not be retorted upon him, though abundant occasion has been given for such retort. I disdain to take advantage of his self-exposure. The ground about my feet is strewn thick with the ugly missiles used in this part of the contest. They were flung with angry violence, and with malignant aim. Doubtless it was meant that they should do fatal execution. And so they probably have done; but not upon their mark. They have utterly failed to inflict the harm intended. And now they lie, scattered and spent, on every side of me. It would only need stooping to pick them up. But it is better to leave them where they are. If Dr. Nevin, or those disposed to imitate his taste in such archery, should feel inclined to use them again, they may come and gather them. I shall not touch them, even with my feet.

But apart from the phraseology employed in presenting the accusation, it amounts substantially to what is stated above. I am violently charged with having indicted the Committee for a *conspiracy to defraud the Church*. And by what means is it attempted to sustain this charge? By any fair and tangible proofs from any thing really uttered or published by me? Nothing of the sort was heard on the floor of the General Synod, and nothing is furnished in the tract entitled a "Vindication," which, by any candid and legitimate interpretation, can be construed into such an expressed or even implied indictment of conspiracy. Admonished by some things said on the floor of the Synod at York, of a purpose to give this false and unwarranted significance to the position taken against the majority of the Committee, I was especially careful in my tract, subsequently published, to disclaim, in the most positive terms, any such design. (See History and Criticism of the Ritualistic movement, &c., p. 9.) That disclaimer is now as positively reiterated; and I deny most unqualifiedly, that any paragraph or sentence of said tract, fairly considered, justifies this bad sense. And unless we are to take Dr. Nevin's opprobrious denunciations for proof, unless labored and extreme exaggerations shall be allowed to pass for argument, unless to decry a man, as a felon, is demonstration that he purloined his neighbor's goods, the accusation brought against the tract has not been substantiated. It is easy to produce temporary excitement by sueing a man at law for a libel or for slander. But not every such suit prevails. The prosecution may seek to make out its case in the strongest terms, may invoke the aid of the most violent epithets,* may make the most inflammatory appeals to those sitting in judg-

---

* The law of association of ideas will readily explain how the perusal of some portions of Dr. Nevin's tract served to remind me of the following incident recorded in *Macaulay's History of England*, vol. I., pp. 386, &c: Boston ed. It is an account of Baxter's trial before Lord Jeffries, the notorious tool of the extreme High-Church party, under that equally notorious persecutor of the Puritans, James the Second.

Baxter had begged for some delay, to allow him time to prepare his defence.

"Jeffries burst into a storm of rage. 'Not a minute, he cried, to save his life. I can deal with saints as well as sinners. There stands Oates on one side of the pillory; and

ment upon the charge. But all that will not sustain it. And unless equity is made subservient to passion, and justice is degraded into a minion of partizan rancor and arbitrary tyranny, the failure to sustain the charge by clear and unquestionable proof, must ensure the defendant's acquittal.

The only charges which can be said to have been made, even by implication, against the course of the Committee, were the following: 1, disobedience to Synodical instructions: 2, persevering efforts to work out their own ideas of ritualism, rather than prepare such a Liturgy as the official action of the successive Synods called for: 3, a desire to secure, by delay, time and opportunity to have the Church educated to their standard of worship, and thus to ensure its ultimate adoption. These points, moreover, were not brought out in any formal way; it was not within the scope or design of my tract, that they should be. That part of the tract in which they incidentally occur, was avowedly a history of the movement

---

if Baxter stood on the other, the two greatest rogues in the kingdom would stand together.

"When the trial came on at Guildhall, a crowd of those who loved and honored Baxter, filled the court. At his side stood Doctor William Bates, one of the most eminent of the Non-conformist divines. Two Whig barristers, of great note, Pollexfen and Wallop, appeared for the defendant. Pollexfen had scarcely begun his address to the jury, when the Chief Justice (Jeffries) broke forth:

"Pollexfen, I know you well. I will set a mark on you. You are the patron of the *faction*. This is an old rogue, a *schismatical* knave, a *hypocritical* villain. *He hates the Liturgy.* He would have nothing but long-winded cant, without the book: and then his lordship, turning up his eyes, clasped his hands, and began to sing through his nose, in imitation of what he supposed to be Baxter's style of praying, 'Lord, we are Thy people, Thy peculiar people, Thy dear people.' Pollexfen gently reminded the court that his late majesty had thought Baxter deserving of a bishopric. 'And what ailed the old blockhead, then,' cried Jeffries 'that he did not take it.' His fury now rose almost to madness. He called Baxter a dog, and swore that it would be no more than justice to whip such a villain through the whole city. Wallop interposed, but fared no better than his leader. 'You are in all these dirty causes, Mr. Wallop,' said the judge. 'Gentlemen of the long robe ought to be ashamed to assist such factious knaves.' The advocate made another attempt to obtain a hearing, but to no purpose. 'If you do not know your duty,' said Jeffries, 'I will teach it you.' Wallop sat down; and Baxter himself attempted to put in a word. But the Chief Justice drowned all expostulation. 'My lord,' said the old man, 'I have been much blamed by dissenters for speaking respectfully of bishops.' 'Baxter for bishops,' cried the judge, 'that's a merry conceit, indeed. I know what you mean by bishops, rascals like yourself, Kidderminster bishops, factious, snivelling Presbyterians.' Again, Baxter essayed to speak, and again Jeffries roared: 'Richard, Richard, dost thou think we will let thee poison the court? Richard, thou art an old knave. Thou hast written books enough to load a cart, and every book as full of sedition as an egg is full of meat. By the grace of God, I'll look after thee. I see a great many of your brotherhood waiting to see what will befall their mighty Don. And there is a doctor (Bates) of your party at your elbow. But by the grace of God Almighty, I will crush you all.'"

Other apt illustrations might be added from the style in which *Heeshuss* denounced the Reformed faith and practice, as advocated by Ursinus; but the above will suffice.

which had reached its climax in the Revised Liturgy. But no one could write that history in accordance with actual facts, as furnished by official documents and the course really pursued by the Committee, without bringing into view those very points. That history shows most conclusively that the Synod gave a definite expression, after mature deliberation, of its desires and purpose in entering upon the work of providing the Church with more settled forms of worship, and that its instructions were not carried out by the Committee intrusted with the work (myself, I regret to say, included, for which I am ready to be reproved.) That history proves that instead of laboring to prepare and furnish such a Liturgy as Synod had plainly and positively declared to be desired and demanded, the Committee persistently worked according to its own theory of cultus and worship, laboring to produce a Liturgy after its own mind and heart; at least that this was the ruling aim of that portion of the Committee which favors the new "Order of Worship." For Dr. Nevin, as their foreman, declares that all those larger parts of the Provisional Liturgy, which *seem* to have been wrought after "the pattern according to which our fathers worshipped," were not meant to be in harmony with that pattern, but are really of the same order with the opposite system, and subordinate to it. And that history, once more proves, that the Committee, or rather those members favoring the new "Order of Worship," did oppose the work of revision from time to time, because they did not think the Church prepared as yet for the adoption and introduction of such an order of worship as they hoped the revision would produce, and because they hoped that by various means the Church might be educated into a state of mind and feeling which would ultimately be favorable to its adoption. (Vindic. p 25.)

Even Dr. Nevin, with a measure of cool self-contradiction which he himself may explain, admits all this substantially, in the tract of 1862–3, (The Liturgical Question, pp. 62, 69), in his speech at Dayton, and in his so-called "Vindication." On p. 13 of this last tract, after denouncing me in his own peculiar style for asserting this very fact, he concedes it all by saying: "The movement inaugurated at Norristown in 1849, he (Bomberger) says, contemplated no such Liturgy as we have now offered for our use. *This is very true and needs no argument.*" But when this very same thing is affirmed by another writer or speaker, the statement is pronounced *erroneous*, though in *somewhat different terms!* An offender acknowledges his fault, but denounces the mention of its name!

Is it denied that the Committee did not proceed in their work according to instructions? Then I refer to the resolution of the Synod of Norristown, 1849; to the action of the Synod of Baltimore, 1852; and to the resolution of the Synod of Easton, 1861. Taking these together, they enjoin, to say the very least, that equal regard shall be paid to Reformed Liturgies of the 16th centuries with what may be shown for earlier Liturgies. But the majority of the Committee come forward in the face of all this, and declare that their Liturgy "*was constructed throughout on another theory altogether*" from that of those early Reformed Liturgies. Was this, then, obeying or disobeying instructions?

Is it, again, denied, that the majority of the Committee labored persistently to work out their own idea of ritualism (whatever its source or basis may be), rather than to produce such a Liturgy as the instructions of Synod demanded? Then I appeal once more, 1, To the plain tenor of those instructions themselves, which, if they mean any thing, distinctly call for the preparation of a work which should be in essential, material harmony "with the devotional and doctrinal genius of the German Reformed Church," and to the almost universal desire and expectation that, in the Revised Liturgy especially, no other would be offered to the acceptance of the Church, 2. To the confessions of the Committee, that in allowing themselves to be "*brought more and more under the power of an idea, which carried them with inexorable force its own way*," instead of heeding the rule which the Synod had prescribed, they produced a Liturgy which involves "a question of very material change in our Church practice, if not in our Church life," and to the fact that their new "Order of Worship" has been drafted and compiled without the least ruling regard to any of the earlier German Reformed Liturgies. Is this a misrepresentation (Dr. Nevin uses other terms in speaking of the matter, which had as well not be quoted), of the Committee's course? Does this charge them with any thing beyond their own concession, and at which Dr. N. has a right to grow so excessively indignant? (See Liturgy. Q. p. 39—62, *et passim*.)

Is it, finally, denied, that the authors and advocates of the new "Order of Worship," desired to secure, by delay, time and opportunity to have the Church educated to their standard of worship, and thus to ensure its ultimate adoption? Then I appeal 1, in proof of their effort to retard or delay the work of final Revision, to the fact that *they steadily and uniformly opposed every attempt made to have the Revision undertaken.* They did so at the Synod of Easton, in 1861. They did so during the year that followed, notwithstanding the action of the Easton Synod, ordering the Revision, and notwithstanding the earnest entreaty of that obstinate, intractable member of the committee, who would not bend his knee simply because five other members bent theirs, that as they saw their way clear, they should take it regardless of his "obstinacy." They did so at Chambersburg, in 1862, arraying their entire force, and struggling for three days to prevent the adoption of any action by which they would be required to go on with the work; until at length the matter was referred to a special committee, of which the President of Synod (the Rev. Dr. *Gerhart*), I think, appointed the Rev. Dr. *Nevin* Chairman, and that committee reported a *resolution of indefinite postponement*. This resolution was, after further discussion, adopted, largely through the influence of a remark made by a lay member of the committee, to the effect, that the further agitation of the matter might involve the Synod in difficulty with the publishers of the Provisional Liturgy.* Again they opposed the Revision at the General Synod of Pittsburgh, in 1863. And I am persuaded, that, could they have prevailed, they would have prevented the accomplishment of it until this day.

2, I appeal to the manifest and avowed *reasons* for this opposition. These I affirm to have been twofold. *First*, those involved in *a desire* that their theory of worship should be adopted. That such a desire animated, and was cherished by them, must be evident from their having personally embraced the theory, from their having recommended it to Synod, from their repeated and extravagant declarations in praise of it, and from their vehement defence of it against all opposition. If the zeal thus displayed in its favor during the course of many years, does not prove the intensity of their desire to secure its ultimate adoption, it would be hard to find evidence of such a desire in any other case. Has it not been proclaimed again and again, that the new Order of Worship they have produced on this theory, is so transcendantly excellent, that in comparison with it, that framed by our fathers, according to the pattern received by them from the Mount, does not deserve to be called a Liturgy? Do we not read their eloquent laudations of its inimitable merits (although it is their own work), set forth in avowed disparagement of such "pulpit handbooks," as our fathers used, on many an offensive page of the notable report of 1862-3 ("The Liturg. Question")? All that Dr. Nevin has said at different times, and reiterates in this "Vindication," of his lack of heart in the matter, is no offset to this evidence. It is not to be wondered at, that his courage often failed him in regard to the final success of the movement. He seems to have had from the start a comprehensive and penetrating view of what it involved; at least he seems to have known for some years past, what *he* meant by it. He had a clear vision of the "essential and material changes in our Church practice and life," that is in her mode of worship, and of holding some vital fundamental doctrines, which it demanded, and sought to effect. And that, with these fairly before his eyes, he should often be tempted to despond or despair of success, is not at all amazing. There was good reason for despondency, if

---

* These facts were not mentioned in my former tract, because I wished to avoid as much as possible every thing which might seem offensive. But Dr. Nevin knew them all, for he participated in what was done.

he had any proper conception of the deep and sincere attachment of the general membership of the Church, to her time-honored evangelical doctrines and customs. A cedar of three hundred years growth, and which has so firmly entwined its roots about the Rock of Ages (the foundation other than which no man can successfully lay) is not so easily to be plucked up and cast into the sea. But the prevalence of despondency does not prove the absence of desire. It is simply beyond contradiction, that for many years, the ritualistic members of the committee have strongly desired the success of their scheme, and have labored with a constant aim to this end. Hence, in part, their strong and persistent opposition to the Revision.

Further reasons, corroborative of all this are furnished by the *arguments* employed by the committee in favor of delaying the Revision. These must not simply be fresh in the memories of those who have attended Synods at which the subject was discussed, but are a matter of record. Immediate revision was urged by those who desired it, because the Provisional Liturgy had proved a practical failure, especially as to its more ritualistic peculiarities; because, on actual trial, one of the forms most needed, that for the administration of the Lord's Supper, was found to be objectionable, both on account of its length and complications; because, through the growing zeal of those who desired the introduction of "material and essential changes" in our mode of worship, the Church was becoming exposed to the perils of increased liturgical diversities, and of internal dissensions; and finally because it was believed to be desirable that the whole question should be settled as soon as possible. On the other hand, however, such immediate revision was opposed, and mainly by that portion of the Committee which advocated extreme ritualistic forms, because the Church was not yet thought ready to appreciate their theory of worship, and, therefore, to pass an intelligent judgment upon it; and because they claimed time and opportunity to educate the Church into an approval and acceptance of their theory.

That the former of these reasons was correct, is too obvious to admit of a doubt. It has been demonstrated practically by the almost universal unwillingness of congregations to admit the ritualistic forms, and by the dissatisfaction which has been occasioned, with possibly two exceptions, in those congregations into which it has been attempted, cautiously to introduce the novelties even in small part, and by slow degrees. And in these cases, the thing has been done without affording the congregation, or perhaps even the consistory, an opportunity to take formal action upon the matter. No; the Church has manifestly not been ready to appreciate the ritualistic "new measures" in the Committee's sense. But it is equally evident that the Church was thought ready to reject them. Or else why has there been so persistent an effort on the part of the advocates of those measures, to evade and prevent a fair and square vote upon the real merits of their scheme? And why was this done with such consummate skill even at the General Synod in Dayton, the action of which Synod Dr. Nevin claims, most erroneously as shall be shown, as a complete triumph of ritualism?

Of the other plea, that time should be allowed for the ritualistic *training of the Church*, it is difficult to speak without ridicule or reprobation. It involves such absurd sophistry and a begging of the question, on the one hand, and so much of design and artifice on the other, that it seems incredible how the fallacy and deceptiveness of it should have escaped the discernment of the Committee. Grant time and opportunity to educate the Church into an acceptance of the "new measures"? Who does not see that in this way the most orthodox and evangelical Church might, in the course of a single generation, be converted into a very synagogue of heresy and superstition? Let our schools come under the reigning influence of Unitarianism. Let our congregations be supplied for successive years with pastors inculcating Unitarian views. Let the children and youth of the Church have Unitarian books of devotion and for reading, placed in their hands, and be taught Unitarian doctrines. How long would it take, by this method, for Drs. Bellows, Furness, and Osgood, to kindle in the Church such ardent zeal for their theory of Christianity, that its general adoption would be insured? And an experiment tried in the same way, with any other system of error, would lead to the same result.

Can Dr. Nevin have been ignorant of this fact, or have overlooked it? Could he have forgotten the history of the Anxious Bench innovations, and its significant lessons? It was by the application and success of this very scheme of *education*, that those innovations gained the ascendancy and power in the Church, which they enjoyed thirty years ago. And it was largely upon their supposed deceptive and mischievous influence in an educational view, that Dr. Nevin so vehemently denounced the system in his tract on the Anxious Bench System, in 1842–4. So far, also, he was right, if that system was pernicious, and subversive of the evangelical doctrines and customs of our Church. But is this educational theory, applied to innovations, to "material and essential changes," any less unfair and deceptive now than it was then?

Evidently, therefore, before such innovations are attempted, their true character and their necessary tendencies should be ascertained and decided upon. They should be carefully examined, and properly authorized in the constitutional way. To prevent or evade this, lest they should be rejected, even as an experiment, is wrong, and must expose the Church to danger. Are they so profound in their principles, so transcendantly excellent in their spirit and organism, that the Church is incompetent to pass an intelligent judgment upon them, even after years of opportunity to examine their merits? Then an evangelical Church, fully conscious of the intrinsic and tried worth of those spiritual blessings which it actually possesses, had better let the innovations, with all their mysterious and incomprehensible superiority, alone.

But by what means was this educational success of the new order of worship to be secured? The answer to this question is obvious. It is well known what agencies the advocates of ritualism have had under their control, and how diligently they have been used. And it must be equally apparent, that with such use of those means, the success of the movement would be only a question of time. Not all the specious plausibility with which Dr. Nevin may plead the case in his tract, or Dr. Wolff in his articles upon the subject in the *German Reformed Messenger*, during the months of January and February, can blind the eyes of considerate persons to these facts. Neither can any fail to see, that by the natural course of things, the final result thus gained would be, not the decision and choice of the German Reformed Church as such, but of that Church as ritualistically educated, and converted to the new faith—both in regard to her worship and her life. Of course, after having had time thus to educate and convert her, the formal entire adoption of the "new measures" would be virtually secured.

This, then, is what was implied or said, and no more than this, in those portions of the historical section of my former tract, which Dr. Nevin allowed so greatly to infuriate him. And it is this, no more than this, which has been so unjustly and violently exaggerated and distorted into an accusation, the very sound of which might excite indignation, and inflame bitter passions against me. But what becomes of all these vituperations now?

Another grave *mistake* committed by Dr. Nevin in his assault, is the attempt to make out a special point against me on the ground of *my alleged inconsistencies*. Both in the speech at Dayton and in his present tract, humorous and exultant allusions are found to a supposed absurd contradiction between my views in 1853 and 1857, and my present opposition to the new Order of Worship. As it will be shown, presently, that Dr. Nevin himself seems to make little account of ecclesiastical and theological vicissitudes, this point may be very briefly disposed of. Regarding the articles in the Mercersburg Review for 1853, he has by some strange error, overlooked or forgotten three facts:—(1.) That with but one exception, and that in a modified form, the charges of error involved in the discussion, were altogether different from those involved in the present controversy. (2.) That whilst *defending the Church* against the reproach of endorsing doctrines at variance with evangelical orthodoxy by her toleration of Dr. Nevin's views, *decided dissent from some of those views is expressed* on pp. 169, 170, especially the foot-note, and 177-8. It is a pity that *these* pages were not consulted before the ridicule was indulged in. (3.) That prior to 1853 Dr. Nevin had written no such tract as the Liturgical Question of ten years later. At that time yet, his great aim seemed to be, to have the Church fully brought back to her historical character, and true, legitimate usages; not to introduce into her midst a new order of things, "not after the pattern strictly of any system of worship which has prevailed hitherto (1863) in the German Reformed Church, either in this country or in Europe." See very particularly the closing chapter of the "Anxious Bench."*

With reference to the article of 1857, in which the general character and contents of the Provisional Liturgy (issued that Fall), are commended, it will be sufficient to reply: That the commendation was meant to apply to what many considered the main, as they were by far the larger portions of the work. Those are forms framed after the pattern according to which our fathers, from the first, did worship. Let them but be examined. There are four different forms for the Lord's day. The *first* is after the new system; but it was said that even *it* might be used without the ritualistic peculiarities. So I supposed it mostly would be. And so, with but eight or ten exceptions, it has been, at least until last November. The *second* has simply five amens, and even these are not directed to be used responsively by the people. It has no formal confession and declaration of pardon, calls for no recital of the Creed by the people, but only by the minister, and expressly allows free prayer at the close of the service. The *third* provides merely an invocation and a general prayer, without an amen, and gives no concluding prayer at all. The *fourth* is like the *third*, excepting that even a prescribed invocation is wanting. There are *fifteen* prayers for Festival seasons. They are not short collects, but long prayers. *Not one of them has responses, not even an amen, excepting the second form for Good Friday.* Thus far, then, we have seventeen non-responsive, simple forms, to two of the other kind, and one of these two is applicable to but one day in the year. Whose statement, then, is open to the charge of "miserable special pleading" in this matter; mine, in affirming that the Provisional Liturgy was for the most part a book of forms, like those used in past years in the German Reformed Church; or Dr. Nevin, in claiming it as a book predominantly ritualistic in his sense?. The form for the administration of the Lord's Supper, and the first form for Baptism, with

---

* As this interesting work may be out of print, and but few of our members may possess copies, the desirableness of re-publishing the chapter referred to, and even some other portions is respectfully suggested to the editor of the *German Reformed Messenger,* and of the *Mercersburg Review.*

some others for *such special occasions,* have indeed prominent ritualistic peculiarities. But does Dr. Nevin, does the Committee, forget, that when objections were made to these, it was commonly answered: They can be used without those peculiarities, and contain enough that is good even when those are omitted? And do they not know that they have been almost generally so used by our ministers?

In regard to some doctrinal peculiarities of the book, I have only to say, that if they had been explained and understood, as they now are, I would never have even qualifiedly approved of them. There are members of the Committee who know that I never held the views now believed to be contained in several of the forms of the New Order of Worship.

Especially does Dr. Nevin know this to have been the case. From my entire course as a member of the Committee, he could not have failed to be convinced that I was at no time committed to his peculiar views, doctrinal or liturgical. If he cannot recall more than one occasion on which I decidedly objected to those views, his memory is much more treacherous on this point than on some others connected with my course. And he could not have been ignorant of the fact, that my conditional approval of the Provisional Liturgy, was based almost wholly on the correspondence of by far the larger portions of that work, with that system of worship known as German Reformed, and upon the supposition that the remaining portions, containing as they did much that was good, might be used without their more ritualistic peculiarities, and objectionable doctrinal phrases. He and I, it seems, viewed the book in essentially different aspects. To him, the innovations it contained were the chief thing. To me, its numerous excellencies, wholly separable and apart from those innovations, were the chief thing. My mind and heart were set on those contents of the book which mainly corresponded with our past faith and practice, and might, after some subsequent modifications, be made to serve for the edification of the Church. His heart was set upon its more extreme and radical qualities. To a man to whom a piece of poisoned bread or a cup of poisoned wine is offered, the wine and the bread are the attraction. To him who offers them, however, the chief thing is the poison they contain.

But even if this charge of inconsistency could not be thus refuted by the facts in the case, it may be fully met by showing the uncertain character of the standard by which Dr. Nevin seems to determine a man's consistency or inconsistency. That standard is assumed, by his allusion to the articles of 1853, to be himself and his views. But it is an essential quality of a standard in such matters, that it should be somewhat uniform and fixed. It seems altogether proper, therefore, to ask whether, and how far, this quality is found in the case in hand? Let the following few contrasts, selected from among many which might be given, furnish the answer.

DR. NEVIN IN 1840-47.

"*The more we can be brought to commune familiarly and freely with the spirit of the Reformation,* as it wrought mightily in the deeds, and uttered itself powerfully in the words of our ecclesiastical ancestry, *the better is it likely to be with us in all respects, at the present time* * * * Let us have progress, by all means; but let it be progress *upwards, within the sphere of the original life of the Church itself,* as a tree unfolds itself in growth, and is the same tree still; not progress *outwards,* by which *the life of the past, together with its form, is renounced,* and "another gospel introduced in the room of the old."—(History and Genius of the Heidelb. Catech., by J. W. Nevin, D.D., Prof. of Theology in the Seminary of the G. R. Church in Mercersburg.—Ger. Ref. Messenger, Dec. 9, 1840, Revised, &c., 1847).

DR. NEVIN IN 1862-3.

"Must our new Liturgy be of one kind in manner and form, *in genius and spirit,* with the Reformed Liturgies of the 16th century, having these only for its basis, and following them as its rule? * * * Let the answer be in favor of a new order of worship, more liturgical in *the old sense* of the term than the Liturgies of the 16th century, and involving a *reform of our past practice, answerable to the genius and spirit of our Church at the present time.* * * * The Provisional Liturgy has not professed at all to be of one order, simply with the Liturgical practice of the German Reformed Church in the 16th century; * * *it was constructed throughout on another theory altogether;* * * it makes common cause with the Liturgies of the ancient Church. * * It is a question *of very material change in our church practice, if not in our church life.*"—(Liturgical Question, pp. 61, 62, 69).

DR. NEVIN IN 1844.

"The *Second Century* shows us the *whole Christian world* brilliantly illuminated with rival systems of quackery, under the name of Gnosticism, which for a time seemed to darken the sun of truth itself by their false but powerful glare. *Afterwards,* under a less idealistic garb, the evil fairly *enthroned itself in the Church.* The Reformation was the *resurrection of the Truth once more, in its genuine original life.*"—(Anxious Bench, 2d Ed., p. 51. See also p. 53).

DR. NEVIN IN 1866-7.

"A modern confessionalism in this way made to rule out the sense of the older confessionalism in which, nevertheless, it professed to have its own root and ground! Did we not hear this nonsense gravely held forth at Synod? Were we not told there that we are to take the creed only in the sense of the fathers of the 16th century, and not in the sense of *the fathers who used it in the second and third centuries, if this last sense should be found not to square exactly with the sixteenth century sense,* as it was quietly granted, might be the case? * * * *How superlatively absurd!*—(Vindication, &c., p. 74).

DR. NEVIN AGAIN IN 1844.

"If * * * *genuflections* and *prostrations* in the aisle or around the altar, * * * * * * have no connection in fact with true, serious religion, * * * let the fact be openly proclaimed."

"The Romish Church has always delighted in arrangements and services animated with the same false spirit. In her penitential system, pains have been taken to produce *effect* by means of *outward postures* and dress, till in the end, amid the solemn mummery, no room has been left at all for genuine penitence. Yet *not a ceremony was ever introduced* into the system, that did not seem to be recommended by some sound religious reason at the time."—(Anx. B. pp. 28, 39).

DR. NEVIN IN 1862–3

"Where the sense of the Liturgical prevails in this sort * * there must *be gestures* and *postures* significant of faith in what the service thus means."

"Let it be considered a part of religion to do bodily reverence, in all proper ways, to the *sacramental holiness which is felt to inhabit the house of God.* Let *all* faces, in the time of prayer, *be turned towards the altar.* Let there be risings and *bowings*, where it may seem to be meet, in token of the consenting adorations of the people."—("The Liturgical Question," pp. 33, 35).

DR. NEVIN IN 1866.

"*I stand now where I did while a Professor at Mercersburg.*"—(Liturgical Discussion at Dayton. See GERMAN REF. MESSENGER, Jan. 2, 1867.)

From these contrasted quotations it is very evident that Dr. Nevin has, in the course of some years, materially "changed his mind. This he had a right to do; but his testimony of the past is of some value in accepting that of the present." In the face, however, of such marked contrasts, no one, surely, should be held chargeable with unpardonable inconsistency, for agreeing on some points with Dr. Nevin in 1853, and then opposing some of his favorite measures in 1867! The fault or folly of such inconsistency rests rather on himself, and upon those who so closely follow in his steps, that they adhere to him through all these variations! "A truce, however, to this pleasantry!"

A *third* unfortunate *mistake* committed by the offended author of the "Vindication," is that of stigmatising his opponents with "*factiousness.*" The delegates from the Eastern Synod, who could not support his extreme ritualistic measures, or endorse those of his doctrinal views which are manifestly at variance with the Heidelberg Catechism, as interpreted by its authors and the early fathers of the Reformed Church, are rather rudely styled a "factious element," "a miserable faction of the Eastern Synod." The "brethren of the Western Synod" are charged with having "joined hands" with that "miserable faction," and so made themselves partakers of its sin. All attempt, therefore, to arrest the progress of the new measures, and prevent their adoption, is denounced as *factiousness.*

Now a "*faction*" is an unlawful and disorderly combination against the constitutional acts of a government, civil or ecclesiastical; a party that seeks, by such combination, to excite or promote discord and contention. And Dr. Nevin plainly means to say, by his application of this term to those who oppose his measures, that they are guilty of being engaged in such an unlawful combination.

But before there can be any factious combination like this, there must be constitutional acts to be opposed. So before any members of the Synod could be guilty of such factiousness, Synod must have adopted, in the constitutional way, the ritualistic peculiarities opposed. The General Synod had, of course, not done so, and did not by its action taken upon the subject. That the Eastern Synod never did, was demonstrated by the official evidence presented in that tract, which furnished the advocates of the new measures, with so much matter in their debates at Dayton; and will be shown still more fully under the "historical" section of the present tract. Dr. Nevin's sweeping and unwarranted assumption to the contrary, will then be satisfactorily disposed of.

It may be said, however, that the factiousness consisted in the attempt of the delegates accused to foment discord and contention in the Church. That is, then, because their opposition to proposed new measures produced some excitement and controversy, they are to be blamed for any such unhappy effect of that opposition! An effort is made "materially and essentially" to change the Liturgical usages of a Church. There are many in the Church who feel fully convinced that the changes advocated are radically revolutionary, and would prove hurtful. But those who proposed the changes, and who advocate them, are strongly determined to secure their introduction, and any attempt to arrest or resist the movement, will produce excitement and dissension. Therefore no such attempt can be made without rendering those who make it liable to the charge of factiousness! And hence, the new measure party should be allowed to have their way!—Such seems to be Dr. Nevin's argument. Would any intelligent man, writing or speaking with the calmness of conscious truth, stake his reputation on reasoning like this?

But however absurd the logic of an argument like this may be, the policy which it implies is sufficiently clear and ingenious. For it demands just what all innovations, however subversive of established principles and practices they may be, most need to ensure their success. Only let them alone. Let no one expose their true character, or attempt to arrest their progress. Give them full scope and sufficient time for a trial of their merits, and for educating the Church into their peculiarities. Place the children under their influence. Teach the youth of the Church their excellence. Introduce them gradually and cautiously into the public services of the congregations. Train candidates for the ministry in the Theological Seminary, and even incidentally during their collegiate course; by this method, to look upon the old order of the Church with contempt, and to regard this new order of things as incomparably superior and more profound. Use largely the papers of the Church in advocating, defending and recommending them, especially by carricature contrasts of the principles and customs which are to be abrogated in favor of the innovations. Only allow this, nothing more; and this, too, for but a single generation, say thirty years! Then, after such quiet and peaceful trial of the new system, if it is not liked, it may be set aside!

Shall an exposure of a policy like this, and opposition to its measures, be stigmatized as factiousness? Shall those who, being zealously and intelligently attached to the system of faith and worship received from their fathers, and convinced that the new order urged is but the revival of old, exploded and pernicious errors, contend for the maintenance of the established system, and resist the encroachments of the new system, be denounced as seditious troublers in Israel, and indicted for treason? The mere questions must show how preposterous are the demands of the new measure policy, and how unjust are Dr. Nevin's sarcasms and maledictions.

It is, furthermore, to be distinctly kept in mind, that the delegates thus stigmatized, *represented*, in the General Synod, *not the Eastern or Western Synods, but the Classes, and the Church*. Dr. Nevin, therefore, has erred again in his great excitement, in designating the members from the East, as "a miserable faction from the Eastern Synod." They were not, properly, the representatives of the Eastern Synod, and were consequently under no obligations to defend or support its measures, even had that Synod adopted and recommended the new system, which it did not. On the contrary, it was their right and their duty to do what they could, in every lawful and proper way, to defeat the desires and policy of the new-measure party. And they may confidently appeal from the unjust condemnation of an angry anathematizer, to the calm and impartial judgment of their constituents, for a reversal of his sentence.

But the censured faction is also denounced as "*miserable*." This term of contempt cannot apply, of course, to the personality of those referred to; for they were severally, as said before, the equals of Dr. Nevin and his associates, in every essential respect. His contempt for them does not at all abate from their private or official worth, and will, probably, have no disparaging effect upon the estimation in which the Church at large may be kindly pleased to hold them. According to the standard by which he weighs or measures his opponents, they may be set down by him as "a miserable" set, "a clique," "a junto," as dupes of "ultra-montane jealousy." But that standard has been found somewhat unreliable when applied to the charge of *inconsistencies*, and possibly may not be admitted here.

It must be noted, also, that this "faction," with those Brethren in the West who more actively joined it, were Dr. Nevin's own pupils, with but a few exceptions. They were trained for the ministry by his own hands, and taught theology by his own lips. Nay more. While under his tuition, they had largely imbibed the doctrines which he then taught, and the precise tenor of which they have better means of knowing than their mere remembrance of them. More than one copy of carefully written notes of his earlier lectures is within their reach. To the doctrines then taught, they, in the main, adhere. For the principles of ecclesiastical order and church worship then inculcated, they cherish a cordial regard, and now feel constrained to contend. If Dr. Nevin has changed his creed and his views of a truly Christian apostolic cultus, the responsibility of such change rests with him. They do not feel warranted in keeping up with his theological vicissitudes. They stand where he then professed to stand, while a Professor of Theology in the Seminary of the German Reformed Church at Mercersburg. If, for maintaining firmly that position, in antagonism to his subsequent developments, they are to be stigmatized as a "miserable faction," or abettors of a faction, they glory in the reproach. As for his shamefully contemptuous reference to the Brethren from North Carolina, one of them, former pupil of his, the Rev. G. W. Welker, has sufficiently rebuked it in the communication appended to this tract.

It may, however, be the author's design to apply the term "miserable" to the *numerical* strength of the so-called faction. Knowing well the power and influence which numbers frequently possess, an effort is made to produce the impression that those who have felt constrained to oppose the introduction of an extreme liturgical order of worship into the Church, are so few in number, as to constitute only a very contemptible minority, especially so far as the Eastern Synod is concerned. But mark now the method of calculation by which Dr. Nevin struggles to make out his case. First, he asserts that the Eastern Synod "had all along been backing the course of the Committee" (Vindic., p. 39), in regard to these extreme measures. Next, he assumes that *all* the other members of the Committee but myself, were wholly of one mind in regard to all the peculiarities of the Revised Liturgy, so that they stood "ten to one." In the third place, he appeals to the action taken at York last October, as a full and formal endorsement of the Revised Liturgy. Fourthly, he counts all who voted at York for the resolutions adopted there, as friends of the new Order of Worship. In like manner, fifthly, he counts all who voted for the Report adopted at Dayton, by a majority of seven in a vote of one hundred and twenty-one members, as endorsing the new Order. And then, finally, he sets down the fifteen delegates from the Eastern Synod, who voted against the Report adopted at Dayton, as "a miserable faction." Of the first two assumptions, notice will be taken further on. In reference to the third, it will be sufficient, now, to expose its great unfairness and fallacy, by reminding the reader of two significant facts which Dr. Nevin has seen fit to ignore or overlook. One of these facts is, that the 3d Resolution of the Report adopted at York, and quoted in the "Vindication," is not the resolution which was originally presented, and which the advocates of the new Order would have been glad to carry. The original resolution expressed full *approval* of the Revised Liturgy, and *recommended* it to the General Synod. Dr. Nevin knew this very well. Why, then, if the York Synod was so strongly in favor of backing the Committee's course all along, was that resolution not passed? Why, if there was only a "miserable faction" opposed to the book presented by the Committee, was that faction not rebuked, by voting them down by an overwhelming majority? And once more, why does Dr. Nevin so carefully conceal the fact, that after a long debate, the original resolution was so essentially changed into its present form? Is this a specimen of the candor of the advocates of ritualism among us? "But the preamble of the Report was adopted," it has been said, "and that concedes everything to the Committee." It certainly was an unfortunate oversight in those who had resisted the adoption of the original third resolution, to allow that preamble, with its approving expression, to pass. The oversight can be accounted for, to all candid minds, only on the supposition that during the interval of a day and a half which had passed after the reading of it (and if my memory serves me, it was not read again, nor was a separate vote taken on it), and in consequence of the excitement of the intervening debate, and the result of that debate securing the change contended for in the third resolution, the precise tenor of the preamble was overlooked. If Dr. Nevin and his party choose to take advantage of this oversight, they may. Such artifices cannot materially help their cause. For it must be clear that, if the opposition to the third original resolution was so strong that it could secure the modification of it, which they desired, that opposition might have succeeded also, in having the preamble modified, had its objectionable expressions not escaped their attention.

In confirmation of this, another very important fact must be mentioned, a fact which, like the last named, Dr. Nevin has not thought proper to quote. On p. 98 of the Minutes of the Synod of York, immediately under the record of the yeas and nays, (which were taken on the *third* resolution of the Report, not on the *last*, as the Minutes erroneously say) the following official statement may be found: "*In the foregoing action of the Synod, it was understood, that the vote on the adoption of the Report, did not commit those who voted for it, as to the merits of the book.*" How came Dr. Nevin to overlook that statement? Why did he not quote it? It has a plain and direct bearing on the case, and its significance reaches back to the first word of the unfortunate preamble. In words too simple and clear to be mistaken, it exonerates even those of the "miserable faction," who voted for the amended Report, (and all of them including myself,—all but *fourteen*, did so,) from an endorsement of the work of the Committee! One is tempted, in view of such disingenuousness, to stoop, after all, and, picking up one of the foul missiles which have been so freely hurled at us, to fling it back. But it was resolved, that they should not be touched. So let them lie!

The next assumption in Dr. Nevin's method of calculating the strength of the ritualistic party is also swept away by this statement in regard to the significance of the action taken at York. The action at Dayton involved no more than that at York, hence the rule of the reckoning is at fault in this case again. Consequently, then, the smallness of the number of those Eastern delegates who voted against the Report adopted at Dayton, does not fairly indicate the actual strength of the opposition to the extreme liturgical measures of the Committee, and Dr. Nevin's "miserable faction" becomes a miserable fiction of his own agitated fancy.

Assuredly, then, the attempt to fix odium upon those opponents, by charging them with factiousness, is most unjust, and betrays a sad determination to accomplish by personal abuse what might not be achieved by unsound argument.

Passing on to another special point, we find the author of the "Vindication" betrayed by excessive excitement into the grave mistake of charging the objects of his anger, with *partizan manœuvering and intrigue*. But little need be said, beyond a most explicit denial of the charge, in answer to this unfounded accusation.

The right to use all fair and constitutional methods to prevent the success of the innovating measures of Dr. Nevin and his friends, will of course not be questioned by any but those whose partizan zeal may lead them to denounce all opposition to their efforts. Indeed it may be unhesitatingly acknowledged, that it was not only the right, but the duty of those who believed that those efforts involved revolutionary and pernicious changes, to employ all lawful and equitable means of frustrating them. More than this was not done, and Dr. Nevin is challenged to *prove* the contrary. For his mere assertions amount to nothing. And as for the ungainly epithets and terms with which he chooses to characterize the "political game," they amount to less than nothing, excepting as they again serve to exhibit the acrimonious spirit which seems to have gained such complete possession of his mind and heart. What if my former tract was prepared and published (from full notes written during months before) in the interval between the Synod of York and the General Synod at Dayton? The brethren who requested its publication had a right to make the request, and I had a right to comply. And as to the charge of its having been "hastily written," it may be said that in a proper sense that charge is false; and, further, that even if true, the tract need not shrink, either in regard to argument or style, from a comparison with the so-called "Vindication." Of course my tract was prepared for effect. Its design is undisguised. But the design was a just one, and the effect it was intended to produce was one of which all devoted to the established doctrine and practice of the German Reformed Church, to its true historical character, would approve. By the necessities of the case, it could not be published long before the meeting of the General Synod. And yet it did make its public appearance by some days longer than the Revised Liturgy appeared before the Synod of York, which was expected to act favourably upon it.

What all in the way of political manœuvering Dr. Nevin intends to include in this charge is not known. It may be said, however, in a general way, that so far as I know of, there were no consultations, either in person or by letters, among the Eastern delegates opposed to the Revised Liturgy, by which any common course of action was agreed upon; there were no caucusings on the way to Synod, either at Altoona or at Pittsburg, or at any other point, not even in Dayton; and there were no resolutions of Classes seeking to anticipate and forestall free and intelligent action, by laying their delegates under obligations to vote for the Revised Liturgy long before it was completed or published. If, therefore, the accusation is intended to charge the friends of the established doctrines and usages of the Church with any such things, the accusation has been laid at the wrong door. *Verbum sat!*

No. If but a small moiety of the policy employed by the advocates of the innovations to secure their success had been used on the other side, the Church would probably not now be in the peril to which she is exposed, by the manifest determination to make extreme use of advantages conceded to them in the way of temporary experiment, or of fraternal, but conditional concessions. As a single proof and illustration of this, it will suffice to direct attention to one or two facts, with reference to the character of most of the eastern delegations at Dayton. The ritualistic side was represented by the President and Vice-President of Franklin and Marshall College, by the President of Marshall Collegiate Institute, by the Professor of Theology in the Seminary at Mercersburg, and by the Editor of the *German Reformed Messenger*, all members of the Old Liturgical Committee, and all carrying with them such influence and power as their official position in the Church may impart. Was this accidental? Again.

Some Classes in which there are many ministers who are opposed to the ritualistic innovations, possibly one-half, or even more, being of this mind, were wholly, or almost wholly, represented by those who favor the new Order of Worship. This may have been fortuitous. But does it look so? How, then, came the author of the "Vindication" to take no note of these significant facts, especially as he did allow his thoughts to be occupied with such "political" aspects of the "game?"

So far from its being true that those who opposed the innovations had any advantages by manœuvering, the real aspects of the case strongly indicated that such advantages had been adroitly secured by the other side. For reasons, best known to themselves, some of those who may be supposed to have possessed the secrets of their part, boasted most confidently of their expected success at Dayton, a success, however, which it was predicted would be far more overwhelmingly complete than it finally proved to be. So that whatever Dr. Nevin's fears may have been, they did not seem to be shared at all by the friends of his measures. And now, on calmly reviewing the case, in this "political" aspect, it seems surprising, that with all the power of influential position in the Church, (a power which those now denounced as "factious," "dupes," and "ciphers," had helped to create, at a time when those who wield it seemed devoted to the German Reformed Church in its true historical character), and with all the use or abuse of that power in the manner displayed at Dayton, that the revolutionary movement should have but barely escaped an utter defeat.

Let this suffice, so far as concerns a few of the odious personalities of the notable tract before us. Our way has now been cleared of the rubbish of those irrelevant points with which the author has labored in his extremity to embarrass the calm consideration of the vital questions involved in the present controversy, and to rescue his cherished scheme from peril. We are prepared, therefore, to examine again, in a summary way, the leading facts connected with the *history of the new Order* of Worship, and to ascertain through them by what means the ritualistic crisis, with all the dangerous innovations it involves, has been brought upon the Church.

HISTORICAL NOTES.

The great importance of the historical argument seems to have been fully appreciated by Dr. Nevin. It is evident, also, from his violent struggles to escape the grasp of historical proofs demonstrating that the new Order of Worship was not such a Liturgy as the Synod had directed the committee to prepare, how fully he realized the force of those proofs. His manner of disposing of them is most remarkable for a writer of his pretensions, and displays far more skill in the art of Heshussian logic than genuine candor. He deals with the official records of the Synod, in the historical section of his tract, as he deals with the Creed in the subsequent part. Into both he arbitrarily inserts a sense to suit his purpose or his theory, and then becomes so entirely the victim of his own artifice, that he seems actually to believe that sense the true one, and violently denounces every other as absurd and false. Resolutions of Synod, most literally and essentially contradictory of his views, as well as positive and plain definitions of the Catechism, and expositions of the authors of the Catechism directly antagonistic to his fourth century conceits revived, or rather perhaps adopted from others who have revived them, are all but so many flimsy cobwebs before the besom in this arbitrary historian's hand. The wilful course pursued does indeed involve the writer more than once in most glaring and ridiculous contradictions. But who shall dare to challenge such a theologian's contradictions, or to expose the absurd consequences to which they lead? What if he does denounce the accusation of disobedience to Synodical instructions as a slander, and then forthwith acknowledge the fact of the disobedience? What if he does inveigh most violently against the charge that the Committee did not abide by the obligations assumed in the Baltimore compact, or treat it with sarcastic ridicule, and then tacitly admit that the terms of that compact were not honored? What if he does incase the Heidelberg Catechism in a gilded casket of eloquent laudations, and wreathe garlands of flowery compliments for the brows of Ursinus, and Olevianus, and Frederick III, " of noble, pious memory," and then modify the lofty commendations by cooly ponouncing them "rationalistic," by condemning their Liturgy as "pseudo-liturgical at best," "a *hortus siccus*," (*i. e.*, a garden of dead grass), and by perverting some of the fundamental doctrines of their Catechism into errors against which that noble and sacred testimony of their faith was lifted boldly up? Self-contradictions, like these, would be perpetrated by other men to the certain ruin of any scholarly reputation they might enjoy. But Dr. Nevin indulges in them so freely, so confidently, that he seems to feel assured, from what guarantees it would be hard to say, that all will be received not only with submissive acquiescence, but with loud, partizan applause.

And yet in this, as in some other things, he may be mistaken. Men are learning to read both history and theology for themselves, and to exercise their own honest, intelligent judgment regarding their testimony and teachings. The Church has begun to see, that not every utterance or ukase issuing from this dictatorial source, is in harmony with actual facts, or in accordance with actual truth. There may be no disposition to doubt the integrity of those who make the declarations. No one may call in question that they believe what they say. But their liability to change and error has been too often demonstrated to give their mere unproved assertions the authority of law. No stronger evidence of this could be needed than is furnished by the history of the Liturgical movement to the completion and report of the new Order of Worship.

That movement passed through three distinctly marked periods. The *first* began with the Synod of Lancaster, in 1847, and extended to the Synod of Baltimore, in 1852, including the important action of the Synod of Norristown upon the subject. During this period the ruling purpose was, as expressed in the most distinct and unequivocal language adopted as an explicit declaration of the Synod's judgment, that the Liturgy contemplated should contain such "forms as were recognized by our fathers," and that it should be strictly modelled "after the old Palatinate Liturgy as our true ideal." The *second* period began with the consent given by the Synod of Baltimore, in 1852, to the Committee's proposition to construct the proposed Liturgy upon a broader basis than that which had been originally adopted. This change of basis allowed of certain important modifications of the plan upon which the work had been begun. And yet those modifications were of such a character, and were so carefully guarded by special explanations, that a Liturgy might be prepared in accordance with them, which would involve no material or essential departure from established Reformed principles of worship. The Provisional Liturgy was, in the main, such a book. And yet the Synod of Allentown, at which it was received, did not endorse it, much less adopt it, but simply allowed it to go forth on trial, as an experiment. Even the Committee had so lively a sense of the responsibility of proposing the work, though framed strictly, as Dr. Nevin affirms, according to instructions given, that they asked for no more than this, and had misgivings even in asking this. Why these misgivings? To what did this cautious legislation refer? Manifestly to those peculiarities in a few of the services of the book, which contemplated some change in the cultus and worship of the Church. Thus far, then, the Committee and the Synod seemed to agree upon the necessity of adhering predominantly to the established faith and practice of the Church in a genuine sixteenth century sense. Dr. Nevin regarded it as a matter of formal congratulation, that the work would "be found in harmony with the theological life and genius of the Church, for whose more particular use it had been prepared." (See Report of the Committee to the Synod of Allentown, Minutes, p. 81.) Not a word was then breathed of its "not pretending at all to be of one order with the liturgical practice of the German Reformed Church;" not an intimation was then given, that the practice of the German Reformed Church was "from the beginning believed to have been too naked and bald." Assertions like these were reserved for five years later.

Meanwhile, however, the movement entered the *third period* of its progress and development. This was the period of the Revision. Most earnestly was the immediate revision opposed by those who now advocate and urge the adoption of the new measures. The only probable, and partly avowed reasons for this opposition, have been given on a previous page. It did not avail, however. The Revision was ordered. The principles on which it was to be made were explicitly stated. They were those of the Baltimore basis. Dr. Nevin himself acknowledges this. Moreover, in connection with these principles, the Committee was directed to have regard to the suggestions made by several Classes, in regard to certain changes and modifications of the Provisional Liturgy. Of these, the Classes of Mercersburg and of Lancaster, in whose midst, Drs. Nevin, Schaff, Wolff, Harbaugh and Gerhart, all members of the Liturgical Committee, resided, declared with special emphasis their desire that such modifications should be made. As an additional guide in the prosecution of their work, the Committee had before it the very significant fact, that the novel peculiarities of that Liturgy had been almost universally repudiated by the Church. With all the influence of Professors and the schools in their favor, with all the strong desires of many worthy pastors who had been sedulous'y taught to admire those peculiarities to introduce them, and with all the careful and quiet efforts made by a few zealous friends to introduce them "without observation," they had signally failed to prove acceptable. The book was largely used as a pastor's hand-book, and very much that it contained in this form was admired. But beyond this, it met with but exceedingly limited favor. All this the Committee knew when the work of revision was commenced, and whilst that work was being prosecuted. And from all this it should have been easy for them to determine upon the course to be pursued, if they desired to conform their work to the plain instructions of Synod, to the expressed wishes of the Classes, and to the obvious desires of the Church at large. It may be unhesitatingly affirmed, also, that it was the general expectation and hope, even of most of those brethren in the ministry who may have theoretically agreed with the majority of the Committee in their peculiar views, that due regard would be paid to these facts, and that material modifications would be made, both in the form and doctrinal expressions of the more ritualistic services of the Provisional Liturgy.

To all this, however, little or no regard was paid, as may clearly be seen by simply holding these rules for the revision in one hand, and comparing with them the Order of Worship as submitted to the Synods of York and Dayton. It requires no profound learning; nothing but that plain good sense which every lay member of the Church possesses, to see that the two things do not tally, but are in material and essential disagreement. To exhibit this diversity distinctly to the reader's view, the points of flagrant disagreement are here placed in parallel columns.

THE INSTRUCTIONS OF SYNOD DIRECTED:

1. That the Revised Liturgy should be framed after the pattern of the worship of "the *Primitive Church*, as far as this can be ascertained from the Holy Scriptures, the oldest ecclesiastical writers, and the Liturgies of the Greek and Latin Churches of the 3d and 4th centuries."

2. Synod required that "among later Liturgies, special reference ought to be had to the Old Palatinate and other Reformed Liturgies of the sixteenth century."

3. The Committee was directed to provide "several forms for those portions of the Liturgy which are most frequently used, as the regular service of the Lord's Day, and the celebration of the Lord's Supper, some shorter and some longer, some with and some without responses."

4. It was most explicitly enjoined that the new Liturgy should recognize and encourage the use of "*extemporaneous prayer*," nay, that it should seek to promote the exercise of the gift, by leaving sufficient room for it in the several services.

5. The Synod of Easton reiterated substantially the directions of the Baltimore basis, laying very special stress upon the necessity of so prosecuting the revision, that the proposed Liturgy should not be "inconsistent with *established* Liturgical principles and usages, *or with the devotional and doctrinal genius of the German Reformed Church.*" It was further ordered that due consideration should be given to the suggestions of the several Classes, calling for fewer responses, and for a modification of certain doctrinal expressions in the sacramental and some other services.

THE COMMITTEE ON THE CONTRARY:

1. Made the Liturgies of the Latin and Greek Churches of the 3d and 4th centuries their ruling pattern, although it is universally known that the worship of the *Primitive Church* had then become materially modified and seriously corrupted.

2. In the Revised Liturgy scarcely a single trace of such reference can be found, excepting in the case of some co-incidence of those Reformed Liturgies with 3d and 4th century services.

3. The Revised Liturgy or new Order of Worship, shows that this direction was utterly disregarded by the Committee. It contains but one form for each of the services named, and that in the fullest sense responsive. The service for the Lord's Supper, also differs totally from any known in the German Reformed Church, and much more closely resembles the Romish mass.

4. The new Order of Worship ignores free prayer, evidently discourages its use, and contemplates its ultimate, total exclusion. Its reigning spirit is essentially incompatible with extemporaneous prayer.

5. The new Order of Worship shows that instead of following these reiterated directions, the Committee steadily persisted in carrying out their own views, interpreting instructions given to suit those views, or wholly disregarding the instructions. There is no diminution of the number of responses, but an increase of them, and a multiplication of services containing them, to the entire exclusion of the many non-responsive forms of the Provisional Liturgy. There is no real modification of objectionable doctrinal expressions. And the book is flagrantly at variance with the established Liturgical principles, and with the devotional and doctrinal genius of the German Reformed Church.

It will serve to increase the real significance of these strong contrasts between what the Synod directed the Committee to do, and what has actually been done, if another fact is remembered. The Synod and the Church *had every reason to expect* that the Liturgy in the course of preparation, would in all material and essential respects, be truly and genuinely a German Reformed Liturgy. Whatever may have been the thoughts or desires of a few individuals here and there, who held doctrinal and ritualistic views at variance with established historical Reformed standards and principles, there is not the least doubt that the general expectation of those ministers and lay members of the Church who paid any attention to the movement, was, that the Committee would prepare and report a book which would be found in full substantial harmony with the instructions given, and therefore with the prevailing faith and practice of the German Reformed Church. There was every reason for cherishing such an expectation. No intimation had ever been given by the Synod, of a purpose or wish radically to change the old cultus of the Church, or materially to modify any of her fundamental doctrines. She was not known, or suspected even, to be dissatisfied with her peculiar denominational characteristics. More than once, indeed, in years past, when assertions or intimations were made which seemed to charge the Synod with countenancing doctrines or tendencies which involved revolutionary results, those who made them were denounced as false witnesses, and declared to be enemies of the Church. Can it be forgotten, that it was then boldly and unqualifiedly affirmed, that nineteenth-twentieths of the Church repudiated the doubtful things of the peculiar views, as an argument sufficient to silence the tongues of those who were said to be defaming us?

Furthermore, the Committee was composed largely of members whose official position in the Church laid them under special obligations of strict fidelity to her traditional genius and spirit. There was good ground to suppose, therefore, that of all her ministers, they would be most zealous in their efforts to maintain and defend the integrity of all her doctrines and legitimate usages, and that they would be the last to propose or advocate any material or essential modification of either. Even the memorable report of 1862 ("The Liturgical question"), with all its strange pleadings, could hardly have then been taken by the Synod of Chambersburg, to mean what it is now seen to have meant. Notwithstanding its very extreme positions and offensive statements, the belief was still cherished, that the Committee would not, could not carry out the principles advocated in that report, to such an extreme degree as is exhibited in the new Order of Worship. Excepting, perhaps, a few more intimate and zealous disciples of the radical movement, or a few opponents of that movement, who were regarded as false alarmists, who dreamed that the Committee really intended to produce a book which would be so utterly at variance with some of the fundamental principles of the past faith and practice of the Church?

These are not fictions, or even facts founded on fictions. They are matters of official explicit record, and of actual occurrence. Their authority, therefore, in the case before us is indisputable and final. If the purpose and the desires of the Synod are not to be mainly ascertained from resolutions adopted, and from instructions given, to what source can we look for positive and certain information? Is it not obvious and just, that whatever else may have been done or not done, said, or simply acquiesced in, must be interpreted in conformity with such resolutions, and such instructions! The Committee, therefore, has no right to go back of the actual record to find a sense to justify their course, at variance with the plain import of the record itself.

From this historical review two things are evident: 1. That the Synod and Church at large never contemplated or desired the preparation or introduction of any other system of worship but one which would be in full undoubted harmony "with the devotional and doctrinal genius of the German Reformed Church," and gave no authority for the preparation of any other. 2. That at least during fifteen years of their labors, down to the Synod of Chambersburg in 1862, the Committee professed and seemed to be prosecuting their liturgical labors in full accordance with the expressed wishes and purpose of the Synod. Some things, indeed, were said and done, which foreshadowed evil, and excited apprehensions in the hearts of those who saw in them indications of a purpose to make the liturgical movement a means of introducing serious changes in the "devotional and doctrinal genius" of our Church. But all intimations of the existence of such a purpose were silenced for the time by ridicule or indignant disclaimers, and all the fears expressed were pronounced preposterous. Why should the work be condemned before it was done? How unjust, it was said, to create suspicions against the book, by such unfair charges, before it was completed and could be carefully and calmly examined in all its parts? Why excite doubts as to the intentions of the Committee faithfully to perform the work intrusted to them according to instructions given, and given largely in compliance with their own suggestions and recommendations?

Meanwhile that work was actually progressing with steady, unyielding determination, according to the principles and plan now fully developed in the new Order of Worship. Meanwhile, also, influences and agencies were zealously employed to prepare the Synod and the Church, if possible, for a favorable reception of the work which was thus performed.

It is in the light of such facts as these, that the true character of the course pursued by the Committee becomes apparent. The "Vindication" may defend or extenuate that course as it pleases, all will not avail to exculpate the Committee from the charge of disobedience to express Synodical instructions. The Synod ordered a certain work to be done in a certain way. The Committee did the work in quite another way, and in a way "materially and essentially" different from that prescribed. Dr. Nevin may call this what he likes. I know of but one name for it, and that is disobedience to instructions. The endurance by Synod of such disobedience, its patience and forbearance towards it, its occasional seeming tacit concessions, may be capable of explanation or not. All this does not change the real aspect of the case, any more than a parent's leniency towards a disobedient child, changes the fact of its disobedience. Absalom was none the less blamable for all David's pliancy. The Revised Liturgy is "essentially and materially" a different Order of Worship from that contemplated and called for by the actions of the Synod under whose direction it was to be prepared, and is so because those actions were disregarded. And now, as a consequence of this course of the Committee, we are shut up to the dilemma, either of contending earnestly for the maintenance and defence of our long established faith and practice, against radical and subversive innovations, or, of timely and recreantly surrendering evangelical denominational principles, to the sweeping demands of ultra-high-church sacramentalism.

Such, then, is the theory of the course of the Committee and of the way in which the Liturgical movement was carried forward to the present posture of things, which is furnished by a careful and candid consideration of the history of the movement. And this review of the case with its obvious lessons and inferences, is the only reply I will make to the distorted caricature drawn by the author of the "Vindication" on pp. 11–13 of his tract.

But what, now, on the other hand, is Dr. Nevin's account of the matter? How does he explain the fact, that while the Liturgical movement began with most distinctly avowed purposes of a faithful adherence to German Reformed principles and usages, it ended with the presentation of a system, devotional and impliedly doctrinal, too, subversive of that system? How does he attempt to justify the course of the Committee in avowedly prosecuting its work according to instructions given, and yet in the end producing a book for which it is not claimed even, that it is in real harmony with those instructions? Let us see.

1. He begins with an unreserved repudiation of those instructions, so far as their details are concerned. "*Let no one imagine*, however, that I propose to follow him in the details of his pretended historical argument. That would be, indeed, both time and labor thrown away" (p. 10). No, truly. It would have taken a great deal more time, and a vastly larger

amount of labor, than Dr. Nevin could well spare from his main purpose, to have done this. Only "imagine" that he had attempted to follow "the details of that historical argument." Those "details" were a literal citation of the acts and resolutions of Synod, setting forth, as has been shown, in distinct and unequivocal terms, what the Committee was directed to do in the preparation of the work on hand. The original plan and principles adopted by the Synod of Norristown, need not be pressed. Allow them to have been superseded by the basis to which the Synod of Baltimore assented by way of experiment in 1852. Only suppose our author endeavoring to show that the Committee had faithfully and strictly adhered to the principles of that basis, and that his new Order of Worship was in full essential harmony with it. He would have found himself called upon to solve some exceedingly vexatious problems, and to answer some very impertinent, annoying questions. Possibly, from some vagueness in the phrase, "worship of the Primitive Church," employed in the first principle of that basis, the flagrant disagreement of the leading forms of the new system with the spirit and genius of any mode of worship known to Apostolic and strictly primitive times (*i. e.* during the first century of the Christian era), might have been plausibly and dexterously defended. Possibly it might have been shown, to the satisfaction at least of those who may be somewhat captivated by the innovations, or tempted to favor them without fully perceiving or considering what all they involve in the way of surrendering fundamental principles of evangelical Christianity, that the term "primitive" covered the third and fourth centuries, and permitted the Committee not simply to ascertain as well as they might through "the Latin and Greek Liturgies," of those centuries such elements of primitive worship as might be culled from them, but to adopt, in large measure, the peculiarities of those later Liturgies. Difficult as it would be to prove all this, and greatly as the difficulty might, if possible, increase his mournful irascibility at being balked at all in his "Vindication" by so paltry and contemptible a matter as this,—suppose he be relieved by conceding what it might be so troublesome to make out, in regard to this point.

But what would he do with the *second* principle of the Baltimore basis? It requires, as has been seen, that "*special reference ought to be had to the old Palatinate and other Reformed Liturgies of the* 16*th century.*" Now, only "imagine" Dr. Nevin writing a *true* historical "Vindication" of the Committee's new "Order of Worship," grappling with this *law* for the preparation of the work. "Imagine" the author of the "Liturgical question," and of all its calumnies upon such "pseudo-liturgical" "pulpit hand-books" as the venerated fathers of our Church prepared, recommended, and used, endeavoring to show how much earnest and respectful reference had been made by him, for instance, to those early Reformed Liturgies, and how largely their scheme of worship, forms and prayers, were used in the preparation of the new "Order." Imagine him striving to show how fully the forms of that "Order" for the regular service of the Lord's day, for preparation for the Lord's Supper, and for the Lord's Supper itself, harmonized in their "devotional and doctrinal genius," with the forms of the Palatinate or any other old German Reformed Liturgy for those same services. Imagine him attempting to demonstrate by an actual comparison of their general structure (I do not say details, for Dr. Nevin dislikes "details"), how cordially they harmonize, and how beautifully they agreed.

Or suppose, once more, we picture to our mind this same author, endeavoring to prove the agreement of the "Order," in all essential respects with the *third* principle and the *fourth* of that same basis. Those principles require provision for non-responsive forms for all the leading services, and for free prayer. Any "Vindication," worthy of the name, of the Committee's work, must show, therefore, that this law again has been faithfully obeyed; that the new "Order" complies with its demands. Now let us see how astutely, how triumphantly the obedience called for, can be shown to have been rendered. Where will he begin? Where will he end in the demonstration? He takes up the new "Order." He searches for the non-responsive forms required. He seeks for some such recognition of free prayer as is called for, and as may be found repeatedly in the Provisional Liturgy of 1857,—that book which he most earnestly contended was a unit of perfectly harmonious parts. Can he find, what yet must be there, if the book shall be fairly vindicated against the charge of not being such a Liturgy as the Synod ordered the Committee to prepare, and as the Committee has a right to ask the Church to adopt? No, it is not to be found. What! not a single instance? No, not one. These two principles were utterly ignored, boldly discarded in the actual production of the new "Order." They were incompatible with the principles and system of doctrine and worship which had come to prevail in the third and fourth centuries, through the influence of such ultra sacerdotal prelatists as Dr. Nevin's great model *Cyprian* (see "Dr. Nevin and his Antagonist," by J. H. A. Bomberger; "Mercersburg Review," Vol. V., 1853, pp. 177–8).

What a dilemma! A vaunted defence of an "Order of Worship," supposed in the course of preparation to be proceeding according to principles laid down by the Committee itself, and demanding adoption unless the Synod would stultify itself, while that defence dare not bring the work to the test of those very principles! A defence professedly based upon historical evidence, and yet shrinking from a fair application of that evidence as derivable only from authentic official records! No wonder Dr. Nevin lost patience with those "details"—those insolent, audacious details, which from the calm pages of that obnoxious tract, dared to confront him with their quiet but irresistible reproof. The testimony which they bore against a course which had issued in the Revised Liturgy, plainly, unqualifiedly condemned that course, and the pernicious issue. And there was no way of escaping the force of the testimony, but by obliterating it. This was the easiest method of disposing of the offensive thing. Set the details aside. Or let them be shorn of their force by ridiculing, caricaturing them. If they cannot be met and answered, they may be laughed at, and their testimony may be drowned by the noise of sarcastic derision.

But by what right, it may well be asked, does Dr. Nevin affect so summarily to dispose of what bears against his cause? On what authority does he so arbitrarily rule out the only reliable and official source of proof in the case? Other Committees or members of the Synod have never presumed to claim or to exercise such liberties. When certain duties were assigned to them, they were expected to perform those duties as far as possible in accordance with the spirit, at least, if not the letter of their instructions. And they would have been deemed deserving of censure had they pursued a contrary course. Why then should a matter of such vital moment as the preparation of a Liturgy, and in reference to which there has been so much explicit ecclesiastical legislation, be allowed to form an exception? Why should Dr. Nevin be permitted to claim exemption from faithful compliance with Synodical instructions, and to scatter them as chaff, by tempest of his displeasure?

2. Thus rid of the annoyance of those historical details, the author of the "Vindication" proceeds to construct his defensive argument upon quite another basis. This is not done, indeed, in any direct, frank, and comprehensive way, by which the reader might see at a glance the facts or assumptions on which the theory rests, and of which it is made up. If the theory was sound, and in harmony with the record, it would, or should have been as easy for the author to put its parts together in a summary way, as it was for him to manufacture the caricature given on pp. 11-13 of his tract. Then it might have been seen in its true character, and judged according to its merits. It seems, however, to have suited his purpose better in this case, to scatter the assertions or assumptions on which the argument is based, over most of the pages of the historical section of his tract, now in one connection, than in another, and always in such a way as to cover their weakness, and to conceal their inconsistencies. Professing to take a broad and profound view of the case, the breadth is found, nevertheless, to be like that on which airy castles rest, and the profundity a shallow depth of thin transparent fictions. And

yet, all is done in so self-confident and defiant a manner, that less scrutinizing minds may be tempted to regard all as real, substantial truth, simply by the unblushing boldness with which it is asserted.

But let these scattered parts of the pretended argument be gathered together. Let them be fairly considered in their connection, and in their consistency or incompatibility with facts. Subject them to such tests as they must be able to endure if they shall be allowed to stand for what they are given. By this just process, let us see how much, or how little they are really worth, and whether they can, indeed, bear the structure which is so confidently built upon them.

Four items seem to be comprehended in Dr. Nevin's basis, and these, though given disconnectedly, are so dependent upon each other, that if one fails, all fall through. The first of these points is, *that the Synod had a clear and distinct knowledge of the plan and design of the Committee, as those have been executed in the Revised Liturgy.* It is asserted, not only by Dr. Nevin, but by others on the same side, that the Synod well understood, especially after the assent given to the principles of the Baltimore report, what the Committee intended to do, and was doing, in the prosecution of the work assigned to them. This was known, it is affirmed, from the tenor of those principles; from the character of the Provisional Liturgy in which those principles were carried out; and from the avowals of some of the members of the Committee publicly made from time to time. And yet, with all this full knowledge and distinct understanding of the case, the Committee was allowed and encouraged to go forward with their work in the very way in which they executed it.

What, now, does all this imply? Evidently, either that the Synod started out in the Liturgical movement with the fixed purpose of revolutionizing its cultus and worship in the radical way now advocated and proposed, or, that, though starting with the design of simply improving its established system in a manner consistent with itself, this purpose was afterwards made to give way to revolutionary measures, subversive of the established liturgical system and usages of the Church. It is assumed, therefore, that, whatever may have been the *original* design, the Synod consented, with a full understanding of the case, to the prosecution of a scheme by which the German Reformed Church would be "essentially and materially" removed from that apostolic primitive foundation, both in doctrine and liturgical practice, on which she had been planted in the 16th century, and be relaid upon a foundation whose chief stones should be gathered from the third and fourth centuries. Ignoring the three hundred years of her history since the Reformation, overleaping the Reformation itself as a sort of illegitimate* birth, closing the eye to the "general mass of Romish corruptions" (Anxious Bench, 2nd. ed., p. 9, 10), which "abounded" during the many centuries of Romish dominion preceding the Reformation, the Synod, with full knowledge and apprehension of what was meant, permitted and encouraged the Committee to cast themselves at the feet of the renowned fathers of the third and fourth centuries, and obtain from such as Athanasius, Basil, Cyprian, and Tertullian, not only some suggestions in regard to worship, nor merely some such prayers or collects of universally acknowledged excellence as that of Chrysostom, but the ruling principles of their entire system.

Could any assumption be more preposterously absurd than this? It seems incredible that Dr. Nevin himself, in calmer hours, can believe it; still more incredible, that he should expect it to be accepted for truth by others. That a Synod, representing a Church whose doctrinal standard, whose spirit and genius, whose constitution, whose entire previous history, and whose actually predominant faith and practice, were a most positive and decided protest against those essential departures from primitive Apostolic Christianity, which characterized the Church of the centuries named, and from which, as poisonous germs and seeds, the still grosser errors and abuses of subsequent centuries sprang; that such a Synod should have been persuaded by the propositions of a single report, read once, or at most, twice, by the published views of Dr. Nevin and two or three disciples of his views, or by any other considerations, to give up the liberty wherewith Christ had made the Church free, and to let her become entangled again with the yoke of bondage; this is incredible.

And it is, likewise, so utterly at variance with the facts of the case, that the author of the Vindication repeatedly contradicts himself in trying to make out this point. Unable to defend the course pursued by the Committee, on the ground of special instructions given, he takes refuge to this general view of the case. Hard pressed for sufficient evidence, he boldly assumes that the Synod knew how the work was being done, and approved of the plan.† And yet, in other connections, he concedes the very point at issue, by confessing that neither the Committee nor the Church foresaw whither matters were tending. On p. 32, 33, of the "Vindication," we read in reference to the tract of 1862–3, entitled, "Liturg. Question," and in which the principles subsequently carried out in the Revised Liturgy are set forth: "I hardly *expected* or wished the Synod to fall in

---

* Who cares for rhetorical compliments bestowed, grudgingly, if not from policy, upon the Reformation and the fathers of the Reformed Church of the 16th century, when their principles are denounced, and their practice is discarded?

† "The Synod knew perfectly well where the Committee stood in regard to the whole subject." Vind., p. 36.

with the high view of altar worship presented in the tract." On p. 38, below, we read in reference to the Revised Liturgy, that the Committee "*felt that they had been successful* in bringing the book into a form suitable to the wants of the Church, *and likely now to come into general use.*" On p. 46, however, we read that, to a large extent, the entire Western portion of the Church was "in profound ignorance of the subject." And once more, in strange forgetfulness of what was said on p. 38, as quoted above, Dr. Nevin says, (p. 48): "how far the work itself, in the form in which it is now before the public, may prove satisfactory to the Church, *remains yet to be seen.*" What does all this mean? The Synod knew what the Committee was doing. It approved, substantially, of the radical course they were pursuing, and was impatient for the completion of the work in such style and form, that the Church might be led, without delay, into the new Eden which would thus be opened to her. And yet, after all the faithful toils of the Committee, according to the mind of Synod and desires of the Church, after all their success in bringing the book into the very form proposed and longed for, a form entirely "suitable to the wants of the Church," and "likely to come into general use," it "REMAINS TO BE SEEN how far it may prove satisfactory to the Church!"

Nor is this all. Notwithstanding the bold assumptions in regard to the Synod's clear knowledge of the Committee's position and doings, and notwithstanding the Committee's consciousness of having succeeded so satisfactorily in doing their work, as Dr. Nevin is fully persuaded the Synod wanted it done, only see with what extreme anxiety, trepidation even, that completed work is laid before Synod, and what excessively modest and moderate hopes are entertained concerning its acceptableness. The work, we are told (p. 41), came to Synod, "asking barely permission to live, and nothing more." And this is literally true. Whether we turn to the reports of the permanent Committee on the Liturgy, or to the reports of special Synodical Committees from time to time, or consult the speeches made and articles written in favor of the work, the same timid, lowly, half-hoping spirit meets us. Like the Pope on Maundy Thursday, it seems to bow as a very servus servorum, and beg the privilege of being allowed only some little opportunity of doing some small service for the dear Church of that most incomparable symbol, the Heidelberg Catechism, and of trying, merely by way of experiment, whether it may possibly be able to improve its doctrines and worship, its spirit and life, by a few modifications of these made, in conformity with third and fourth century Cyprianic, Athanasian, and Ambrosian principles! Is this the language, is this the suit of a movement which feels confidently assured that it has been carried forward faithfully according to instructions, and in essential harmony with the knowledge and understanding of the Body by which that movement was inaugurated, and under the direction of which it professedly reached the desired result?

But there is still another fact, showing how utterly groundless this assumption is. The Committee acknowledged more than once in the course of their work, *that they themselves did not foresee where they would end.* "Their studies, conferences, and experimental endeavors, shut them up, *in a very slow way,* to this finally, as the only proper conclusion of their work. They were themselves brought more and more under the power of an idea *which carried them with inexorable force its own way;* so that they were compelled to change again and again what they had previously prepared, till all was brought *to take at last its present shape.*" This confession may be found on p. 39 of the "Liturgical Question," published in the Fall of 1862. A similar confession is reiterated on p. 21 of the "Vindication." Taking these admissions in connection with other hints of like import occasionally given, do they not most clearly prove, that even the Committee was moving forward more or less hap-hazard, and walking uncertainly in dim twilight at least, if not groping in the dark? Do they not concede that Dr. Nevin and his coadjutors, felt themselves at the mercy of a current which, for aught they knew, might carry them, "with inexorable force," up the muddy Tiber, as well as up the limpid Rhine? And yet, forsooth, we are asked to believe that the Synod knew perfectly well what the Committee was doing, how they were doing it, and where the doing would end; and, with such knowledge, fully approved of all. Will Dr. Nevin reconcile this palpable contradiction?

For my own part, without laying claim to any greater discernment than belongs to most common men, it has seemed clear to me for at least six years, that the movement was tending towards a result essentially and materially at variance with the original design and expressed desires of the Synod. And I think that Dr. Nevin deludes himself, through excessive modesty, when he says that the Committee, including himself of course, were mere passive instruments in the hands of an inexorable ritualistic power, which carried them, whether they would or no, its own way. He may disclaim the credit, and yet many will give him the credit of supposing that the author of "Early Christianity" and "Cyprian," in the *Mercersburg Review,* could hardly have been so much in the dark, as he meekly imagines himself to have been, upon the points involved in the liturgical movement. It is true, that nothing suggested by me, in the Committee, or set forth in the long series of articles published in the *Messenger* in 1862, showing the irreconcilable disagreement between the established cultus of the Reformed Church, the instructions of Synod, and the radical ritualistic course which the Committee seemed then determined upon pursuing, might give him any light or satisfaction. But it will not

4

be easy to persuade any one that he needed light, or was sailing without compass, in the dark. He saw clearly what he regarded as the utter misery and outrageousness of the free-prayer system, and gave a most forcible exhibition of his views upon that subject, in 1862. At the same time he had gained a perfect insight into what he considered the worthlessness of "mechanical directory" "pulpit hand-books," such as our Church, and others, had always used, when forms were used at all. And surely, it will be concluded, that he must have seen further into the import of the only ritualistic alternative left, than he seems willing to think he did. And yet, as he disclaims this, it may be proper to accept of the concession. But is it any wonder, that amidst conflicting testimony, and contradictory facts like these, the mind of the Synod should remain unsettled and somewhat confused? Is it not rather far more in accordance with reason, and all the circumstances of the case, to suppose, *that Synod took it for granted, that* whatever might be said on the one side, or on the other, *the Committee would no doubt, in the end, produce a liturgy in essential and material harmony with instructions, and suited to the historical genius of the Church.*

It will serve to expose still further, how gratuitous and groundless this assumption is, if one more fact is considered. The Synod, after 1857, possessed a means of ascertaining what seemed to be the mind and purpose of the Committee, which was far more tangible and reliable than mere floating rumors or vague suppositions could supply. That means was furnished in the Provisional Liturgy published that year. In the Provisional Liturgy, the Committee gave a full exemplification of the ideal Liturgy recommended in the Baltimore Report of 1852, and of that sort of a Liturgy which they thought "the Church needed, and which would satisfy the expectations and wants of the German Reformed Church." (Report of the Committee in the Minutes of the Synod of Allentown, p. 80.) Now the Synod had a right to take that Liturgy as a fair exponent of the utmost extent to which the Committee thought the Church should go, in its Liturgical developments. The work, they said, was most carefully prepared, was the result of mature deliberation, and was declared to be, in the judgment of the Committee, "in harmony with the theological life and historical genius of the Church for whose use it had been prepared." Where, then, could the Synod have gone to learn the views and designs of Dr. Nevin and the other members of the Committee, so properly as to that book. But suppose the Synod derived its knowledge of the subject from the Provisional Liturgy, as the best source for obtaining such knowledge. To what conclusion would this lead? Was it calculated to produce the impression that the Revised work would be prosecuted on a basis essentially different from that on which the Provisional work was constructed? Most assuredly not. If the Provisional Liturgy, therefore, was to be regarded as a declaration of Dr. Nevin's views in the case, nothing could well have been better calculated to mislead the mind of Synod as to the manner in which the work of revision would be carried on, or as to the nature of the result to which that work has come. The material and essential diversities between the two books will be more fully set forth in the next section of this tract. But they are so broad and deep, that it is not surprising that so many should be disappointed with the result. And this especially in view of the fact, a fact not to be forgotten, that the result, such as it is, was reached in disregard of the expressed wishes and suggestions of the Classes, as shown on a previous page.

How evident, in view of these facts, that Dr. Nevin has been deluded by his own assumptions. The "broad exposition," therefore, instead of demonstrating the "universal falsehood" of my historical analysis of the detailed instructions by which the work should have been governed, proves itself to be most false and deceptive. And so sure am I that he has fallen into error on this point that I appeal most confidently to those brethren who constituted the several Synods concerned, in confirmation of the fact given above. Whatever may have been the impression of a few who desired a book like the new Order of Worship, the expectation of the large majority was, that the Committee would prepare and offer a liturgy with less responsive services, and such positive modifications both as to form and doctrinal expressions, as would bring it into closer conformity with the established faith and practice of the Church, than even the Provisional Liturgy was, upon full trial, felt to be.

A second item in Dr. Nevin's theory seems to be, *that the Synod from time to time approved of the course which the Committee was pursuing, and thus conditionally committed itself to the adoption of their work when done.* After what has been said in exposure of the fallacy of the point just disposed of, but little need be added to prove the error of this item. For as it rests mainly upon the same assumptions, it falls with them. The means however, by which it is attempted to fortify this assertion, serve to show how great a mistake was made by the author, in abandoning the substantial ground furnished by official records, and taking refuge to a visionary conceit.

First of all a general appeal is made to the fact that the Synod from time to time adopted the reports made by the Committee of the progress of their work. Such reports were made at Martinsburg 1850, Baltimore 1852, Chambersburg 1855, &c. A sufficient answer to this is, that in the adoption of such reports, it is never thought or intended that a Synod should commit itself to the endorsement of all the statements they may contain; and then, so far as the reports in question are concerned, there is nothing in them to indicate the purpose of the Committee to produce such a work as the Revised Liturgy.

But, in the next place, special stress is laid upon the action of the Synods of Chambersburg in 1862, and of Lewisburg in 1865. Both those Synods met during the period of the Revision. To save repetition, the reader is referred to pp. 21–40 of this tract for an account of the action of the former of these Synods upon the report of the majority of the Committee then rendered. But the members of that Synod will no doubt be greatly astonished to learn that the vote finally taken upon the Liturgical question, then discussed, committed the majority to an endorsement of the extreme sentiments set forth in the tract entitled the "Liturgical Question." They will be likely to repudiate this assumption most earnestly, and to declare that they were not called upon at all to vote upon the sentiments of the report of the majority of the Committee as set forth in that tract any more than upon the sentiments of the minority report, as presented by Dr. E Heiner, Dr. S. R. Fisher and myself. The truth of the case is that the only point gained by Dr. Nevin and his friends at the Synod of Chambersburg, was that of the indefinite postponement of the work of revision. That the Committee had, indeed, spoken very boldly in their report, no one denies. Nor will any one deny that it was remarkable that some of the views they proclaimed were allowed to pass without some decided expression of disapproval. Certainly no Synod of the German Reformed Church could now be induced to endorse those views. But it is a most unwarrantable assumption for Dr Nevin to conclude that because the sentiments of that report escaped formal rebuke, the Synod approved of them, or of the Committee's utterance of them. And just as little was the Committee justified in assuming, that because no such rebuke was administered, they were authorized subsequently to carry out the work of revision, in accordance with the extreme principles advocated in that report. For to all intents the Baltimore basis was still in full force.

The reference to the Synod of Lewisburg, in 1865, is of still less account for our author's argument. For that Synod not only expressed no opinion in regard to the work as it was going on, but had no opportunity to do so, as only a few copies of the specimens then completed were circulated, and those privately.

At most, therefore, all that can be claimed on this point is, that Synod held its judgment in reserve until the whole work should be completed, and a full opportunity should be afforded to judge of its real merits. Meanwhile the matter was confided to the hands of the Committee, in the hope that it would discharge its duty in faithful conformity with wishes distinctly expressed, and with instructions definitely given.

If the successive Synods of the Eastern portion of the Church meant by their actions, what Dr. Nevin claims was meant, those Synods were consciously committing themselves to a most serious violation of the Constitution of the Church, and to such a fundamental change of some of her essential doctrines and usages as is expressly forbidden by that charter of spiritual right, without the previous consent of the Classes. With the careful, explicit wording of that Constitution before them; with a knowledge of the jealousy with which the Synod has ever guarded its articles against violation; with a conviction of the prevailing agreement of the mind of the Church with the principles laid down in those articles, and of her sincere, intelligent attachment to the denominational peculiarities which they exhibit; can it be for a moment really supposed, that the Synod nevertheless meant to clothe the Committee with unqualified, discretionary power, to make whatever radical changes they pleased and to give assurances that those changes would be as unqualifiedly approved and accepted? Who can believe this? Implicit, if not blind, as the confidence of the Church in any of her members might be, it is a reproach upon her good sense, her self-respect, and her obligation to regard her constitutional law, to assume that she could be guilty of such folly.

But the author of the "Vindication" ventures boldly upon *a third assumption* in support of his historical theory. He *interprets the action of the Synods of York and Dayton last Fall, as a virtual endorsement of the Revised Liturgy.* This is indeed not categorically asserted. But the declarations made on pp. 40–47, in regard to what was done by the Eastern Synod at York, last October, and on pp. 46–47 in reference to the action of the General Synod in Dayton, last December, are plainly designed to produce this impression. The only evidence in support of the assumption that the Synod of York endorses the Committee's course is derived from the *preamble* of the special report there adopted. But until Dr. Nevin can explain why the original third resolution of that report was stripped of every expression commendatory of the Revised Liturgy, and reduced to the simple form in which it was adopted, this appeal to the preamble cannot help his argument (See p. 32 of this tract.) His inability to explain this is only too manifest from his utter silence in regard to it. He would have the reader believe, that the special report in question, was adopted pretty much as it now stands on the minutes of the Synod at York, though he knew how materially it had been amended in what was, for his purpose a vital point. And then to show how little the Synod meant to commit itself to the Revised Liturgy by anything the report in question may contain, we find, at the close of the action in the case, the very explicit and significant statement: "*In the foregoing action of Synod, it was understood, that the vote on the adoption of the report, did not commit those who voted for it as to the merits of the book?*"

If Dr. Nevin meant to be perfectly fair and candid in discussing this subject, why did he, not only make no allusion to the change of the third resolution above referred to, but wholly ignore this official qualification of the action of the York Synod? And why, furthermore, does he withhold the fact, that the Report, as so materially amended, *was carried, at last, by the votes of those very members of the Synods who had opposed it in its original form*, because in that form the Revised Liturgy was approved and commended? For in the fifty-three votes found in favor of the Report, there are at least twenty-four names which would not have been given for the full adoption of the Revised Liturgy. Is the concealment of known facts, ingenuous or the opposite?

How little ground the action of the General Synod at Dayton furnishes for Dr. Nevin's sweeping and boastful assumption, may be sufficiently seen from the following explanation of the import and intended bearing of the report there adopted, as given immediately before the vote was taken. "It is said that the adoption of the majority report would exalt this Liturgy to an article of faith. We deny this. It is not the case. We do not propose to give it any binding force. *The object is simply to let the Liturgy live. We want no authority to go with the book. No endorsement is sought. We are not yet prepared for that point.* We ask that decision may be postponed—that the book may be made an object of inquiry and investigation, *so that when we are called upon to act with reference to its adoption, we may do so intelligently. There are doctrines appertaining to the Liturgy; there are customs not in present harmony with the Church.* The discussion we have had shows that we are not agreed as to the doctrines contained in it. * * * Our object is simply this, to let it live. A child is born into the family—let it breathe—give it a chance for its life. It may have something wrong in it, but you do not know that it has. So let it run its chances. We ask nothing more; we can ask nothing less." These remarks were made by Rev. Dr. Gans, one of the most intelligent, and at the same time, extreme advocates of the peculiarities of the new measures, made immediately before the vote was taken. Taken in connection with the great modesty and moderation of the majority report prepared and thus explained by himself, they no doubt had great weight in securing the adoption of that report. The same sentiments are reiterated in the "Vindication," p. 47. How then can Dr. Nevin appeal to this action, so explained, in support of his broad assumptions? And how could some friends of the extreme ritualistic movement, on returning home from Dayton proclaim in the face of such facts as the above, that the General Synod had virtually endorsed and adopted the new Order of Worship? True, the majority report does allow of it "as an Order of Worship *proper to be used*," and much account has since been made of this last phrase. But if that phrase was really intended to express the meaning now put into it by some zealous friends of the new Order, must not those, who voted for the report, have been deceived by the explicit declarations of Dr. Gans, to the contrary?

Surely then it is a great misrepresentation to assert that the work of the Committee as presented in the Revised Liturgy was ever endorsed by any Synod of the German Reformed Church. That Liturgy possesses no more Synodical authority than did the Provisional Liturgy. It has simply been allowed to go forth with a chance for its life. It is put on open trial. All are at liberty to examine and criticise it; any minister, congregation, layman of the Church, may object to its use. Reasons against its introduction may be freely expressed. Those who as yet do not know what its doctrinal and devotional peculiarities are, may ascertain them, and then approve or disapprove, according to what is believed to be right and truth. Nor should any one be discouraged against the full exercise of this liberty. The General Synod did not by any means enjoin an actual trial of the book.

And still less was its action designed to forestall or forbid a thorough and searching dissection of the new system. That action is not absolute and final. It does not say that the book may not contain the very errors with which it is charged, or that it is not open to the ritualistic objections which are brought against it. There is nothing in that action which makes it factious or seditious for any one who believes the new Order to be materially at variance with the life and spirit of our Church, and dangerous in its character and tendency, to say so, and to say so, if he chooses, (that would be a matter of taste) in terms as violent and scurrilous as those employed in the "Liturgical Question" against free prayer and such "mechanical directories" as the Palatinate Liturgy, or in the so-called "Vindication" against scores of ministers of the German Reformed Church. Why should more leniency be shown to this new "Order of Worship," than its authors show towards the liturgical legacies which our fathers have bequeathed to us? Upon what grounds can it be thought entitled to greater respect than the Agenda of earlier, and I will add, better days? Surely, therefore, the General Synod of Dayton could not have meant for a moment to tie the tongue or to stay the pen of earnest and honest criticism. Nor can it be fairly understood to have bound the highest judicatory of the Church never to pronounce decided judgment against the new "Order." The most that can be made out of the language adopted is, that in the opinion of the Synod at the time, and so far as it had the means of knowing the general character of the book, it might be allowed for use in an experimental way. For satisfactory reasons pastors, consistories and congregations may refuse to permit this, believing its doctrines and service subversive of our legitimate faith and practice, and likely to do harm wherever they may be circulated. All therefore may enjoy equal freedom to examine the matter and to decide upon it for themselves, and all should be bold to use their liberty, in spite of any bitter denunciations or fierce anathemas to which they may be subjected for so doing. No such threats as were thrown out by correspondent A. in the "Messenger" some time ago against the exercise of full freedom of speech and pen in exposing what may be considered a scheme subversive of our denominational faith and practice, should intimidate any, or have the force of a puff of a child's breath, in deterring them from the severest criticism and condemnation of that scheme—provided this be done, as it may be, without violating Christian principles or propriety. And if this be thus done, so far from there being reason to fear Synodical reproof, it is certain that in the end the courage and fidelity so displayed will be commended.

One more point in the historical theory of the "Vindication" remains to be disposed of. It is the assumption that *the Church at large was developing with the Committee in liturgical views, and demanding some such book of public devotions as the new "Order of Worship."* ("Vindication," pp. 8, 13, 15, 38. Liturgical Question, pp. 63, 71, &c.) It seems to be a favorite delusion of the author to suppose that the Church has all along been not only permitting him and those who may agree with him, to give free utterance to their peculiar opinions, and patiently listening to them, but that she has been cordially imbibing and embracing them. He finds manifest pleasure in cherishing the hope that he has not only succeeded in training many pupils placed under his tuition to the belief of those views, but that this success extends widely into the Church at large, so that her membership generally are not only willing, but anxious to exchange the faith and practice, genius and spirit of the Reformed Church of their fathers, for the new scheme now pressed upon our acceptance. And so confident does he become at times of the correctness of this fancy, that he defiantly asserts that the opponents of the new measures resist their introduction as earnestly as they do, because they are afraid the people would eagerly adopt them, if they were but afforded an opportunity of doing so.

Now this assumption is so flatly contradicted by well-known facts, that instead of feeling called upon to show its absurdity, we are rather led to inquire by what strange hallucination the author of the "Vindication" could have been tempted to adopt it. He knew how anxiously some disciples of his progressive and changeful views desired to secure their general acceptance, and the adoption of the peculiar measures growing out of those views. He knew how zealously those views and measures had been advocated with more or less variation and confusion, in the press and in many of the pulpits of the Church, for years past. He knew that the "phenomenal" S. S. Hymn Book of 1860, had been furnished as a most effectual propagandist of those views and measures, by training the pliant minds of unsuspecting youth, ever fond of novelty, to the use and love of them. And yet he must or might have known, also, with how little actual effect all this had been done. Considering the nature of the agencies employed to promote the scheme, he might and should have seen and estimated the true significance of its practical failure. Was he ignorant of the fact, that the new mode of worship, "not after the pattern of our fathers," that is the mode exemplified in the first form of the Provisional Liturgy, had made next to no advance since 1862, when he wrote: "Such as it is, however, the Provisional Liturgy has not come thus far, as we know, into any general use in the Church; * * * has failed to get into any wide use. * * Our congregations generally have refused to go into the use of it?" Did he not know that there were not ten congregations at the time he wrote his "Vindication," in which the full forms were employed, least of all that for the Lord's Supper? And did he not know that some of those few into which it has been somewhat fully introduced, but without the consent of the Consistories or the people, are not favorable to the innovations, and would gladly see them dropped? It is about three years since I assisted at a communion season in one of those congregations. Dr. Nevin himself was present. From what I had heard, I supposed the Lord's Supper service of the Liturgy would be followed closely. But to my surprise little more than half the service in the book was used, and that half in a manner which made it very strongly resemble one of those pulpit hand-book services on which Dr. Nevin had cast so much ridicule and contempt. Has all this been forgotten—and that by one whose memory held so tenaciously what transpired many years before? It seems incredible. How then shall the self-betrayal into an assumption so utterly at variance with well-known facts be explained? But one solution suggests itself to our minds. It is the fatal error, an error which appears to have gained complete ascendancy over him, of supposing that he and those who more closely follow him, fully represent the Church. This solution may possibly not be the correct one. But until a better is offered, it must suffice. (See my former Tract, p. 33.)

There is an easy method, however, of testing this matter in a most practical way. Let those brethren in the ministry, having pastoral charges, who wholly endorse Dr. Nevin's views and measures, try in an open and fair way to introduce the New Order into their congregations. Let them plainly tell the people all the differences between this new mode of worship and that which the German Reformed Church has hitherto authorized and practised. Keep nothing back. Tell all frankly and truly. Ask them whether they desire that henceforth their pastors should be priests in the specific high-church sense; whether they are willing to consent to the doctrine that there can be no full pardon of sin, until common confession be made before the minister, thus converted into a priest, in the Church, and he declares their sins forgiven. Let the people have intelligent opportunity to say, also, whether they desire these multiplied responses, with enforced forms of prayer to the exclusion of all free prayer. Ask them about "*all* faces, in time of prayer, being turned toward the altar; about *risings* and *bowings*, in token of the consenting adorations of the people." Show them plainly the broad difference between the Lord's Supper and Baptismal services of the new Order, and those handed down to us from the 16th Century, differences which recent developments and explanations now prove to be as broad and as deep as those between the 4th Century "mummeries" of a corrupted Church in which "quackery in its worst form had enthroned itself," and the pure and simple worship of the primitive Apostolic Church. And having fairly shown them these things, let them choose freely whether they will hold fast to the old, or take instead the new Order of Worship. Does it need prophetic vision to foresee what would be the result of such a submission of the case to the people? Cannot every layman say what would be the effect, if Dr. Nevin, or any of his more devoted disciples should start out upon a mission thus to reconstruct and renovate the Churches, after this ultra-Mercersburg model? If there be any doubt in his mind, let him try it, and learn by experience what he seems reluctant otherwise to believe.

And yet, who but one blinded by his own desires, could have failed to discern that the cause of the practical failure of the ritualistic movement of the past ten years, lay in the extreme innovations it proposed? As a theory, that system of worship might seem very attractive to minds of a certain cast and training. But when it came to putting the theory into practice, it was found to be quite another thing. The people would not have it. Earnestly as they desired the restoration of the proper and legitimate usages of the Church, their pastors felt instinctively that they would not endure such an overturning of their faith and practice as was aimed at and proposed by Dr. Nevin's new Order. And yet so complete and persistent is his self-deception, that the cause of failure is supposed to have been, *not* that the Provisional Liturgy went too far, was too radical in some of the changes it proposed, *but that it was not radical enough.* The concessions made in the larger portion of that work to "a mechanical, pulpit hand-book, pseudo-liturgical" style of worship, such as was provided by "the Church of the Heidelberg Catechism" of glorious Tercentenary commemoration—those unfortunate concessions are supposed to have done the mischief. The way to manage children, is not to humor them. Such humoring only spoils them, and makes them refractory. Hence the remedy must be to recall those concessions in the revision of the work. The new order must be a unit, and that unity must consist in its extreme and exclusive radicalism. The Church that will not have a log for its king, must take a serpent. The people that murmur at tasks imposed with straw, must be silenced by being compelled to perform those tasks without straw. So Rehoboam, the foolish son of Solomon, argued that subjects who complained of his rule, did so because his demands were too lenient. The reader knows his remedy, and the ruin which that remedy wrought in Israel.

Summing up, then, in a few sentences, this review of the history of the Liturgical movement, we get these results. (1.) By the explicit instructions of Synod, and the confession of Dr. Nevin himself, the Revised Liturgy should have been constructed and prepared, mainly, in accordance with the principles of the Baltimore basis. (2.) Any modifications made of the Provisional Liturgy of 1857, were to combine a simplification of the more ritualistic forms of that Liturgy, especially of those for sacramental and special occasions, with such alterations in certain doctrinal phrases as would bring them in more literal harmony with the standards of the Church. (3.) The Synod and the Church had a right to expect that their wishes in these respects would be complied with, and had no reason to suppose that a course contrary to the instructions given, and to known wishes, would be pursued by the Committee. (4.) The new "Order of Worship" is not in harmony with the principles of the Baltimore basis, or with the suggestions of the Classes, but exhibits a material and essential disregard of those principles and suggestions, in containing full responsive services *only*, in retaining the objectionable doctrinal phraseology of the Provisional Liturgy, in utterly excluding free prayer, and in presenting a system of worship which shows no proper regard to Reformed Liturgies of the sixteenth century, and which is not "consistent with the doctrinal and devotional genius of the German Reformed Church." (5.) The course of the Committee, as indicated by the result reached, has never been endorsed by the Synod, and their "Order" has not been adopted. To these points may be added—(6.) As an inference fairly warranted by the history of the case, that notwithstanding their prosecution of the work in a way not justified by the instructions given and wishes indicated by facts or expressed in words, the Committee nevertheless hoped, and have most zealously endeavored, to secure a favorable reception for their work, and its ultimate adoption and introduction, by bringing such influences to bear upon the case as circumstances placed under their control.

And they have so far succeeded in their measures (I mean, of course, those five members of the Liturgical Committee who display special zeal, and who at York or Dayton took the most active part, in defending and furthering the movement, viz., Drs. Nevin, Wolf, Gerhart, Harbaugh, and Rev. T. G. Apple) that the case now stands where the Synod at Dayton left it. An "Order of Worship," so "materially and essentially" different from anything ever known to the German Reformed Church either in this country or in Europe, and known to be so contrary in some of its leading features to the predominant wish and taste of the Church, that its advocates and friends would not let it come to a fair vote upon its merits, has been allowed to go down to the congregations for examination or use, and thus to become either a means of revolutionizing the constitution and customs of the entire Church, or an occasion of dissension and strife, through a most natural and justifiable resistance to such revolutionary innovation. Historically, therefore, it is a question involving the maintenance of the traditional evangelical life and character by which the German Reformed Church has been from the first distinguished, or the surrender of all to the extreme and sweeping demands of a system of doctrine and cultus the paternity of which may be traced directly to Dr. Nevin himself. For, as shown, already, the new "Order of Worship" is not built upon the Baltimore basis, as mainly prepared by Dr. Schaff, but upon a very material modification of that basis. And that modification was made chiefly in accordance with the views of Dr. Nevin, and through the force of his personal influence over ardent disciples of those views. What all this new scheme involves, the radical revolution in the devotional usages of the German Reformed Church which it purposes to effect, and its essential disagreement with her established principles of public worship, next claim our attention.

THE LITURGICAL QUESTION.

Amidst the din and confusion of the present controversy, there is great danger that the main point at issue may be forgotten, or be made a matter of secondary moment. It is one of the frequent attendants of warm and exciting discussions, that side issues, raised incidentally or with design, and pressed with violence and bitterness, produce so much distraction, that the minds of those concerned are diverted from the interest really at stake, and become absorbed with other matters. Such distraction and diversion have, no doubt, been caused in the case before us, by the manner and style in which the debate has been largely conducted by the leading advocates of the new Order of Worship. Dr. Nevin, especially, both at York, at Dayton, and in his "Vindication," has helped, whether intentionally or unintentionally to produce this result. Among the objections urged against the new scheme, the objectionable character of some of its *doctrinal* expressions has been exposed, and pressed as a reason why it should not be adopted by the Synod, or recommended to the Church. This objection, however, has been raised and argued as one involved simply in a subordinate way, in the Liturgical movement. Its great importance has indeed been admitted, but it has not been set forth so as to lessen *the primary question of the proposed revolution in our entire mode of worship.* But now an attempt is made by those favoring that revolution, to treat the matter of such radical Liturgical changes as something of comparatively small account, and to make the whole controversy turn chiefly upon doctrinal points. It is quite easy to see what would be gained by effecting this change of base. Doctrinal points are more or less abstruse, and can be discussed in such a manner that those not familiar with the subtleties of scholastic or mystical theology, are unable to discern their real import, or to detect the sophistries and errors which they involve. Those errors may even attempt to vindicate their orthodoxy by texts of Scripture, and by quotations from standard Church authorities which, in sound and in superficial form, may seem to substantiate their evangelical pretentions. Why then, should they be denounced or rejected? Who will undertake to pass judgment upon them as subversive of true evangelical faith? If they can thus defend themselves by the same Scriptures and standards of Church doctrine from which proofs of their falsity are drawn, how shall the Church at large, or any representative Synod of the Church decide who is wrong or who is right? Although, therefore, the doctrinal objections made to the movement now agitating our Church, are believed to be as obvious as they are serious,—a point which will be taken up in the concluding section of this tract,—it may be found more easy to confuse the proof of those objections by such means as adroit debaters are mostly skilled in using.

Sometimes theological phraseology is ambiguous, or lacks precision. Certain terms employed may have one sense in one connection, and a different sense in another. An author, consequently, like Calvin or Ursinus, whose system, taken as a whole, is clear and definite enough, may make statements which, taken alone and out of their proper connection, may seem to furnish grounds for doctrines diametrically opposed to those which they really hold. That their writings should be liable to such perversions, will, of course, not surprise those who remember that Papists and Puseyites, as well as Phrygian Montanists and Gnostics, all quote the Holy Scriptures for their purpose, and pretend to prove by inspired testimony that their condemnable heresies are most heavenly truths. But this very liability of all writings, inspired or not inspired, to such misuse, can be made the occasion of misleading the minds and disturbing the judgment of men, and of thus securing, perhaps, a temporary ascendancy of error over truth.

But whether this be so or not, it is simply a matter of fact, that the

Liturgical Question, in the proper sense of the term, is of primary importance in the present instance, and claims the most earnest consideration of the Church. The movement began professedly as a liturgical movement. The changes which are now most urgent in asking for ecclesiastical sanction, and in seeking to become predominant, are liturgical changes. The revolution which is striving to establish its ascendancy, is a revolution in our mode of conducting public worship. Even, therefore, if not a single doctrinal point of any moment were at stake, it is a matter sufficiently serious to justify an earnest challenge, and to demand most careful consideration, whether such a mere liturgical or ritualistic revolution should be allowed to prevail. Taking the question as amounting simply to this: Shall the German Reformed Church adhere substantially to the mode of worship by which she has been distinctively characterized for three hundred years, or shall that mode, with the principles on which it rests, be abrogated, discarded, and another mode "essentially and materially," in principles, and in form, different from it, be substituted in its stead? it may well be expected that the Church would hesitate long before giving an affirmative answer, if she did not promptly and indignantly reject the very proposition.

A Liturgy may exert greater influence than a formal Creed, not only upon the moral character, but upon the doctrines of a Church. The moulding power of national poetry is proverbial. What is said or sung, in prayer and praise, at least by those who take any devout and earnest part in both, must, in the very nature of the case, possess vastly greater power. Such prayers and hymns are most potently educational, and soon insinuate the truths or errors they may contain into the worshipper's inmost life. Whatever, therefore, may be the import of the articles of their Creeds, people really, heartily believe what they sincerely sing and pray, or practice in any other form in their private and public devotions. No religious system better understands this than the Romish papacy. There is scarcely an error in that monstrous perversion of Apostolic Christianity which did not gain currency, and secure final adoption, in this way. The dreadful idolatry of the mass can be historically traced to this source. It was by gradual changes in the mode of celebrating the Lord's Supper, by introducing a peculiar phraseology into the liturgical forms used in its administration, and by adding one ceremony after another to the service, that the mind and heart of the Church, during the third and fourth centuries, were slowly trained to those views of the Sacrament which soon developed into the abominable error which *subsequently* became a leading article in the heretical Creed of Rome. This is certified by all evangelical Protestant Church Histories, and is most convincingly demonstrated in *Ebrard's* Dogmengeschichte I., 186–197. And what history shows to have been thus effected in regard to the error of the mass, it also proves was the actual course of development and adoption in reference to the veneration paid to saint's relics, the worship of the Mother of our Lord and of saints, prayers for the dead as associated with a purgatory, and well-nigh every other false doctrine peculiar to the Romish Church. Those errors were not primarily taught in the preaching, or proclaimed by the Creed. They were inculcated by means of the liturgies and ritualistic ceremonies, which became more numerous and complicated as the Church was carried further off from Apostolic times and allowed herself, through the influence of such men as Cyprian, Cyril, Ambrose and Gregory of Nyssa, (A.D. 384,) to be led away from the spiritual simplicity of Apostolic worship. (Beside the Church Histories above referred to, see Dr. Nevin's " Anxious Bench, pp. 9, 10, 29, 39, 50, 51, 53. Also the articles, Anglican Crisis, Early Christianity, and Cyprian, Mercersburg Review for 1851, 1852.)

All this too, let it be most distinctly noted, possibly took place without any previous design or preconcerted plan on the part of those who first introduced those liturgical and ritualistic changes, into the services of their respective churches (for they were mostly introduced in an independent and limited way.) Greatly as Dr. Nevin may overrate Cyprian and others of like spirit in that early age, not only in regard to their learning, but also other qualities—and who does not know that distance, and darkness too, often magnify objects long gazed at through them—it may be admitted that they were at least ordinarily devout and honest men. When they made figurative and rhetorical allusions to the *oblation*, (oblatio) as the bread and wine were called, which members of the churches presented for use in the Lord's Supper and the attendant "love-feast," and where they spoke of the duty of renewed self-consecration to the Lord, in the sense of Rom. 12 : 1, in connection with the offering (oblation) thus presented; and when, to enforce this exhortation they appealed to the propitiatory offering which He voluntarily made of Himself, once for all, and which they were assembled solemnly to commemorate, and as they did so *lifted up the plate* (a custom first practised in the *fourth century*,) containing the sacramental bread ; they may not have most distantly thought of inculcating the idea of even a symbolical reënactment, an *antitypical* repetition of the atonement. And yet the impression produced in this way upon the popular mind, especially as such modes of representing the matter were amplified by their successors, resulted in that false contemplation of the sacred service which soon perverted the sacrament into a sacrifice, and the sacramental sign and seal of the believing spiritual union with the Lord Jesus Christ, into a means and channel of the literal communication of His substantial flesh and blood to all who participated in the sacramental ordinance.

Whilst, therefore, the few ritualistic changes which, by slow degrees, were admitted into the Church during the latter part of the third, fourth and immediately succeeding centuries, may have been originally designed to promote the spirit of true devotion, and so to serve for the better edification of her members; they proved a most perniciously efficient means of sowing error, and propagating corruptions of the primitive Gospel faith and practice. And the mischief thus wrought, possibly by a gross abuse of the original design of those changes, was greatly increased and intensified, by the multiplication of liturgies in later centuries, characterized by those changes in their most objectionable form, and by "improvements" even upon them, for which greater currency was gained by ascribing their authorship to some famous Church fathers of earlier times. Such, for instance were the Coptic Liturgies which bore the names of Basil, Gregory of Nazianzen, and Cyril, though they were certainly not produced earlier than the seventh century. (See *Ebrard's* D.-Gesch.)

With such proofs before us of the *educational power* of liturgies, it would not be easy to overrate the doctrinal significance of the ritualistic movement, into which the desire and effort of our Church to provide herself with an order of worship suitable to her historical character and spiritual wants, have been turned. Let us, therefore, not permit our attention to be diverted from the extreme and radical nature of this movement in its primary ritualistic aspect, by any doctrinal discussion which may be incidentally associated with it. The first question now before the Church is whether this new ritualistic scheme of worship, prepared in disregard of the plan and purpose of the Synod, and confessedly at variance with any style ever known in the German Reformed Church, shall be allowed to usurp the place of worship in its legitimate evangelical Reformed type and spirit. After having for three hundred years maintained an order of worship possessing as much authority and entitled to as sincere regard as the Heidelberg Catechism, with which that order stands in the closest affinity, shall we let the Church be exposed to all the hazards involved in such a ritualistic experiment as Dr. Nevin and the more zealous advocates of the new scheme would persuade us to make? This, assuredly, is a matter which should be weighed with great deliberation. Especially must it be admitted that the Church should pause a long time before giving her consent to changes so radical, that they would make her entirely different, not only in her outward dress, but her inmost spirit from what she now is. Does the new scheme guarantee to her any certain adequate compensation for changes which would wholly sunder her historical relation to her past life, and attach her to the peculiar life of the third, fourth, and subsequent centuries?

When the real design of this movement became manifest more than six years ago, and its extreme tendencies were then exposed, it was common for its advocates *to deny that it involved the radical innovations charged upon it*. In reply to whatever was said or adduced, in proof of its revolutionary nature, efforts were made to show that the extreme peculiarities of the more ritualistic portions of the Provisional Liturgy, were in essential harmony with authorized Reformed antecedents! Zwingli's Liturgy of 1525 was appealed to in a most disingenuous way, as justifying the use of numerous responses, and even the strong phraseology which occurs in the sacramental forms of the Provisional book. By this means it was hoped not only to furnish an excuse for the extreme course which some members of the Committee were then bent on pursuing, but to reconcile the Church to that course, and secure its formal approval. (See *Ger. Ref. Messenger* for April 1862.)

Soon, however, it was felt that such appeals could not be fairly sustained. Whatever seeming countenance might be given to the extreme forms advocated, by the first Swiss order of services, the Committee were conscious that the resemblance was mainly external and superficial, and also that no peculiarities of those early Swiss forms could be honestly pressed as of authority for the German Reformed Church. Hence this line of argument has been almost entirely abandoned. Occasionally some feeble pen endeavors to take it up, and re-echo what was erroneously asserted five years ago, at least in a modified form. But the disagreement, not to say antagonism, between the New Order of Worship, and that mode which is distinctively German Reformed, is too broad and obvious to be denied. Hence in the notable tract of 1862, the Committee summoned courage, frankly to confess, that if the Synod or the Church had been expecting that the New Order would be in essential harmony with the historical cultus of the German Reformed Church, they were greatly mistaken. Thus they (including Dr. Harbaugh) acknowledged that all attempts to vindicate the peculiarities of the new Order, as then proposed, on the ground of their being in unison with the spirit and genius of the historical Reformed Church, such attempts as Dr. Harbaugh and one or two others had made during that very year (1862) in the "Messenger," were in contradiction of facts, and calculated to deceive the people. No such agreement between the new Order proposed, and our old mode of worship, was claimed. The new Order, it was then avowed, "made no such profession or pretence."

But now to suit this very significant change of front on the part of the leading advocates of the new measures, a new line of defence or assault must be established. And this is immediately done. Hence we hear no more of any "material or essential" *agreement* between the ruling spirit and structure of the new Order and our old cultus; but, along with concessions of "material and essential" *disagreement*, we have arguments, labored and specious, to justify this disagreement. And what is the burden of these arguments? Why that *the age of the Reformation was unfavorable to the productions of true liturgies, and that the fathers of our Church were not qualified for the work.*

Thus one of the main points in the controversy is changed. Instead of being required any longer to prove that the cultus which Dr. Nevin's advocates is "materially and essentially" at variance with any recognized German Reformed cultus, it becomes necessary to vindicate the qualifications of the Church, and of her leading theologians of the sixteenth century, to provide a liturgy worthy of the name, and suitable to the wants of her members. Happily, the opponents of the ritualistic innovations have as abundant means of vindicating their Church, and the founders of that Church, against this accusation, as they had to show the radical diversities of the new style of worship from that approved and practiced by the Church.

In their allusions to worship as distinctively characteristic of the German Reformed Church, the advocates of the new measures frequently involve themselves in contradictions which are very absurd and irreconcilable, but which are nevertheless calculated to confuse and mislead the minds of some who may read their statements upon the subject. At one time they acknowledge that our Church has had from the beginning a true system of worship. That "*worship is not a new thing* in the Reformed Church," is most graciously admitted. Nay, they go farther, and, with at least, implied approbation, confess that the "prescribed forms" used in such worship, were consistent with a true idea of worship. Indeed, to serve the purpose of a certain line of argument, the faith and practice of our ecclesiastical ancestors is sometimes warmly commended, and set in most flattering contrast with the usages of later times. Even the old Palatinate Liturgy comes in for a share of compliments in such connections, and in comparison with it, the forms *said to be used* by our ministerial fathers* of the last century, here in America, are pronounced "jejune formularies."

On the other hand, however, when the advocates of the new "Order" come to descant upon their own theory of worship, and wish to exhibit its superior merits, their whole tone is changed. Then both the Liturgies, and the worship of the Church conducted more or less fully according to the order of those Liturgies, are spoken of not only in terms of disapprobation, but of sarcastic disparagement and strong contempt. Such directories for public worship, as were originally provided for our Church, are freely denounced as "a bastard conception of what a liturgy means," as

---

* Dr. Nevin should certainly have known that the earliest ministers of our Church in this country, almost invariably brought the Palatinate Liturgy with them and used its forms in worship.

"an outward fixation of forms which must almost* necessarily seem to be formal only, and therefore slavish also and dead." Or they are sneered at as "dry forms," "mechanical helps," and altogether "not worthy of respect." And in full harmony again with the contumelious style of criticism we find apt imitators speaking or writing of our old established Order of Worship in the most disparaging terms, and comparing its peculiar services to "beggarly elements" which should be promptly forsaken, and cheerfully cast out to the dogs. (See Liturg. Question.)

In the same contradictory way Dr. Nevin puts face to face, on directly opposite pages of his remarkable tract, a commendation and a condemnation of the Liturgy prepared by Dr. Mayer. Thus on p. 8 he refers quite approvingly to that book as "the respectable work of a truly respectable man." And yet on almost parallel lines of p. 9 we read in reference to this same work: "But what have we here? Dead forms only, bound together in a dead way; from which it was vain to expect, therefore, that the breath of life should be kindled in the devotions of the sanctuary." That in this case, as in his allusions to the earlier Liturgies of the Church, the censure should be expressed in so much stronger terms than the praise, may be perfectly natural. Only as the Liturgy of Dr. Mayer had been adopted by the Synod, and is still so far as formal official action goes, the Liturgy of the Church, Dr. Nevin should have alluded to it in more decorous terms, and not have so rudely denounced it, under cover, too, of the honored name of a departed friend.

But through all these contradictions, it is the manifest aim of the writers to excite disgust and prejudice against that mode of worship which for three centuries has been distinctively Reformed; and to create a taste and desire for that style of Liturgy which has now, in the latter half of the nineteenth century of the Christian era, been discovered to be the only one worthy of respect, and for which the Christian Church is indebted to Dr. Nevin and his more active associates in the work. To put the argument in a favorite logical form, it furnishes the following significant syllogism:

No book of devotional forms for public use, which does not correspond in its principles and structure with the new Order of Worship, can be considered a true Liturgy, and worthy of respect.

The earlier Liturgies of the Reformed Church do not thus correspond with the new Order of Worship.

Therefore such Reformed Liturgies are no true Liturgies, and have no claim to our respect.

To this scandal upon the character and reputation of the Reformed Church has the Liturgical movement been driven by the anti-Reformed spirit to which, as to an "inexorable force," the advocates of the new measures have been surrendering themselves. Dr. Nevin uses all the influence with which a confiding Church has been investing him, to produce in the heart of her members feelings of disgust, aversion, contempt for her own historical character, and legitimate peculiarities of worship. With all his profound "respect for the sixteenth Century," he not only sees no reason to be bound slavishly by all its opinions, but tells too patient listeners that the Reformers of that period "had no proper insight into the true conception of a Liturgy, regarded as an organic scheme of worship; and no active sympathy therefore with the idea of worship in any such form." Who will thank him for his frigid professions of respect for the Church, after such condemnatory criticisms upon the labors of her devout and learned fathers? He may pour with lavish profusion harsh and ribald accusations of slander, libel, and whatever else comes freely to a vituperative pen, upon obnoxious individuals, and no one will be seriously disturbed, excepting for the prosecutor's reputation. But when a man called into the Church from another denomination to aid in maintaining and defending the established faith and practice of that Church; one most warmly welcomed to her inner sanctuary, and long honored with more than moderate regard and homage, allows himself to assail and ridicule that Church in matters pertaining to her inmost life and most sacred usages, it may well excite deep indignation in the breast of every member of that Church to whom her true character and reputation are of more account than the fitful Theological vagaries of a comparative stranger. It may be safely asserted, that there is not another minister in the Reformed Church, whether in this country or in Europe, who would have written a tract so defamatory of Reformed Liturgical principles and usages as that of 1862, now again endorsed in this "Vindication." And it is more than doubtful whether another Synod could be found which would so patiently endure such presumptuous defamation. Considering this endurance, manifested in the face of the provocation given for a severe rebuke, it is hard to suppress feelings of burning shame for the seeming want of self-respect evinced. And there is good reason to believe that the time will come, before many years have passed, when the lenient toleration displayed on the occasion referred to, will excite not only amazement but regret. Future generations will not know the circumstances under which all took place, and which may now serve to palliate if not to justify the forbearance of the Church.

Inasmuch, however, as Dr. Nevin and his school so freely indulge in such reproachful animadversions upon the mode of worship originally established and more or less faithfully maintained in the Reformed Church, especially in the German branch of that Church, it becomes necessary to inquire somewhat carefully into the matter, and see whether those animadversions are just or unjust; whether they spring from ignorance, or from a worse source. Such an inquiry, we may feel assured, will lead to a very different judgment as to the respectableness of the Liturgical legacies bequeathed to us by our ecclesiastical fathers, from that passed upon them by the author of the "Vindication."

Among the first things which claimed the attention of the Reformed Church, whether of Switzerland, the Palatinate, or of other countries, was the importance of making suitable provision for the observance of public worship. Dr. Nevin perpetrates an inexcusable mistake, when he affirms that the leaders of the Reformation, especially of that section of the great and glorious work which received the specific designation *Reformed*, in distinction from the Lutheran, were too much occupied with the adjustment of doctrinal matters, to give proper attention to the cultus of the resuscitated Church. He may have been betrayed into this strange error by the fact that doctrinal questions were discussed more publicly, and so came out more frequently and boldly into open view on the arena of controversy. Or he may have allowed himself to be misled by the absence of much strife on points pertaining to the cultus of the purified and renovated Church, and thus to conclude falsely, that the subject received but little earnest attention. But, in regard to the former of these points, it was perfectly natural, that doctrinal contentions, as affecting the public confessional life of the Church, should place themselves in the foreground, and occupy a more prominent and observable position. And in reference to the other point, an entirely satisfactory explanation of the comparative absence of strife is furnished by the fact of the substantial agreement of all the leading Reformers, both of the first and second period upon the principles and order of public worship.

It is far from being true, therefore, that but imperfect limited attention was paid to the subject of worship by our Reformed fathers. All the more thorough Liturgies of that period concur in testifying that the opposite was the case. The rupture with the Church of Rome had no sooner become a fact, than immediate provision was made for Liturgical services suited to the new state of things. Such forms as were deemed needful for properly conducting public worship were at once prepared. Liturgies appeared almost simultaneously with Creeds and Catechisms. And quite as much attention was bestowed upon the preparation of the one as of the other. Neither was the product of a single year. To both, and perhaps equally, diligent and prayerful study was devoted! The Heidelberg Catechism and the Palatinate Liturgy were published, as is well known, during the same year. And yet it is just as well known that both were the result of several years antecedent labors. Those bestowed upon the Liturgy were of course prosecuted more quietly, and their results when made public attracted less exciting observation. But it would be very wrong to conclude from this that they were less earnest and thorough, and therefore "not entitled to our respect" as fully as the confessional productions of that period.

And any one who duly considers the points which were involved in the Reformation, and the condition of those portions of the Church which became separated at that time from Rome, can readily see why such immediate and special attention should have been given to liturgical matters. The corruptions of the Romish apostasy pertained fully as much, to say the least, to its cultus as to its creed. Its system of worship, root and branches, was as degenerate as its faith; indeed, the departure of the former from primitive Gospel spirituality and simplicity had largely led, as was shown on a previous page, to doctrinal defection from Apostolic truth. It was not simply the article of justification by faith, for the perfect restoration of which the Reformers contended; but that article as involving a purification of the Church of ritualistic abuses, which had been multiplied in proportion as Rome had profanely substituted justification by works for the true Gospel doctrine, or as the growing tendency of Judaizing Galatian self-righteousness developed more and more into the prevalence of those anti-Apostolic ritualistic services, which, by their natural influence, wrought such doctrinal defections. It was not simply for the restoration of the supreme authority of the Sacred Scriptures as the highest rule of faith, that the Reformers contended; but for the abrogation of those abuses in practice, and most especially in worship, which had been introduced simultaneously with the elevation of human traditions to a position of authority equal with or superior to that of the Sacred Scriptures, and which were vindicated by appeals to such traditions.

For it is a most significant fact, corroborated by the entire past experience of the Church, that a lowering of the standard of evangelical faith in regard to these two cardinal doctrines, is uniformly associated with the advocacy and prevalence of extreme liturgical or ritualistic conceits and observances. There seems to be an inseparable natural affinity between the two evils. High-Churchism, hierarchal sacerdotalism, and complicated, multiplied ritualistic services, including the scrupulous outward observance of numerous saints' days, "æsthetic" rites and ceremonies, are commonly, so commonly that it might be truly said always, found abiding together, and locked in the most cordial embrace. Neither appears to be compatible with the grand and blessed theme of Apostolic preaching and teaching, or with the unreserved recognition of the Bible as a supreme rule of faith and practice. It was so in Galatia. It was so in most of the seven churches, addressed and warned in the Apocalypse. It has been so in the Greek and Romish Churches. It is so with the high ritualistic portion of the Anglican Church. And why should not like causes produce like effects elsewhere? But matters pertaining to the doctrinal section of this tract must not be anticipated.

Such, then, being the actual state of things in the Church as separated from Rome, it was most obviously one of the first necessities to provide for pure worship, as well as for a pure faith. And it is equally manifest that the importance of making this provision in the most careful manner, must have been fully realized by the leaders of the Church. It may be safely assumed that they had quite as earnest a sense of this, and fully as profound a conviction of the significance and solemnity of the work, and of the vast spiritual interests it involved, as Drs. Nevin, Harbaugh, and others of their mind, as that mind is expressed in the unjust and disparaging criticisms of the Liturgical Question (pp. 40—42). If proof of this is demanded, the history and the results of their liturgical labors, as those results are set forth in the Agenda of that period, may be triumphantly appealed to. Let the various services of those Agenda be tried by a fair and reasonable standard of criticism; let them be examined, not through glasses borrowed from fourth century fathers, but through a more Apostolic medium; let them be judged, not by fanciful Christocentric conceits, but by the light of New Testament principles, and of genuine primitive practice; and they will be found to bear the most convincing testimony to the diligence and care with which they were prepared.

But the framers of our early Reformed cultus, and authors of our first Liturgies, had not merely a due sense of the importance of the labors thus imposed upon them. They possessed eminent personal qualifications for the work; and they had at their command ample means, and abundant opportunities for performing it in a worthy and acceptable manner. Of their personal qualifications it ought not to be necessary to speak in this controversy. But they have been directly or indirectly assailed and disparaged, and this imputation of the comparative unfitness of the Reformers for satisfactory Liturgical duties, must be repelled. No proof need be given, of course, of their literary and theological qualifications. These are not only admitted by our opponents, but are in part appealed to in evidence of their lack of proper fitness for Liturgical labors. It is assumed that as theological combatants, and champions of Gospel orthodoxy against errors of all sorts, they must have been necessarily disqualified, by the very excitement and animosities connected with their sharp conflicts for the production of suitable devotional services. They were mighty men of valor, it is insinuated, and potent controversalists, on the field of theological warfare. They wielded pens like sharp two-edged swords, in hewing giant heresies to pieces, and fighting for the faith once delivered to the saints. But for this very reason, it is argued, were they unsuccessful in other offices. They lacked, it is affirmed, the calmly devout and quiet spirit which is most especially indispensable to those who would provide the

Church with unctious forms of worship. Furthermore, it is broadly suggested, they were too much under the influence of opposition and aversion to the ritualistic practices of the Papacy, and were too anxious to get away as far as possible from those practices. Hence the extreme, radical, bald simplicity of their Agenda; their lack of decorous and impressive "ritual action in worship" (Liturg. Ques., p 60); hence also the absence of all ritualistic "risings and bowings, and turning of all faces towards the altar in time of prayer" (Liturg. Ques., p. 35). Hence, again, their inability to perceive that only such "life like worship" (in distinction from their own dead "mechanical productions" Liturg. Ques., p. 61), was "comely and most becoming at the same time to the Lord's house." And hence, finally, their "opposition to the constraint of fixed religious *rites and ceremonies*," (such for instance as began to prevail from the fourth century onwards, and with which some brethren of our day have become so warmly enamoured) "which could hardly fail to exert an injurious influence on any work of this sort" (L. Q., p. 40).

For assumed reasons like these, Dr. Nevin would persuade us to believe that the founders of the Reformed Church particularly, were constitutionally unfitted for the work they undertook, and which they handed down to posterity, with the same authority with which they transmitted the Heidelberg Catechism. He seems to know of no other cause as more powerfully operative in their minds and hearts; he can assign no other reasons for what he regards as the predominant characteristic defects of such pulpit hand-books as the Palatinate Liturgy. So carelessly and so one-sidedly has the history of the case been studied, or so "hastily" has judgment been formed and "written" in reference to it, that no more complimentary account of the matter could be given. It is the *deliberate decision* of this ritualistic censorship, 1. That the Liturgies of the 16th Century, especially those of the Reformed type, are mere "mechanical directories," not deserving of respect, etc., etc. 2. That they are so because their authors, such men as Ursinus and Olevianus,—in high praise of whom nevertheless so much is said in Dr. Nevin's introduction to the Commentary on the Heidelberg Catechism, and in the Ter-Centenary Monument, were not qualified to produce any thing better. 3. Therefore the German Reformed Church in this country should ignore those Liturgies, repudiate the principles on which they were constructed and the sort of worship they present, and should adopt the new "Order of Worship" which is in all respects, and naturally enough, so incomparably superior to those original "pulpit hand-books!"

But the premises on which all those objections to the Palatinate and other Reformed Liturgies of that period, as well as the suspicions raised against the proper qualifications of their authors for the work, rest, are utterly at variance with facts, and must consequently be rejected as false.

Those Liturgies were indeed prepared during a period of exciting conflicts. and the men who performed the task were often involved in severe theological contentions. But the ecclesiastical strifes and agitations amidst which the Reformed Agenda of Germany, Switzerland and Holland were brought forth, were not more unfavorable to the proper execution of the work, than the dissensions and conflicts which disturbed England when the "Book of Common Prayer" was in course of preparation. And the authors of the former were not more deeply or violently involved in the ecclesiastical warfare which agitated the Churches of the Continent, and therefore more unfitted for the work of providing a suitable order of worship, than were Cranmer, Ridley, and their associates in the preparation of the Episcopal Liturgy, during the reigns of Henry VIII. and Edward VI. And yet the Book of Common Prayer is recognized as answering very fully to Dr. Nevin's idea of a true Liturgy, and has been honored by a remarkably close imitation in the new Order of Worship urged upon the acceptance of our Church; the chief points of difference between the two being, that the latter outdoes the other in its extreme high-church tone and pretensions.

It is equally erroneous to assert that the authors of the Reformed Liturgies of the 16th Century were too much influenced by extreme and fanatical aversion to the peculiarities of Romish worship, to be duly competent for their work. This was indeed charged against them by their Popish opponents; and for them to bring the accusation may have been perfectly natural. But the charge has been so often refuted, that it may well excite indignation to have it reiterated in our day; and that, too, in our own Church, and by those who should not only know that it is unfounded, but promptly repel it whenever an enemy might attempt to revive it. It is not true that the acknowledged leaders of even the first period of the Reformation, were swayed by such extreme and fanatical opposition to Rome. Still less can those of the second period, and most especially the fathers of the German Reformed Church, be convicted of it. *Even Zwingli was no radical,* if the facts and arguments set forth in a long article published in the Mercersburg Review of 1849, and of which Dr. Nevin is the author, may be regarded as correct. And the representatives of the Reformed Church who lived and labored after the first excitement of the Reformatory struggle had subsided, proved themselves to be still more conservative, in a true sense, than the Reformation hero of Switzerland.

That they earnestly and zealously opposed and denounced the errors and superstitions of Rome, is freely admitted. They are to be honored for it, not reproached. It is to their great praise, that regardless of all personal consequences to themselves, they laid bare the gross idolatrous corruptions which defiled the apostate Papal Church, and had especially accumulated in the service of the mass. And no less are they to be commended for having labored so faithfully to purify not only the creed but the cultus of the Church of all those vile corruptions, sparing none of them,—not even the exorcism and unction which Zwingli had retained in his Baptismal service. But in all they thus did they were animated, not by a spirit of mere fanatical opposition to Romish practices as Romish, but by their conviction that those practices were utterly opposed to the Word of God, to Apostolic order, and to the pure primitive customs of the Church. And unless the rebuke and abrogation of errors and usages which are flagrantly irreconcilable with the doctrines of Christ and His Apostles, and with that pure worship which He instituted, can be stigmatized as radical fanaticism, the fathers of the Reformed Church are not liable to this reproach. Unless the earnest and faithful endeavor to liberate the Church from the bondage of degrading hierarchical superstitions, and to restore to it freedom to worship God as the Apostles and earliest Christians worshipped Him, can be branded as extreme spiritualistic bigotry against the rites and ceremonies of the Romish Church, those fathers deserve better at our hands than to have their reputation tarnished by such damaging reflections as have been cast upon them by some of the more ardent advocates of the ritualistic measures. Not only the Heidelberg Catechism, but its most intimate fellow the Palatinate Liturgy, prove by their pervading spirit and tone, by what they say as well as by their silence, that those condemnatory criticisms are most unwarranted and unjust.

So far from there being any real ground for such charges or imputations, it is only necessary to know the history of those men, their life and character, their aims and works, to be convinced that they not only were free from such prejudices and revolutionary radicalism, but that they possessed the most important and desirable qualifications for the particular duties which the times and wants of the Church imposed upon them. By their pure Christian spirit as well as by their entire course of training, education, habits of thought, and studies; they seem to have been specially prepared for the offices they were called to perform. It need not be regarded as an invidious disparagement to say, that the German Reformed Church in this country has not now two men as fully fitted for the work of preparing a truly evangelical Reformed Liturgy, as were Ursinus and Olevianus. They had always been accustomed to liturgical worship, that is to what all but extreme ritualists have ever been willing to recognize as such. There was *no period in their history* when they were not liturgical. Hence there was no necessity for their conversion in this respect. Hence, also, they were less liable to be carried to such unwarrantable extremes as are frequently run into by new converts, whose zeal is apt to outstrip knowledge. For them the subject was not one whose captivating novelty overpowered their judgment and "carried them by an inexorable force" its own way. In this, already, it must be admitted that they possessed a great advantage.. Very susceptible, and especially unsettled minds are likely to be overwhelmingly impressed by a first attendance upon an elaborate ritualistic mode of worship, conducted in Romish style. And persons of this temperament and peculiar frame, particularly if they were under the influence of a morbid dissatisfaction with the simpler and less sensuous services of an evangelical Church, would be in danger of quite losing their heart and reason both amidst the gorgeous ceremonial, the chorals and antiphonies, the sacerdotal chantings and intonations, and all the multiplied æsthetic accompaniments calculated to delight the eye, to ravish the ear, and bring their entire sensational being under a spell of enchantment.

But the ruling spirits of the Reformed Church during the latter half of the sixteenth century, were men of quite a different character. From childhood they had been familiar with Romish worship in all its most elaborate ritualistic arrangements. Some of them had often personally officiated, or at least participated in it all. The antiphonies, the litanies, the Gregorian chants, they knew by heart. With the order of the Romish mass they were perfectly acquainted. But they also had learned to know that for none of the distinctive parts of this elaborate ceremonial worship, could there be found any warrant in the New Testament, or in the practice of the Apostles and the primitive Church. They were the sad witnesses likewise of the many pernicious moral consequences which, as bad fruit from a corrupt tree, had sprung from those extreme ritualistic departures from the simplicity of original Apostolic worship. And they had carefully and honestly traced all those mischievous departures to those innovations upon primitive worship which had gained ascendancy during the third and fourth centuries; that period when, already, the Church had begun to *delight in arrangements and services which were designed and calculated to produce effect by outward means, "till in the end amidst the solemn mummery no room was left at all for genuine piety."* Whilst, therefore, they were not so blinded by prejudice or animosity against the Romish system, that they fanatically abolished every thing, simply because it might stand in some connection with that system; they were able to discern its errors and corruptions, and had both courage and intelligence to reject them. They could prove all things; they held fast only to that which was good. There were fanatics in those times who pursued a more destructive course; "Gnostics, Phrygian Montanists," &c. But our Reformed fathers were in no sympathy with any such wild fanatical revolutionizers. What they attempted and accomplished, was undertaken in the spirit of a calm, dispassionate conservative faith in the Lord Jesus Christ, and in the Church as He established it; and was carried out with a docile conservative determination to restore His Church, as far as lay in their power, to original order and purity, in faith and practice.

There is yet another fact to be emphasized in this connection. Those who were commissioned to provide the original Order of Worship for the German Reformed Church in the sixteenth century, *had access to many Protestant Liturgies then already in use.* And it is known that in the preparation of the Palatinate Liturgy, of 1563, those earlier Orders of Worship were carefully consulted. With the distinctive characteristics of the more strictly Lutheran mode of worship they were perfectly familiar. They knew, especially, how closely its service for the Lord's supper adhered to the Romish mass, including the major and minor doxologies, the litany, and a certain amount of ritualistic ceremonial. With the peculiarities of the Episcopal services in England, as set forth in the Book of Common Prayer, as then in use, they were also acquainted, and probably were well aware of the alterations which had been made in those services at the suggestion of Bucer and Peter Martyr, such as the omission of the use of oil in Baptism, the unction of the sick, the prayers for the souls of the departed, the invocation of the Holy Ghost in the consecration of the Eucharist, the prayer of oblation, and some other things which seemed to savor of Romish superstition. In a word, they were thoroughly informed in regard to the entire liturgical literature and labors of their times, and had all at their command in the preparation of their work.

How unjust, therefore, to represent them, whether by assertions or insinuations, as lacking the requisite means and qualifications for such a work! And how wholly unwarranted the disparaging criticisms passed upon the Liturgy which they furnished for their Church, on the assumption of their want of qualifications. Surely such criticisms are not entitled to much weight, and should not be allowed to prejudice our minds against the Reformed Agenda of the sixteenth century, or to lessen our estimate of the competency of their authors for the liturgical labors performed by them. On the contrary, the facts above stated, and of which we defy contradiction, prove them to have been abundantly fitted for the work, and to have possessed ample means and opportunities for its faithful performance. Of course, no reasonable critic will lay stress upon any peculiarities of style or phraseology which may be found in Liturgies prepared 300 years ago, and in which the main thing is the matter they contain, and the principles on which they are based.

To those who are aware how often and vehemently the author of the "Vindication," and a few who have followed his unhappy example, have written and spoken in terms of disapproval and depreciation of some of the more distinctive features of Evangelical Protestantism, this defence of the qualifications of such men as Olevianus, Ursinus, and their more active associates, will not seem superfluous. Confidence in their ability to do well what they were required to do, is indispensable to a due estimate in the results of their labors, and to confidence in those results. To shake this confidence, efforts have been made to exhibit them as disqualified for what they undertook, especially in the department of Church cultus. Their Liturgy is condemned because they are affirmed to have lacked the ability and the means for such a work. That this mode of argument has been honestly employed, may not be questioned. No one may doubt for a moment that Dr. Nevin and Dr. Harbaugh really believe that Ursinus and Olevianus, as well as Farel and Calvin, were not competent to prepare "true liturgies" for the Reformed Church; that they had no proper idea of liturgical worship; that their whole education and all their circumstances were insuperable barriers in the way of their rising to the true celestial height of a genuine Christian cultus. But whilst the sincerity with which this opinion is held by them may not be challenged, we beg leave to pronounce the opinion itself erroneous, destitute of all foundation in facts, and not very modestly entertained or avowed.

This point then being settled, we can, with unbiased minds, enter upon an examination of the manner in which the fathers of the Reformed Church proceeded with their liturgical labors, and will be able to form a more correct and impartial estimate of the character and merits of the system of worship which they established. And I think that the system will not be found that bald thing, "collection of dry forms," of miserable "mechanical helps," which Dr. Nevin has the presumption and irreverence to style them now again, after four years' reflection, in this misnamed "Vindication."

A very remarkable fact meets us at the outset of this particular inquiry. Let us approach it by way of supposition. It will be admitted now, that the authors of the first liturgy of our Church, in 1563, would be likely to avail themselves of all the helps within their reach. As earnest, honest, thoughtful men, they would seek counsel of all the pious and learned men of their day in sympathy with the Reformation, and above all would carefully study any existing liturgies at hand. What, then, if among the liturgies of that particular period there was one closely resembling in spirit groundwork, and special structure, the new "Order of Worship," for whose success Dr. Nevin struggles so desperately? What if they not only knew of a service-book of this character, but also its authors or compilers; and what if they were well acquainted with all the arguments employed in "Vindication" of its peculiar character? Would it not be very significant *for us* if, though well acquainted with such an order, with its numerous responses, its alternating recitation of the Psalms, its Lord's supper service, so closely patterned after the Romish Mass, &c. &c.,—they should have totally discarded its type of worship, and have adopted another *only* " materially and essentially" different from it ?

Such, however, was exactly the case, and that is precisely what they did. In 1550, bp. Cranmer, the primate of the Church of England, yielding to some objections made against the Liturgy then in use, undertook a *revision* of the work. The book thus revised was adopted in 1551. This early Episcopal Liturgy, as intimated above, must have been known to Frederick III., and to his favorite theologians, Ursinus and Olevianus. *Bucer* and *Peter Martyr* had assisted in the Revision, and it was published, as shown by the date, twelve years before the Palatinate Liturgy. Moreover, there was frequent correspondence between the Reformed Churches of the Continent and the chief theologians of the Church of England. And yet Ursinus and Olevianus did not follow the Book of Common Prayer, either in its general plan or in any of its details. It is true it had not then yet attained to its present form. Notwithstanding the important modifications of the first edition, procured by Bucer and Martyr, in the way of purging it of some Popish superstitions, not all of these were removed. Here, then, was an " Order of Worship " which came strongly commended to the consideration of the Palatinate Reformers. Outwardly considered, there might seem to have been many reasons for adopting it as a model. Men of great learning, influence and renown had labored on it. The adoption of its scheme would have served to promote ecclesiastical unity, and would have won favor for the little Church of the Palatinate with men of high position and great power in England. But none of these things moved our fathers. They were so blind that they could not discern the superior beauties of a cultus whose model Dr. Nevin extols as the only one deserving the name. They were so foolish as to discard the opportunity afforded them of escaping the scorpion lash of his sarcasm, and of being regaled with the nectar of his benign approbation. Had Ursinus and Olevianus but enjoyed the light which, after so long and mournful an eclipse has now at last illumed the wretched " pulpit handbook," "mechanical dictionary," " hortus siccus," worship of the poor misled, benighted Reformed Church ! But, alas, they lived and died *three centuries* too soon ! Or else, it might be suggested, the radiance of that light was too long withheld. Too long, especially, for the generations of our fathers and brethren deprived thus of the privilege and joy of worshipping their God and Saviour in the only fit and decent way, the only acceptable and edifying way. Only imagine Dr. Nevin's estimate of their mode of worship to be correct, and then think of that estimate applying to all who have gone before us in our Church back to the days of Frederick III., and to the time when our fathers worshipped in their sanctuaries in Heidelberg! Without a vicarious priesthood, (for it must be kept in mind that Dr. Nevin holds in derision the declaration of pardon used by our fathers), without an altar of propitiatory sacrifice, without grand services like those in the new "Order of Worship," they are set before as objects exciting our deepest commiseration. Wretched Palatines! What had they done that those set over them for instruction and guidance should only prove blind leaders of the blind, causing both to plunge into the ditch! For what Dr. Nevin says of that style of worship, which was adopted by our Church in 1563, involves all this. And he himself makes no exceptions. (See Liturgical Q., and "Vindication" p. 51). Doubtless, it is a grievous offence to "slander" the living, and no one should be excused for wilfully committing it. But is it not a vastly more heinous thing to cast dishonor on the dead? To speak lightly or contemptuously of a brother is reprehensible. But what is it to hold up a Church to mockery?

Still another fact of similar import must be noted. Besides having the Anglican cultus before them, the fathers and founders of the Reformed Church were perfectly familiar with the cultus which prevailed in strictly Lutheran Churches. Many considerations would prompt them to copy closely after the Lutheran pattern. The Reformers of the Palatinate, especially, might feel themselves urged to do so. Their country had just rejected extreme or rigid Lutheranism, and might even have been regarded as in some sense Lutheran still. By their national and ecclesiastical relationships to Lutheran German States around them, as well as by a desire to conciliate as many friends as possible, they would no doubt be inclined to avoid all diversities in the mode of worship not deemed essential. Furthermore, though in some of the leading forms the Lutheran Liturgies bore a strong resemblance to those of the Book of Common Prayer, both having followed the same model, they were more simple, and so far approximate more closely to the primitive practice. That considerations like these would have prevailed, had not stronger convictions of truth and right prevented it, there can be no doubt. If Ursinus and Olevianus, and other Reformed theologians of that period, could have incorporated in their Liturgies a Lord's Supper service like that practised in strictly Lutheran Churches in their day, they would have done so. Their adoption of an order "materially and essentially" different, proves how deep and strong their convictions must have been, that the Lutheran cultus even was not in accordance with the only pattern and principles which should rule in the case. And it must be acknowledged by all whose mind and heart are not so wholly prepossessed against the plain testimony of facts, that this refusal to follow a model, by the adoption of which they might have escaped contumely and reproach as bitter as that now heaped upon those who are striving to vindicate their course and to keep their Church from repudiating the principles which they adopted, is of very great significance in the present controversy.

Let these two facts then be distinctly borne in mind. The fathers of the German Reformed Church were perfectly familiar with an order of worship similar in all essential respects, though in some important points less objectionable, on evangelical grounds, to that so vehemently advocated by Dr. Nevin. But although so familiar with it, and with all the considerations which might be urged in its favor, they unqualifiedly rejected it.

Having thus seen how inconsistent with historical facts, and therefore how unjust and indefensible the disparaging criticisms of Dr. Nevin upon the authors of our primitive Liturgy are, we are ready to inquire more particularly into the precise character and basis of that cultus, and to estimate its merits with unprejudiced minds. Why did the fathers of the Reformed Church, not only in the Palatinate, but in all other countries, refuse to adopt a mode of worship like that of the Anglican and strictly Lutheran Churches? And why did they prefer one of a more simple, less ritualistic type?

The first thing that arrests attention in the inquiry is, that *the same fundamental principle was adopted* in providing an Order of Worship for the Church, as in drawing up a system of doctrine. Both were made to rest upon divine authority, and to be in essential, and as much as possible, in formal harmony with the Sacred Scriptures. The testimony of tradition was not discarded. But it was of secondary authority, and strictly tried by that touch-stone of truth, which tradition itself declared to be the standard. Even the Romish Church acknowledged the divine inspiration of the Bible, and admitted its authority, though not its sole authority, in matters of faith and practice. But if the Holy Scriptures were what the Church had all along declared concerning them, an inspired revelation of the grace and will of God, it was legitimately assumed that their authority must be supreme in reference to all matters pertaining to religion. And as the true meaning of the Scriptures must be the same in the sixteenth century as in the first century, and that meaning could as well be ascertained, at least in regard to all essential points, in the later as in the earlier period, it was fairly assumed by the founders of the Reformed Church, that it was possible for them to discover what doctrines and customs of their time were in harmony with the Word of God, and what were not. They maintained also, and with equal propriety and justice, that true submission to Church authority did not require them to accept of any arbitrary interpretation which might be put upon the acknowledged divine standard of faith and practice, in manifest contradiction to the plain and obvious import of that standard. If, in the course of time, the faith and practice of the Church had degenerated through perversion or corrupt additions, the Reformers held that they were not only not bound by such departures from the truth, but that it was their duty to expose, and, as far as possible, to correct them. Hence, in matters of doctrine, they went to the fountain-head, and derived directly from the Word of God those truths and facts which were deemed necessary to Christian faith. Even whilst accepting of the Apostles' Creed, and of the Nicene and Athanasian symbols, they refused assent to the errors which pretended to be based upon those symbols, and contended for such an interpretation of their several articles as was warranted by the Scriptures, and by the primitive faith of the Church. In like manner in matters pertaining to public worship, they made the Word of God their rule, and held that it furnished instructions and examples in accordance with which the worship of the Christian Church should be regulated and arranged. They did not arbitrarily and radically discard the testimony and practice of the ages immediately succeeding that of the Apostles and primitive Church. But instead of taking the traditions of those later ages as a rule for determining the principles and mode of Apostolic worship, they reversed the process, and made the latter the test of what should be rejected or allowed in the former. With such subordinate helps as the second, third and fourth centuries might furnish, they endeavored to ascertain the true Apostolic order. But in pursuing this investigation they did not allow themselves to be blinded or captivated by the garish attractions of those false systems of worship which met them on their way. They ever kept in mind that the true object of their search was, *not* a cultus which might be vindicated by appeals to the third and fourth century, or commended by a "highly cultivated æsthetic taste," but that order of Christian worship which was originally instituted in the Church, and which had the sanction of apostolic and primitive precept and example.

Guided by this just and safe rule, a rule furnished and approved by the infallible Word, if not by an arbitrary and arrogant but fallible church, our ecclesiastical fathers soon and easily found what they sought for. Not only did they discover some broad and general basis of worship, which by its very breadth and vagueness might justify the exercise of a great variety of taste in rearing a superstructure upon it. In numerous declarations of the Lord Jesus Christ, such as those in Matth. vi. 5–18; xviii. 20; Luke iv. 16, etc.; i. 43; vi. 6; John iv. 19–24, and in many directions and incidental statements recorded in the Epistles, such as 1 Cor. i. 21; xiv. 15; Gal. i. 6, etc.; Eph. v. 19, 20; Col. iii. 16; Heb. x. 25;

xiii. 15, as well as in frequent illustrations furnished of the actual practice of the primitive Church, such as are met with in the account of the services connected with the institution of the Holy Supper, and in passages like Acts i. 13, 14, 24; ii. 1, etc., 46; iv. 23, etc.; vi. 4; xviii. 4, and wherever allusion is made to the mode of public worship, they found both in the form of precept and example, distinct and explicit intimations in regard to what the Head of the Church and His immediate Apostles wished to be considered essential to true Christian worship.

Above all, they saw the very marked distinction at once established and made prominent between the *formal ritualistic character of the Jewish cultus* and the *freedom, spirituality* (Dr. Nevin might call it "spiritualisticism"), and great *simplicity* (Dr. N. would condemn it as "baldness") of primitive Apostolic worship. They saw not only that the latter was not modelled, *in any respect*, after that of the Temple, but that even so far as it adopted *the usages of the synagogue*, it was done in a free way, and not in exact slavish imitation of those usages, done also at the time to a large extent in the spirit of accommodation to the habits and prejudices of Jewish converts. In the early Christian Church they saw no visible altar of propitiatory sacrifice, no visible sacrifice of propitiation, no priestly caste to mediate with such offerings between the Lord and His people. The people themselves were freely admitted into the Holy of Holies, in a deep spiritual sense, by the blood of Christ shed once for all. Instead of the altar of atonement and bloody sacrifices of the Old Testament, they saw the "*Table of the Lord*" established as a place of sacred commemoration of Him who had given His life a ransom for many, and of hallowed communion by faith with Him who was their Life, "whom not seeing they loved, and in whom * * believing they rejoiced." And in that *sacramental* (*not sacrificial*) table they saw the Church supplied with what was a most abundant compensation for the removal of the ancient bloody altar of atonement (Heb. xiii. 10–16, not verse 10 alone as Dr. Nevin takes it). In the early Christian Church they saw that "the Word of the Lord" read and preached was the *spiritual centre* around which the service revolved, and which was used as the *chief means* of common edification. "Christ *crucified* and *risen* was the luminous *centre* whence a sanctifying light was shed on all the relations of life. Gushing forth from a full heart, the *preaching* went to the heart; and springing from an inward life, *it kindled life, a new Divine life*, in susceptible hearers. It was revival preaching in the purest sense." (Schaff's Hist. of the Chr. Church, I. 119.) This they found illustrated beyond all contradiction by the example of all the Apostles. Wherever the Apostles went they made "preaching the Gospel" their chief work. And this not only in their labors among unconverted multitudes, but in the assemblies of believers.

In the Acts of the Apostles, in the Epistles, whether of Paul, of Peter, of James or John, they found the Word, the truth as it is in Jesus, constantly and unqualifiedly represented as the chief, the most efficient means, as well of regeneration as of sanctification. And although our fathers knew well by what specious arguments the Papists attempted to explain away these plain facts, and endeavored to bind all saving grace to such acts as tied the conveyance of that grace to sacredotal functions; they knew also that those arguments were utterly without Scriptural foundation. Otherwise how could St. Paul have said in language which hyper-churchism tries in vain to explain away : "I thank God I baptized none of you, * * * for Christ sent me not to baptize, but to preach the Gospel" (1 Cor. i. 14–18)? How could have St. Peter have written: "Being *born again, not* of corruptible seed, but of incorruptible, *by the word of God,* which liveth and abideth forever. * * * And this is the word which by the Gospel is preached unto you." "Wherefore, * * * as new-born babes, desire the *sincere milk of the* WORD *that ye may grow thereby?*" How could St. John and St. James both have written epistles, which throughout assume this great and blessed truth, that the *Word*, the Gospel of the grace of God in Jesus Christ, is the chief Divinely appointed means, first of awakening then of promoting the life of God in the soul? Thus it was manifest that however Divine, sacred, supernatural the character of the Holy Sacraments, and however important and essential their office, *they* were not, neither was the table on which one of them, the Holy Supper, was spread, "the *Shekinah*" from which light and grace was radiated and diffused through all the place where primitive believers worshipped.

Next to this our ecclesiastical fathers learned the important and noteworthy fact, that the rigid enforcement of prescribed forms of worship by the Romish Church, though in harmony with fourth Century principles and usages, was not in accordance with the primitive practice. For in the Apostolic Church they found that while some such forms may not have been despised, *there was no certain evidence that they were statedly used;* on the other hand, however, there was *incontrovertible proof that free prayer was the more common practice.* (See passages referred to above Also Schaff's Hist. of the Apost. Church, p. 562, and Hist. of Chr. Ch., I. 120). Indeed *they had abundant reason to believe that whatever forms may have to a limited extent been recognized and used by the early Church they were long regarded as subordinate to Christian freedom.* (See *Ebrard*, Kirchen-u., Dogm.-Gesch., I., 40–42). Putting all these facts together, therefore, the order of early Christian worship, as indicated in the Sacred Scriptures, furnished a full and adequate model according to which the worship of the Church as Reformed might be patterned. That model, in preference to any of those doubtful improvements which the fancy or the folly of possibly well-meaning but presumptuous men, had added to it, was the model adopted in the spirit of docile Christian liberty by our ecclesiastical fathers. And we may challenge the advocates of the new Order of Worship to show any material or essential disagreement between the mode of worship exhibited in the old Palatinate and kindred Liturgies, and that of the primitive Apostolic Church.

With the distinctive features of this mode of worship, it may be presumed that the members of our Church generally are sufficiently acquainted. Besides, the great point at issue in the case is conceded by the advocates of the new Order of Worship. It will only be needful, therefore, to keep the simple outline in view. The regular Lord's day service was opened with an evangelical salutation; then a hymn was sung; next followed an exhortation to prayer, and a prayer which while the Liturgy contained a prescribed form which was at first commonly, if not always used, yet might be free, and which in the course of some years, through the legitimate operation of the Reformed principle and spirit actually yielded to free prayer. As to the *place* occupied by the minister during these devotional services, the old Liturgy contains no direction. But the impression left by what is said concerning the sermon in connection with the directions concerning prayer, is that the minister occupied the pulpit during all the services. And so far as I can learn, this was the common early practice in the Reformed Churches, strictly so called. After the prayer the *sermon* was preached, and in connection with it a portion of the Scripture read as a text. No *lessons* were prescribed, the minister being left free in the choice of his text, excepting that he was directed to adapt himself to special occasions.

The sermon was followed by the public *confession of sin*, which took the place of auricular private confession in the Romish Church, and the *comforting assurance* of pardon, which took the place of sacerdotal absolution. The *confession* was *spoken* by the minister, who included himself in it, the congregation following heartily in silence, ("let every one say with me in his heart," is the phrase used) as the language plainly implies, and as universal practice, so far as known, shows was the case. During this part of the services the *people stood*. In the "comforting assurance" pronounced by the minister, every expression was carefully avoided which might lead people to think that the forgiveness of sin was in any way dependent upon the formal announcement made. On the contrary, the declaration clearly implied, *went on the assumption*, that pardon had already been granted, and that the declaration of it was made *not* as something necessary to the conveyance of such pardon, but only as a proper means of confirming the hearts of timid, troubled penitents in the possession of it. In a word, and this is a fact worthy of earnest consideration in the present case, the Confession of sin, and accompanying declaration of pardon, in the Reformed Church wholly and most designedly *excluded the idea that there was any thing sacramental* in the act, in the specific sense of that term. And as a consequence, the peculiar form of this part of Reformed worship, served, and was undoubtedly intended to serve, as an emphatic practical repudiation of both *ordination* and *pennance* as Romish sacraments.

In regard to this form of confession, etc., it is proper to add, that while it was commonly used every Sunday at the morning service, at least during the earlier years of our Church, the rubrics of the Liturgy seems to have allowed some option in regard to its use, requiring, however, "*especially*" that it be used at the service preparatory to the Communion.

The Confession was followed by singing, and the whole service closed with a benediction.

The *Preparatory* and the *Communion* services are constructed upon the same principles, and pervaded by the same simplicity as that for the Lord's Day. In the former, *after an appropriate sermon* (mark that), the communicants rising in their seats, and sometimes even gathering around the chancel, in which the *communion table* stood, were addressed in reference to the three points laid down in the answer to the second question of the Heidelberg Catechism, viz.: their sense of and sorrow for sin, their hearty faith in Jesus Christ, and their sincere purpose to lead a godly life. Upon each of these they were required to give an audible answer.* Then followed the confession and declaration of pardon, in the form and sense above named. Thus most emphatic prominence was given to a "*subjective*," that is, inward personal preparation, by subjective repentance, faith, and a solemn purpose to lead a holy life, as of the first importance to fitness for celebrating the Lord's Supper.

In full accordance with this were the ruling spirit and tenor, and all the parts of the order for administering the Sacrament itself. The service immediately preceding the Communion proper, consisted of an address in which the *commemorative* design and import of the Sacrament were set forth in succinct, earnest and solemn statements, combined with a tender

---

* Because *answers* are also in one sense *responses*, some advocates of the new order have appealed to the above custom as an evidence that "*responses*" were used in the early Reformed Church. The sophistry is too transparent to deceive any one. It is not even smart. All can see that there is an essential difference between a simple "Yes" in answer to a question, and such "responses" as abound in the services of the Revised Liturgy. To make the attempt to confound the two things still more manifestly absurd, a recent writer in the interest of the new Order of Worship, has very gravely undertaken to prove that the German Reformed Church has always been a "responsive" Church, from the fact that the Heidelberg Catechism has questions and *answers*, i. e. responses! Oranges and crab-apples are fruit; therefore, crab-apples are oranges!

and impressive exhibition of the passion of Him in "*commemoration*"*
of Whom it was celebrated, and an exhortation to partake of the ordinance
in its true spirit. Then followed a prayer "*for true faith, sanctification,
and patient endurance under sufferings*," closing with "Our Father," and
the Apostles' Creed. In regard to the Creed, the wording of the Liturgy
may be understood to require the congregation to unite aloud ("mit
Herz und Mund") in repeating it. If, however, actual practice rule the
import of the language used, the Creed was not commonly repeated aloud
by the people. The prayer and Creed were followed by a brief exhortation, which, being very significant, is here given in full:

"That we may now be fed with the true heavenly bread of Christ, let
us not cleave with our hearts to this external bread and wine, but lift our
hearts and faith above themselves unto heaven, where Jesus Christ, our
Advocate, is at the right hand of His Heavenly Father, whither also the
articles of our Christian faith direct us, not doubting that our souls
shall be fed with His body and blood, through the operation of the Holy
Ghost, as certainly as we receive the sacred bread and wine in remembrance
of Him."†

In the administration of the elements, the sentences used were: "The
Bread which we break is the communion of the Body of Christ." "The
cup of blessing (thanksgiving) with which we bless (give thanks) is the
communion of the Blood of Christ."

After all the communicants had participated, the service was closed
with a prayer of thanksgiving of inimitable beauty.

Thus this service, again, shows throughout how much importance was
attached to the *subjective* element in the public devotions of Christians.
Indeed the entire Reformed type of piety, and consequently the entire
cultus of our Church, assumes the fact of the immediate personal relation
of the believer to God in Christ. Hence public worship, all the divinely
appointed means of grace, are designed as helps to promote this immediate
personal union. The lay believer is as *really* a priest as the officiating
minister. Hence also the indispensableness of a proper frame of mind
and heart, in order to secure the benefits of the means of grace. And
it is simply as absurd, according to the principles of our cultus, to speak
of the objective efficacy of the Sacraments whenever they are administered,
independently of subjective, (personal) preparation and fitness, as it
would be to speak of the nutritive properties of bread independently of
the capacity of the stomach to take up such nutriment. For a *stone* bread
has no more nutriment than another stone. The property is consequently
relative. Bread needs a stomach as much as a stomach needs bread. The

---

* In using the terms, "commemorative" and "commemoration," I follow strictly the language of the old Palatinate form.

† The original has been designedly rendered as literally as possible.

objective is therefore, so far at least, dependent for its *efficacy* upon the subjective. This is also in full harmony with the marked subjective spirit of the Heidelberg Catechism. Let this be called what it may, let Dr. Nevin stigmatize it unrestrainedly as pietism, spiritualisticism, or even Puritanism, its prominence in our cultus cannot be denied. *Such* subjectivism, in which, however, the objective is by no means ignored or even under-rated, is a marked distinctive characteristic of the German Reformed cultus. And it is so, as has already been shown, because that cultus was closely modelled after Apostolic precedent and practice.

How much store was set by this conformity to the Apostolic pattern of worship, by the fathers of our Church, may be further seen in the ruling resemblance of all the other forms of the Old Palatinate Liturgy to those for the Lord's Day and Communion services. Such as they were, also, they were found efficient in serving all the purposes of common edification. They had, indeed, no responses; not a single one is found in any of the services, unless, indeed, the confession of sin, and the Creed, were said aloud by the congregation, which has been shown to be improbable. There were no "ritualistic risings and bowings," there were no "antiphonal concerts of praise." That is true. But there was worship, deep, earnest and devout; such as is mirrored forth in the devotions of the primitive Church, and such as our Lord declared was most acceptable to Him "Who is a Spirit." There were no attempts at reviving or imitating the ceremonials of the abrogated Jewish ritual worship; but there is manifest a sincere and successful purpose of having worship conducted with the spirit and with the understanding also.

And such, furthermore, as that early order and those original forms of worship in our Church were, in 1563, such they continued to be during succeeding periods. For among all the inexcusable errors which Dr. Nevin commits in his turbulent "Vindication," it is altogether inexplicable how he should have fallen into the mistake of saying that the old Palatinate service soon ceased to be regarded or used, either in Europe, or by the fathers of our Church in this country. There are scores of old European Hymn-books, of that very period, during which especially the forms in question are represented as having fallen into decay, which contain those very forms. In my own possession there are three such books, the oldest an edition of 1716, published at Marburg; the next dated 1746, published at Leeuwarden; and the third dated 1784, Marburg and Frankfort, all of which contain these very forms, as forms then still used. So that whatever other Liturgies may have been brought forward from time to time (See Liturg. Question, p. 42), the old Palatinate maintained its place and its predominance in the Church.

In regard to the practice of the fathers of our Church in this country, it might have been supposed that every tyro in her history knew: that those fathers uniformly brought the old Palatinate Liturgy with them, and uniformly used it; that even when what may have seemed like private forms were used, they were mostly, if not always, copied from the old Palatinate, or abbreviations of its services; and that our early Hymn-books in this country, like that now before me, published by Saur in Germantown, 1753, as well as the first English Hymn-book used among us, that of the Ref. Dutch Church, *contained those same old Palatinate forms, and usually in connection with the Heidelberg Catechism.* Nor have they been thus only contained in the Hymn Books, but they have also been used to the present day. Those forms were never objected to on the ground of not being sufficiently ritualistic, and where they were set aside, it was not owing to any inherent deficiency in this respect. And Dr. Nevin might have known this, and thus escaped the blunders into which his oversight or neglect of facts has precipitated him. The old Palatinate forms were *not* objected to in the first place, *because* they served the purpose of merely a pulpit Liturgy, *or because* they did not provide for enough active participation, on the part of the congregation. No one, at first, said a word about repudiating that Liturgy or the theory of worship upon which it was constructed. *The chief and, indeed, only modifications proposed (for modifications only were talked of) had reference to the length and the style of its forms.* Having been written three hundred years ago, and that in the German language, it was believed that some improvements could be made without disturbing the general structure, or violating the spirit of the services. This seemed especially necessary, in order to meet the views and wishes of those of our Churches which had become English. And the reason why the Liturgy of the Rev. Dr. Mayer did not prove generally acceptable was, *not*, as Dr. Nevin says, because "it was the same thing in fact" as our older services, but because it was prepared in an independent way, or because a feeling of entire indifference or opposition to Liturgical forms of all kinds had become predominant in large portions of the Church. *The truth is, that excepting as Dr. Nevin and his school endeavored to produce aversion to our old and simple mode of worship, and have succeeded in disseminating dissatisfaction with German Reformed characteristics of faith and practice, and in exciting a desire for something newer or older, no such aversion, dissatisfaction or desire ever existed or even now exists.* He tells us that he has been laboring to produce this result ever since his professorship at Mercersburg; for he says, he "stands now where he stood then." It is true, many of us did not so understand him then, but rather supposed that his theory and measures contemplated the restoration and confirmation of true historical German Reformed characteristics. Many of us were unsuspicious, and, I may add, simple enough, to indulge a fond but, as it now seems, silly delusion, in regard to the true import and design of the Mercersburg system. Our misunderstanding and delusion, however, did not hinder the process. And that with the confidence of a Church and the influence of a Theol. Sem. and a College to back him, he should succeed in twenty-five years in effecting some change in our prevailing ecclesiastical sentiment, is not to be wondered at. The foundations of Unitarianism in New England were laid in less time than that. But partial success in disseminating such views in a Church does not prove that the Church wished them to be disseminated, or desired to reap such a harvest as they promise to yield.

Such, then, is the ruling spirit, and such are the characteristic features of the cultus established by the fathers and founders of the German Reformed Church, or rather restored by them to the people of God, long defrauded of their spiritual rights by the ritualistic bondage of Rome. And what fault have Dr. Nevin and brethren of his mind in regard to the new measures, to find with this system of worship, so carefully prepared and devoutly introduced in the 16th Century, and so distinctively German Reformed in all its chief characteristics? Is it not faithfully modelled after the Apostolic and primitive pattern? Dr. Nevin will not venture to deny that it is, or that any minor points in which it may not literally correspond with the earliest and purest practice, are not in essential harmony with that practice. Is it not in all its several services earnest, solemn, deeply devout, and are these services not calculated to promote the spirit of true worship in the hearts of all who sincerely participate in them? Let the influence and effect of the system upon the Church in which it has obtained, answer this question. The tree is known by its fruits. And the fruits of this tree may boldly challenge comparison with those of any system which prevailed from the third Century down to the period of the Reformation. If worship is designed to *promote true piety*, as well as to be a medium for its devout expression, and if the merits of any system of worship are to be measured by its fitness to serve this purpose, then the cultus of our Church may triumphantly appeal to the enlightened judgment of all evangelical Christians for a verdict in its favor, against Dr. Nevin's attempts to bring it into disrepute, and to secure its formal rejection and abrogation.

What fault, then, can be found with it? It restored to the people their full Christian rights in public worship. Rome had established the invariable use of the Latin language, as peculiarly sacred to the Church, and thus deprived the laity of the power of uniting intelligently in the services. Our fathers ordained that all public worship should be conducted in the language of the people among whom it was celebrated. Rome had robbed the people of their right to praise the Lord in psalms and hymns and spiritual songs, and allowed a vicarious priesthood the exclusive exercise of this prerogative. Our fathers condemned the robbery, and restored to the people their right in this respect to share the common privilege of the only universal priesthood in the Christian Church. Rome had, in the same exclusive and tyrannical spirit, deprived the people of their common inheritance in the Word of God, and refused even to allow them to hear the glorious Gospel read in the public services of the sanctuary, and expounded and applied for the edification of the people. By the Apostolic system of worship reclaimed from the bondage of a Babylonish captivity, the free Word of God, together with the preaching of the Gospel according to that Word, was reinstated in its legitimate prominent place, so that the people had unrestrained access to it, and might again be "fed with the sincere milk of the Word, that they might grow thereby." Rome claimed that the forgiveness of sins was bound to the formal confession made to her priests, and to their formal sacerdotal remission of those sins, grossly perverting one of the most comforting declarations of our blessed Lord, and one of the most consoling assurances connected with the proclamation of Gospel grace. By the cultus of our Church, as instituted in the 16th Century, the hearts and consciences of sincere penitent believers in the Lord Jesus Christ were rescued from this cruel subjection to sacerdotal usurpations of a Divine prerogative, and assured for their joy and peace, that He who alone hath power to forgive sins, had most certainly pardoned them, if they had truly repented and fully trusted in His merits. The Romish Church had taught the people to rely upon the sacrifice of the mass, for the salvation of the living and the dead, to attach to its celebration such *opuss operatum* efficacy, and to believe that their salvation here, and deliverance from a fictitious purgatory hereafter depended upon the sacerdotal administration of the mass. To quite another source did the cultus of our 16th Century fathers teach believers to look, upon quite another foundation to rest their hope of salvation, as they celebrated the Holy Supper of our Lord after the manner and spirit of its original institution.

Is it with these distinctive peculiarities of our early Reformed worship that Dr. Nevin and some others find fault? Possibly not. But he tells us what he considers their fatal defects. *It was not modelled after the Liturgies of the third and fourth centuries! It lacked ritualistic action. It was too spiritualistic, ran into extreme simplicity.* And all this "*over against the worship of the Catholic*" (*Roman*, of course, must here be meant) "Church," which "stood in the way of its producing a full Liturgical cultus, *in the proper sense of the term*." (Liturg. Ques. pp. 40–1, 60–1). But what is a still more serious defect, in the opinion of those who find fault with our old order of worship, is, that it wholly abolished the sacrificial altar of the Romish style, with an officiating specific priesthood, and substituted in its place the sacramental table of the Lord. This was sufficient to condemn the Liturgies of the sixteenth century, if they had been marred by no other defects. Even the Book of Common Prayer, considered so superior in all other respects to any acknowledged Reformed Service of that period, lacked in this respect an essential element of a true Liturgy. Like the rest it had no altar, in this sacrificial sense, and recognized no specific priesthood as a separate caste. Although, therefore, the new "Order of Worship" so closely follows the Episcopal Service in most of its details, often even literally, that "Order" could not endure the ignoring of the altar and sacerdotal character of the ministry. Consequently we find in the new "Order" that the altar in a propitiatory sacrificial sense is openly restored, and that although the minister is not called a priest, it virtually invests him with priestly functions, as well in the regular and sacramental services, as in the form of ordination. And now, because in the Reformed Liturgies of the sixteenth century, especially that of the Palatinate, there is no such altar of "sacramental holiness inhabiting the house of God," to which worshipping assemblies might "*do bodily reverence;*" because though they breathe a truly sacramental spirit, they do not "*breathe throughout a sacrificial spirit*" (Liturg. Ques. p. 51) in a propitiatory sense; and because they allow no place to a mediating specific priesthood, they are to be discarded. These, substantially, are the objections urged against what has ever been the Reformed type of worship. Again, it may be allowed that these objections are honestly entertained. For myself, I confess my conviction that Dr. Nevin and his disciples believe most heartily that our German Reformed style of worship is not as good as the style they advocate. But that does not make ours bad or theirs better. Their judgment may err. Their tastes may be false. They may apply a wrong standard to the case. The constitutional character of the Reformed Church may *not* have " carried in it a tendency to what we call *extreme* simplicity and spiritualism." (Liturg. Ques. p. 41). It may be much nearer the Apostolic type than " the constitutional character" of the Revised Liturgy. And *that* Liturgy, rather than those of the old Reformed type, may not only be "materially and essentially different from any thing known to our fathers," but may be radically and fatally defective in all that pertains to the ruling characteristics of Christian evangelical worship.

After the severe animadversions cast upon the older cultus of our Church, and the disdainful manner in which our earlier Liturgies are spurned, it is both natural and reasonable to expect that those who indulge in such criticism and contempt have a substitute to furnish, which shall, in every sense, be above reproach, and altogether worthy of acceptance. And possibly, if we could only get into the right position for securing a favorable view of it, it would commend itself to our approbation. As Dr. Nevin says, in the striking astronomical illustration on p. 56 of his treatise, very much depends upon position in contemplating things. It is, therefore, no doubt very unfortunate for ourselves, if not for the Revised Liturgy, that our habit of looking at such things from a Protestant evangelical, *i. e.*, from a Scriptural Apostolic stand-point, is so confirmed, that in spite of every effort to get into a Cyprianic or Gregorian position, we are constantly viewing the remarkable work in quite another light. The true touch-stone by which to test its merit is Apostolic precept and practice, as revived and established again by our Church in the sixteenth century. Not Dr. Nevin, nor a thousand like him at his side, should be allowed for a moment to shake our confidence in the work wrought by our Reformed fathers, as directed and guided by the Spirit of God. And until it is proven beyond all contradiction, by Scripture and Apostolic testimony, that they did their work badly; or until it is proven that the compilers of the Revised Liturgy have done their work better, in the true Apostolic sense, we should not let ourselves be tempted to barter our ancient birthright. The very first thing we have a right to demand of this new aspirant for fame and authority in our Church, is, whether it is honestly and thoroughly Reformed? We have a standard of worship which we should not suffer to be removed or altered, until it is proven false by a stronger kind of evidence than the denunciations and sarcasms of Drs. Nevin, Harbaugh and others. Does the Revised Liturgy come up to the measure of that standard?

With the distinctive features of the book, the readers of this tract may be supposed to be familiar. By the confession of its advocates, it does not pretend to be German Reformed in any true and historical sense. They say that the great defects of the Provisional Liturgy were the large concessions it made to the system of worship known to our Church, and which alone can be harmonized with its true spirit and genius. It was by far too much of a pulpit Liturgy; could be, and, with three or four exceptions, was used as a pulpit hand-book. "The Revised Liturgy is now relieved of its first defects, and brought into easy working form," says Dr. Nevin. Hence to be made perfect in his judgment, the Provisional Liturgy had to be purged most thoroughly of every element which it possessed in common with old Reformed Liturgies. And this we find done to the extremest degree in the new "Order of Worship." In every respect it is made to differ as widely as possible from the Reformed type of worship. *Spurning the very order which our fathers adopted and established it takes up that order which they knowingly and designedly rejected*, and even "*improve*" upon it by sundry additions and variations. Under pretence of elevating the cultus of the Church, and this in compliance with her own instructions, this new Order seeks wholly to subvert the true cultus of the Church, and to *force* itself upon her members and congregations by the use of unworthy means. For what Dr. Nevin says about *freedom, liberty* &c., in regard to the introduction of the new Order, is too manifestly one-sided, to deceive any cautious reader. He means that there ought to be full *liberty to introduce the book, to laud and commend it*, and to use whatever methods "cautious and prudent pastors" may think best suited to secure its success. But he is intolerant of liberty to expose and resist the movement; to tell the people fairly and candidly that it involves a complete metamorphosis of their Church; the utter forsaking and, repudiation of her past history; a change from all that is distinctive of us as a Church, into what would convert us, *not* indeed, into a *genuine* Episcopal Church, for *true* Episcopalians whom we highly esteem denounce the new Order of Worship as inconsistent with evangelical Protestantism, but into what would convert us into a Church whose closest affinities would be with what the Reformers condemned as the harlot of Rome. Dr. Nevin may say what he pleases, and others may take up and reiterate his words, in misrepresenting and decrying the spirit and genius of our Church; for doing this full liberty is claimed. But when the nakedness of his views or schemes is exposed; when the reproach put upon the fathers is repelled, and reasons are urged why the Church should not accept of or allow the innovations, then the cry is raised: you deny us our liberty. Because men, awaked in time to a sense of the evil threatening our heritage, resist the attempt to sow tares over the field, and endeavor to let others know the danger, those men are enemies to congregational liberty! If Dr. Nevin were a pastor, and the Rev. C. G. Finney should pass along, would he throw open the doors of his church to the renowned revivalist, and let the stranger have fair play for a year or two? Or would Dr. Nevin think it an infringement upon the *liberty* of his congregation, not to let them have the opportunity, and enjoy the privilege of hearing Mr. Finney, and seeing whether his views might not be thought more acceptable, or more "live theology," than those of their old Pastor?

Talk of liberty! Is it not a well-known fact that in the majority of cases, where the responsive and other peculiarities of the New Order are used, they were introduced without the consent of the congregation, and are used to the offence of many members? And is not Dr. Nevin perfectly familiar with at least one illustration in point? Or apart from that illustration, so near home, is it forgotten that an attempt made by an elder at Dayton to protect the people against having the New Order forced upon them against their desire and will, was at once frowned down? Why, if all this cry for liberty is sincere, not require every pastor and consistory to submit the question to the congregation in full assembly (not with but fifteen or twenty members, out of two hundred, present, as is said to have been the case at Jonestown not long ago), instead of permitting the innovations to be introduced "on the sly?" This, however, by the way. As we have already stated, the new "Order of Worship" is freely acknowledged to be "materially and essentially different from any mode of worship known to the Reformed Church." And yet the real extent of this diversity is probably not fully realized, even by those who have given some attention to its peculiarities. But before we consent to the endorsement or adoption of a book marked by such peculiarities, their true nature and effect upon our personal and denominational life should be most carefully pondered, and, if possible, correctly ascertained. Sometimes, it is true, in entertaining strangers, angels are entertained unawares. But whilst the counsel of one Apostle should be heeded, we should not forget that another admonishes us against opening the door to all strangers indiscriminately, or giving them comfort and encouragement. We most cordially accept of Dr. Nevin's rule, as taken from the advice of this same second Apostle. The spirits must be tried. Only he and we differ as to the standard. He says, the fourth century; we say, the first. He says, by patristic authority; we say, by Apostolic authority. He says, by the *Creed* in the third and fourth century sense; we say, by the *Creed* as explained in our Heidelberg Catechism, which gives, in all essentials, the true Gospel sense. He says, by the test, has Christ come in the flesh; we say, the cunning spirits have long since learned to mimic this Shibboleth, and whilst saying most glibly, We believe that Christ has come in the flesh, have glided into the Church and filled her with most abominable God and Christ dishonoring corruptions. For ten centuries before the Reformation, Papal Rome said this, and yet she was an apostacy, the harlot of the book of Revelation. Hence we plant ourselves upon this divine test: *not every one that sayeth Lord, Lord,* i. e., not every one that avows faith in the incarnation, &c., is to be welcomed as sincerely of the truth, and entitled to our hearty God-speed.

There is more to be done, therefore, before the new Order is adopted as the order of worship for our Church, than merely to contemplate its exterior features. It can be shown by the declarations and admissions of its advocates, that it not only *varies* in some material respects from the established cultus of our Church, but that it is utterly *irreconcilable with it.* To how great an extent this is true, may be clearly seen in the following points of disagreement.

A general proof of the fact that the new Order is not simply different from our denominational cultus, but utterly irreconcilable with it, is found in those assertions of its advocates which declare our established cultus *unliturgical,* and pronounce such Liturgies as the Old Palatinate no true Liturgies. Upon this point no men could speak more plainly, to say nothing of justice or modesty, than they have done. But, however successfully the claims of our ancient cultus may be maintained against such reproaches, is it not evident that in the estimation of those who plead for the new Order, it and our old order are in radical and fundamental hostility to each other? And so they unquestionably are. They rest upon totally different theories of Christianity and the Church. They do not pretend even to be based on the same foundation. The cultus of the German Reformed Church rests upon the Apostolic type of worship; that of the new Order upon the fourth century patristic type; the former appeals to the word of the Lord and His Apostles; the latter to the word and example of the fathers of the third, fourth, and, if Dr. Nevin were perfectly candid, he would acknowledge, the fifth and later centuries. To set aside our old order of worship, therefore, and to adopt this new system, involves a repudiation and abandonment of the Apostolic foundation on which our old mode of worship rests. For be it remembered that the advocates of the innovations do not pretend at all to support or to justify them by an appeal to the true original source of authority, but solely to the practice of the Church in the third and fourth centuries. They do not claim that their cultus is Apostolic, excepting so far as it is Patristic. And yet I may have written too fast. I call to mind that Dr. Nevin does appeal in one place (so does Bishop Hopkins in his late defence of Ritualism) to something said in one of the Psalms about all the people saying: *Amen.* Did he forget what is said in another Psalm about "praising the Lord with the timbrel and dance?" Or has he become such a literalistic and indiscriminate interpreter and applier of Holy Writ, that he would justify the dancing Quakers (notwithstanding his dislike of Quakers in general) on the ground of this latter exhortation of the Psalmist? The unfortunate irrelevancy of the few appeals, like that to Hebrews 13: 10, in justification of the propitiatory altar, made by the vindicators of the new Order, to the Sacred Scriptures, only serve to show how little store they set by *inspired* precepts and examples in such matters.

But this general irreconcilable diversity between the two schemes of worship, becomes more manifest if we look at the constituent elements of the cultus of both.

1. The most prominent disagreement between the two systems, that diversity which is likely first to strike the mind, is found in the *responses* of the new Order. It is not said that this is the most important and serious,

by any means. We readily accept the statement, that the great question before us is not a mere matter of "*responses*" or "no responses." None of the opponents of the new measures ever said it was. At the same time this extremely responsive feature of the new "Order" is not to be flippantly set aside with a sneer or a laugh. In the thing itself of congregational responses in public worship, but little may be seen that is seriously objectionable. At any rate we would not ridicule it, or try to make it seem intolerably absurd, as the Liturgical Committee have done with the cultus of the Reformed Church. We have no fault to find with the Episcopal Church, because their Common Prayer is marked with this peculiarity. In that Church there are both clergy and laymen whom we cordially esteem, and are happy to enjoy their regard. Especially has the evangelical portion of that Church the sincere sympathy of those of us who are learning by sad experience how fierce and reckless a foe the spirit of hyper-ecclesiasticism is. But while responses *per se* may be set among things indifferent, and while other Churches which have them may not be denounced or discarded on that account, we must remember that they are not offered to us *per se*, in themselves alone, in the present case. The advocates of the innovations would no doubt confess that they are an essential part of their system *as at present developed*. So the introduction of such full responses, choral antiphonies, *and so forth*, into the fourth Century Church, was the budding or flowering of a theory, a system, "*an organic process*," which by and by surprised the world by its fruit, as much as the first discoverers of some vegetables were to find that the blossoms on the stem indicated fruit under ground.

In these responses, then, as incorporated into the Revised Liturgy, *we discover a purpose and a scheme, to sever completely all historical connection between our Church of the present and our Church of the past and, also between our section of the Reformed Church, and other branches of the Reformed family*. When some conquerors desired wholly to absorb their captives and to destroy their national identity, they forbid their speaking their native tongue, or singing their national songs; and required them to learn and speak the language, and to practice the manners of their new master. It was the very perfection of craft, but no less the refinement of heartless cruelty. In some cases the craft succeeded, and cruelty in progress of time rendered the captives *or their children* callous and indifferent to the destruction of their nationality.

Thus, in a figure, those who are seeking to gain the assent of our Church to be brought under the dominion of this new order, propose, as one of the first things, that we worship the God of our fathers in a form and manner so entirely different from their mode of worshipping Him, that by the adoption of the new scheme, our ecclesiastical affinity with them, and with the descendants of their nearest and dearest ecclesiastical kindred, would wholly and forever cease. And let us remember here, that whilst our legitimate ecclesiastical relationship would thus be severed, there are other features distinctive of this new Order of Worship, which would prevent our finding congenial fellowship in any other denomination of evangelical Christians. For much as we all should regret to lose our denominational identity by being absorbed by the Episcopal Church (and I think that many intelligent and liberal members of that Church, who, I am happy to know, would join in the regret), our greatest peril from the new measures is not that they may lead our Church into evangelical Episcopacy, but into that element of the Episcopal Church which many honest and earnest Episcopalians themselves justly and unqualifiedly condemn. And in corroboration of this truth I may state, that without exception, so far as I know, all the ministers who have, during the last years, abandoned our Church, and united with the Episcopal Church, belong to the extreme high-church party there. Much, therefore, as we have reason to object, on the ground of a commendable regard for our denominational existence, that our mode of worship should be changed into such conformity with that peculiar to another Church, as might lead to denominational loss—there is still greater cause for opposition to such change on the other ground indicated.

It is further to be noted, that the new order not only differs in the use and multiplication of responses from our old mode of worship, but also from the Provisional Liturgy, upon which it is offered as an improvement. In the Provisional Liturgy there are simple non-responsive services. In the Revised Liturgy all such are excluded. It has the merit, at least, of being now unique, though for that reason more radically anti-Reformed. For it will hardly be called in question, that such a studied, persistent exclusion of forms, resembling those to which the Church had ever been accustomed, and the sole use of a new mode of worship, implies irreconcilable antagonism. If not, why did not the Committee propose to the Synod the propriety of dissolving our ecclesiastical organization, and of merging our denominational existence into that of another Church?

Upon this ground then, chiefly do we maintain that the *responses** of the new Order present an insuperable objection to its adoption and place

---

* A correspondent (A.) of the *G. R. Messenger*, for whom I still cherish great esteem, seems so bent upon throwing stones at me that he goes far out of his way to pick them. Thus he persists in arguing that because I am willing to allow the Creed to be recited in the S. School (he might have added in the congregation, also, on special occasions), the whole point of responses is surrendered. Surely the Brother is too old to indulge in such puerile sophistries, with any hope of misleading people by them. Because a congregation may occasionally recite the *Creed, therefore,* it should not object to the Revised Liturgy! What a leap to reach the rock!

7.

it in essential hostility to the historical cultus of the Reformed Church. It is not only our privilege but our duty, to preserve and perpetuate our identity. The introduction of a full responsive scheme of worship like that of the new Order strikes at the root of that identity, and must prove its destruction. Are we willing to submit to such an issue? With all our liberality, our lamentations over the divisions of Zion, and our strong desires for the day when there may be "one fold and one Shepherd," are we prepared, can we think ourselves required, to offer so partial and one-sided a sacrifice to an experiment so unreasonable, so visionary, so unlikely to serve the end of true and sacred unity as this? We hope, we believe, that the day of the general unity of the Church, is not far off. But Ritualism, instead of hastening is retarding it. It is not by zeal to have men say with the lip: "Amen! the Lord's name be praised," and the like; but by the spirit which seeks to have them animated with true inward devoutness, and deep heartfelt aspirations, that the desired result is to be achieved.

2. But if the *responses* of the new Order of Worship place it in rather an external and superficial antagonism to the cultus of the Reformed Church, that Order is strongly marked by another characteristic, and ruled by another principle, which does not constitute a merely outward and "insignificant" objection, but is one which affects the inmost life of our evangelical system.

It was shown, some pages back in the statement made concerning the basis upon which the fathers of the Reformed Church reconstructed her cultus, that *the immediate personal relation of each believer to God in Christ, and of the free personal access of each directly for himself to God, was a cardinal doctrine or principle of their system.* Hence in the order for public worship which they restored, the congregation does not approach the mercy-seat *through* the minister (as though he were a mediating sacerdos), does not pray *through* the minister for pardon, and such blessings as may be desired. Rather are minister and people considered as one common priesthood, and the people as praying in and with the minister as their mouth-piece (not sub-mediator). Their doing this silently, and breathing at the close of the prayer a silent Amen, no way diminished, but rather was calculated to increase, the sincerity with which it was done. But the main point is, that the people themselves had access, in common with the minister, by one and the same Spirit, to the Father. This was especially the case in the service of the Holy Supper. The minister did not stand before them as a mediating priest, offering up on their behalf a memorial propitiation for their sins. It was not to a sacrifice in such sense, but to a spiritual supper they had come, and to full, direct personal participation in all the benefits of that Holy Supper, they had all an equal right with the minister. This, then, was a fundamental distinctive characteristic of the Reformed cultus. Dr. Nevin and the Committee themselves acknowledge this, even whilst condemning what they regard as a serious unchurchly defect. To deny this prerogative to the individual Christian, to set up a cultus, one of whose chief corner-stones is the principle of some sort of sacerdotal mediation, as indispensable to popular worship, is most undeniably, therefore, to set up a system which must be in irreconcilable antagonism both to a ruling characteristic of our Reformed cultus, and to the Reformed evangelical doctrine of the universal priesthood of Christians.

But this is one of those points in which the new Order of Worship differs so "materially and essentially" from all our old Reformed Liturgies. Of course, we find no explicit formal statements to this effect in the book. It is not a text-book of theology. But the principles on which it rests may nevertheless be ascertained, from its ruling spirit and tone, and from the known sentiments of its authors in reference to the points involved. Thus, examined and judged, the Revised Liturgy is plainly seen to be in open conflict with established Reformed principles.

Happily we are relieved of the necessity of sustaining or illustrating this point by elaborate argument. The Committee, speaking through Dr. Nevin, tell us most distinctly that they utterly discarded the Reformed idea of the immediate spiritual relationship of the believer to God, and of his right of direct personal access to the gracious Hearer of prayer and Source of all grace. This is expressed, indeed, in language which might seem ambiguous to those not familiar with ecclesiastical phraseology. But to others, the import of their language is obvious enough, as it was doubtless meant to be. Thus they unhesitatingly declare in the manifesto tract, to which we have so much occasion and such full right to refer in proof of their views and designs,—that a *true* Liturgy "must bear a certain *priestly* character, determined by a proper regard throughout to the idea of a Christian *altar*." Now, as the terms *"priest"* and *"altar"* have a familiar inoffensive sense, a sense in which they are altogether proper and allowable, this quotation may seem to contain nothing objectionable. But those very terms, so evangelical as they are commonly employed by Christians, have also a signification which is utterly incompatible with the Gospel idea of "altar" and "priest," and which renders both virtually synonymous with their import under the ancient Levitical dispensation, and those modern mongrel imitations of it found in the Romish, and Puseyite portion of the Episcopal Churches.[*] Have they this sense in the new "Order of Worship?" Undoubtedly they have, if the following passage

---

[*] What Dr. Nevin says about a "ridiculous fuss," and what his feeble echo says about "Spooks in the garret," and "nigger in the cellar," will receive some little notice by and by.

can be regarded as meaning what the words plainly imply. "We feel at once what the Liturgical means, in this view, in the *old priestly services of the Jewish temple*, WHERE THE TRANSACTION OF THE ALTAR SERVED TO MEDIATE OBJECTIVELY BETWEEN THE HEARER OF PRAYER AND HIS WORSHIPPING PEOPLE. IN THE SAME WAY, it is held, *the true Christian Leitourgia, the substance of which that older service was only a type, must ever circle, as a system of offices, round the Christian altar, as something always mystically present in the Christian Church.*" Here, then, it is frankly declared, though with some mental reservations, that the design of the new "Order" is to restore sacerdotal functions to the Gospel ministry, and a "mystical" propitiatory significancy to the altar. For let it be noted that the language emphatically declares that the Christian altar must be a real, *substantial, visible* centre, corresponding as a full antitype to the altar of the "old services of the Jewish temple, where the *transaction* (i. e., the sacrifices of atonement, propitiation, &c.) *of the altar served to mediate objectively between the Hearer of prayer and His worshipping people.*" It is true that after the phrase "Christian altar," as after the word "altar" in the preceding sentence, no mention is made of "*priest.*" But this is merely an ellipsis, and the word is so clearly implied that it will suggest itself to every reader's mind.

By this new theory of worship, therefore, the old Levitical idea of worshipping God through a visible propitiatory sacrifice offered upon an altar, and through a mediating priesthood, is to be actualized in full antitypal form, in the cultus which Dr. Nevin and his disciples hope to persuade the German Reformed Church to accept. If the declarations of the author and endorsers of the "Liturgical Question" do not mean this, there is no sense in their language. And although the author of that tract may often have said things which were not understood, he seems to have written lucidly enough in this case. To the same effect is the theory of the Church upon which Dr. N. says, the Revised Liturgy rests. According to this theory, the order of salvation is as follows: To be pardoned and saved, and worship God acceptably, men must 1. in the Church, 2. through the minister, 3. be forgiven and 4. have access in the worship of the Church as mediated by the minister (this title has not yet been dropped, though its incompatibility with the rest of the theory is obvious) to God. No one, therefore, can be forgiven, until he has come to the minister at the altar, there confessed his sins, and thus obtained pardon. In proof of this doctrine, the advocates of the theory appeal, just as Episcopal ritualists like Pusey, and Roman Catholics do, 1. to the order of the articles in the Creed, where we have a., the Church, b., the Communion of saints, and then c., the forgiveness of sins. (Is it not the acme of philosophical sagacity!); and 2. to the much abused passages about loosing and binding, and remitting and not remitting sins.

With great propriety might Dr. Nevin acknowledge, in view of this very marked peculiarity of his new scheme as it has now been developed, that it involves a question of very "material change in our Church life." How decided and how hopeless the antagonism between a system of worship which encourages every believer to feel that his access to God, His reconciled Father in heaven, is immediate, direct, free, spiritual, through the one and only High-priest Jesus Christ, by the Holy Spirit; a cultus which seeks to *cultivate* in every believer's heart the assurance of his own priestly prerogative before the spiritual throne of grace, and spiritual altar of praise and prayer, and to embolden each one to draw confidently near to that throne, even as into *the holiest of all, as that is to be found in its true spiritual sense wherever two or three are gathered together in the name of Jesus Christ,* even though the Lord's Supper should not be each time celebrated; and a system which says to God's people that they may not worship their Lord thus *subjectively*, thus *spiritualistically*, thus *Gnostically*, but that they must approach him through the visible altar and its mediating priest!

"Ridiculous fuss," says Dr. Nevin, "Spooks in the garret," echoes the classic Dr. Harbaugh. But let them mock and ridicule. Only we will not be thus laughed and derided into a surrender of "the liberty wherewith Christ has made us free," and into renewed subjection to the "yoke of bondage" cast off by our fathers. I have not forgotten the disingenuousness with which Dr. Harbaugh sought at York to evade the charge that the new "Order" involved the virtual restoration of a propitiatory altar and a specific mediating priesthood. Nor am I insensible how hard it is to get the Church at large to believe that any such radical revolution in our doctrines concerning worship, the Church, and the ministry, is really contemplated and pressed. But I persist in the charge, and the more earnestly as none of the leaders of the new measures have dared cordially to meet it, and still less squarely to deny it. There is indeed a pretence of restoring to the dear people their rights in public worship: to let them orally participate, and so forth. But it is to be hoped, and may well be believed, that the dear people will be altogether too sagacious to be caught by any such specious bait as that. They know too well the old story of sacerdotal aggressions, and the bribes by which they succeeded, in the great Apostasy; they know too well by what gracious concessions to the people, the arrogant priesthood of that Apostasy still contrives to maintain its spiritual supremacy over them.

3. The RITUALISTIC character of the new Order is another element which renders it hostile to the legitimate cultus of the Reformed Church.

As this charge has been pronounced groundless and absurd, it will be well to give it special attention. The first point to be settled is the meaning of the term *ritualistic*.

Although the words "liturgy" and "ritual," with their derivatives, are often used interchangeably in common language, they are not really synonymous. The *former* refers to the act of worship, in the use of suitable forms, or without such forms; while the latter refers to the outward manner, the rites and ceremonies which may be associated with that worship. All worship must, of course, be rendered in some form, and that form might be called a rite, or ritual; and hence it might be said that all worship, even liturgical, must be ritualistic. But this is not the exact and proper import of the term. It refers strictly, to *some special ceremonial*, artistic or æsthetic, superadded to those forms or acts which are indispensable to the performance of worship at all. This is, indeed, conceded in the Liturg. Question (pp. 18, 60). A *Ritualistic* style of worship is, therefore, clearly distinguishable from a simply *Liturgical* mode of worship. The *latter* is characterized by the use of only such forms and actions as are indispensable; the *former* invests these forms and services with extra drapery and ceremonies, for the purpose, avowedly, of making those services more interesting and impressive. The number and character of these additions may vary. The ritualism of the Greek and Romish Churches varies, and that of the ultra high-church Puseyism by which the Episcopal Church is now being so sorely vexed, differs somewhat from both. It is not necessary, therefore, that an "Order of Worship," say like Dr. Nevin's, should minutely prescribe what vestments the "priest" should wear, how the "altar" should be decorated on certain "high days," or go into *nice details* about the "*risings and bowings*," and the "turning of all faces towards the altar," as the "*shekinah forth from which must radiate continually* THE ENTIRE GLORY OF GOD'S HOUSE." (Liturgical Question, p. 29). The "Order" may be exceedingly reserved upon all such minute things. And yet it may be essentially and unqualifiedly ritualistic.

For this term, again, has a *relative* sense. What might hardly be termed ritualism for another Church, may be decidedly ritualistic for ours. That the new "Order," therefore, can not be fairly called ritualistic in comparison with the Book of Common Prayer, may be readily granted. This, however, is no criterion for our Church. The true measure by which we must try the new "Order," is not the Episcopal, but the Reformed standard of worship.

Tried by this standard, our judgment upon it will be found correct, and this, too, by the concessions of Dr. Nevin and his immediate assistants in completing the work. Only let the contrast they themselves have drawn between the legitimate Reformed type of worship, and that which they have adopted, be carefully pondered, as set forth in the following quotations from their own tract:

"It is to be freely admitted that there lay in the distinguishing spirit of the Reformed Confession, as such, from the beginning, a tendency in opposition to the constraint of fixed *religious rites and ceremonies*. It belongs, as we all know, to the Reformed Church, *to represent that side of the Christian life, in which the inward, the free, the spiritual in religion, are asserted against the authority of the merely outward in every view. Such is her historical vocation; such is her genius.* While we honor* then the constitutional character or the Reformed Church, in the general view of which we are now speaking, we ought to be willing to admit that it carried in it a tendency to what *we may call* extreme simplicity and spiritualism, over against the worship of the Catholic Church," etc. (Liturg. Question, 40, 41).

"The Reformed Confession from the beginning, if we except the Episcopal portion of it in England, for reasons which it is not now necessary to consider, *has not been favorable to much outward form or ritual action in worship.*" (Liturg. Ques. p. 60).

Although this does not tell the whole truth in regard to the great simplicity and spirituality of Reformed worship, and although it does not delineate it fairly even as far as the statements go, the picture fully answers our purpose. A man of Dr. Nevin's deep and bitter *"prejudices"* against the essential and material characteristics of Reformed practice, and one of his strong partialities for a very different style of piety and worship, could hardly be expected to describe fairly and truly the cultus of the Reformed Church, or to estimate properly the principles on which that cultus rests. And yet any attempt to do this at all, could hardly fail to let out enough historical truth to answer our end. According to his own admission, then, *every thing ritualistic in worship, was most alien and contrary to the distinguishing spirit of the Reformed Church.*

What now is the distinguishing spirit and character of the "Order of Worship" which Dr. Nevin would persuade this extremely simple and spiritualistic Church to substitute for her old, historical and legitimate mode?

Again we let the advocates of this Order describe it in their own words, that all who are willing to be convinced may see that it is not charged

---

* "The words of his mouth were smoother than butter, but war was in his heart; his words were softer than oil," etc. Is it by such bland flatteries that Dr. N. seeks to manipulate the Church into acquiescence in the revolutionary scheme? "And Joab said unto Amasa, Art thou in health, my brother? And Joab took Amasa by the beard to kiss him. But Amasa took no heed to the sword that was in Joab's hand; so Joab smote him therewith in the fifth rib; and he died."

unjustly with being *ritualistic,* and *that* in a very strong sense for a Church like ours.

According to Dr. Nevin and those who adopt his peculiar views upon this subject, every "true liturgy" must possess such characteristics as are indicated in the following statements: "It must be confessed, however, *that mere forms of prayer are not enough of themselves to make the services of the sanctuary what they ought to be* in the view now brought into notice. * * There must be GESTURES and POSTURES *significant* of faith in what the service thus means, ACTS OF BODILY WORSHIP FITLY SUITED TO CORRESPONDING ACTS OF THE SPIRIT, responses of the tongue to seal and confirm the silent responses of the heart." (Lit. 2, pp. 32, 33.)

What particular "acts of bodily worship," &c., should accompany, precede, or follow the "responses of the tongue," &c., we are left to surmise. It is perfectly easy, however, to discern the direction in which such things point. Among ritualistic practices which high-church Episcopalians are introducing into their services, there is one called "*Orientation.*" That is, whenever the name of Jesus Christ is used in the services, the worshipper, no matter how he may have been standing, turns quite around with his face to the East (the Orient) and makes *one or three low bows.** This, then, to some minds, seems a "bodily act of worship fitly suited to a corresponding act of the Spirit."

"It will not do to call these things the idle mummery of superstition." (Will the reader please refer to one of the quotations from Dr. Nevin's views in 1844, as given on p. 27 of this tract.) "If they seem mummery to any, it can only be, most assuredly, because they have themselves no lively sense of the true nature of Christian worship in the view just described. * * * Devotional forms, then, the *outward actings* and utterings of worship on the part of the people *are not only to be tolerated in the services of the sanctuary,* THEY ARE TO BE ENJOINED as the necessary condition of worship in a truly spiritual form. * * Let the outward and the inward here go hand in hand together. Let it be considered a part of religion *to do bodily* reverence, *in all proper ways, to the sacramental holiness,* which is felt to inhabit the house of God. Let there be *rising* and *bowing,* where it may seem to be meet, *in token* of the *consenting adorations of the people.*"

So much, then, for the verbal declarations of Dr. Nevin and others in regard to their ideal of worship. They seem explicit enough, and quite frank. And, taken in connection with the circumstances under which they were made, interpreted by the contrast which they are intended to

---

* Not long ago, a student of ritualistic fancy in an Evangelical Divinity School, left the institution because such superstitious "mummery," as Dr. Nevin once called this sort of thing, would not be tolerated by the Faculty!

exhibit between this new sort of cultus and that of our Church in past years, they plainly indicate the reigning spirit and certain tendency of the new system. For when they speak of doing "bodily reverence," of combining the outward with the inward, of the superiority of a worship not purely spiritual, &c., it is clear that something different is meant from the mode of worship, which has all along, with more or less regularity, prevailed in our Church. In a very real and true sense, *we have always been accustomed to unite the soul and body, the outward and inward form with spirit in our worship.* Our fathers and their ecclesiastical descendants always attended *bodily* upon the public means of grace; united *bodily* with their mouth as well as heart, in singing the praises of the Lord; and stood up bodily doing *such* outward reverence in the house of God. It is true, *they did not look to the visible Lord's Table*, or outward altar, as, in an evangelical sense, it may be called; they *turned their eyes heavenward, and their hearts too*, as our fathers beautifully and truly say in their old Order of Worship, on which Drs. Nevin and Harbaugh have cast such scorn. But still, they rendered bodily service as far as they thought it necessary and fit.

This, then, is *not* what is meant in the extracts above quoted, by "rising and bowing," and such like things. But if those expressions mean something more, something very significantly different, is it not perfectly plain that they involve the very essence of *ritualism* in the true and exact sense of that term? For ritualism, as shown already in distinction from worship (leitourgia) in the stricter sense, consist precisely in the addition of such rites and ceremonies to that worship. And this, now, is the style of worship found in the revised Liturgy. The above extracts furnish the basis, the principles on which they say that work was constructed, as well as the author's vindication of the work thus formed and fashioned.

It will, moreover, help us to estimate aright these peculiarities of the new Order of Worship, if we remember another significant fact. While the style of worship adopted as the model after which the new Order was fashioned, differs so "materially and essentially" from *our* old mode of worship, its very striking resemblance to *another style* cannot fail to arrest attention and produce a bewildering impression.* That style is not *Reformed*, not *Lutheran*, not Evangelical *Episcopalian*, not *Moravian;* in a word, you search for it in vain among any who care to call themselves Protestant Christians. What is it then? Where may an illustration of it be found? Let me answer as gently as possible, by pointing out again, in its own phrases, a few of the most prominent features or this new

---

* Dr. Nevin will please prepare again to say: "Ridiculous fuss!" And Dr. Harbaugh will get ready to echo, with classic variation: "Spooks in the garret!"—The reader will please remember that I quote their own words.

thing in the Reformed Church, and then by asking two or three simple questions.

1. "*The altar, and not the pulpit, is to be regarded as the central object of the sanctuary*—THE PLACE OF THE CHRISTIAN SHEKINAH *forth from which* MUST RADIATE CONTINUALLY *the entire glory of God's house.*"

2. "Do bodily reverence in all proper ways, to *the sacramental holiness* which is felt to inhabit the house of God. Let all faces *be turned* in time of prayer *toward the altar.*"

3. "Let there be risings and bowings * * in token of the consenting adorations of the people."

Now take these three marks of what Dr. Nevin and his friends call true worship, and which they proclaim essential to true worship, marks without which nothing ought to pretend to be worship—take these marks, the importance of which Dr. Nevin and others unhappily involved in his delusion, magnify so greatly, take them, and go around among the Churches and tell me where do you find them realized? Where do you find the *altar made the central part of the sanctuary, the place of the Christian shekinah forth from which must radiate continually the entire glory of God's house?* Where do you think Dr. Nevin saw the "beautiful" picture which suggested this *brilliant* figure of speech? Can you say? And where, again, do you find the congregation *doing bodily reverence*, to the *sacramental* holiness in the house of God, *all faces being turned toward* the altar? And where, finally, do you witness numerous "risings and bowings in token of the consenting adorations of the people" (still turned with earnest gaze toward the altar)? Does not every reader, who lives within reach of a Roman Catholic Church, or who has ever read of their style of worship, know where these things are to be found?

Will any one deny now that this new Order, embodying such elements as its essential constituents, and marked so broadly by such inseparable characteristics, is *properly* called *ritualistic?* Let a church edifice be built according to its ideal, and the inner structure and arrangements will be found in harmony with that model which makes the Lord's table an altar, sets that altar on high, in some most prominent central place, and locates the Word, or its symbol, the pulpit, below and aside. Enter a church in which the services are conducted according to this new "Order," and you will find the forms and movements all in harmony with the demands of ritualistic action. And now, when we remember that the end is not yet; that the new "Order" bears internal proofs of being but a partial development of the theory it involves; that to carry out the system to its legitimate end, it demands arrangements far more artistic and æsthetic than any thing now openly indicated in the book, we need not shrink from any of the raillery or indignation which may be excited by pronouncing the new cultus *extremely* ritualistic for a Church like ours, and therefore strongly antagonistic to the genius and spirit of Reformed worship. That these ritualistic elements and characteristics may not protrude themselves very boldly, or that many who have looked into the Revised Liturgy, or even been present when portions of its services were used, may not have discovered them, is not evidence that they are not inherent in the system, and essential to it. In order to judge aright in this case, it is necessary to see the thing in full operation, to be present when the service, especially the Lord's Supper service, is performed exactly according to the book. *This I have never yet seen done*, and I suppose that few, if any of our members, have been present at any public service when it was done. At Dayton there was a good deal of it, so much that all but the zealous disciples of Dr. Nevin in this matter, felt that it was extreme and offensive. And yet the whole Communion Service was not used at Dayton, and in that which was used, as far as I saw the "risings and bowings" did not appear. It is often said, indeed, that the full services are used here and there, strictly according to the rubrical directions of the book, and in such instances the people suppose that they have seen the whole of it. And yet I know some congregations in which this is supposed to be done, in which it is not done. So the people are under the impression that they have seen the entire service, when they have really witnessed but a part of it. The "prudence" of this course is not questioned. For those who are intent upon introducing the innovations without exciting too violent and open opposition, without letting the people scarcely know what the design is, it is wise, no doubt, to introduce the thing gradually. They may thus by degrees become accustomed to it, and gradually be able to bear more. Church history, especially from the third and fourth century onwards, furnishes abundant illustrations of the success of such policy. But the "wisdom" of this "policy" is not in discussion just now. The point is, that in this way there may be a great many things pertaining to the system of cultus contained in this book, which the people may not discover. I repeat, therefore, that the cultus of the Revised Liturgy is essentially and really *ritualistic*, and that so far as its ruling principles are concerned, in an extreme degree; especially in contrast with the legitimate Liturgical worship of the Reformed Church.

4. A *fourth* distinguishing characteristic of the new "Order of Worship," which places it in irreconcilable antagonism to our historical Reformed cultus, is exhibited in the *extreme significance and virtue* which it assigns to the *objective* element in worship, to the implied disparagement and repudiation of the *subjective* element. In one sense, this may be regarded as the root of the ritualistic peculiarities. Practically and popularly, however, it is the fruit and effect of those peculiarities

It will be observed that the point is not, that true objective virtue or efficacy is assigned to the means of grace, but that this is done in an *extreme way*, in a manner which involves a virtual setting aside of the importance of personal qualifications, or, to use a favorite Mercersburg expression, subjective conditions. That the means of grace are invested by God with supernatural virtue in themselves, and do not receive their virtue or efficacy from the persons (subjects) using them, is a doctrine held by all evangelical Christians. And when Dr. Nevin, or any brethren who permit themselves to reiterate his views without duly examining them, say that this is denied by any evangelical Church, the Lutheran, the Moravian, the Presbyterian, the genuine portion of the Episcopal, or even the Methodist, Churches, it is simply bearing false witness against sister denominations. It may serve very well to amuse Dr. Nevin and his unqualified adherents and admirers, to display their skill in casting down and hewing to pieces men of straw thus shrewdly set up. Our unhappy friend seems to have found special delight in this sort of gladiatorship for many years. But all will not avail in the end. We who dare to differ from Dr. Nevin on some important points, hold just what we hold, and not whatever erroneous or absurd views he may impute to us. His mere declaration cannot make heretics out of those who cleave honestly and firmly to the essential doctrines of all the Evangelical Reformed Confessions, any more than he can make those Confessions of faith harmonize with and justify the high-church, sacerdotal ritualistic theology, in whose knotty meshes he has allowed himself to become entangled, and by which he has unfortunately ensnared so many who trust unsuspectingly to his guidance and follow with docile obedience his footsteps.

But whilst all evangelical Christians believe in an objective virtue in the means of grace, they hold to this in full harmony with what the *Holy Scriptures* teach, and what the *true* Church has always maintained, concerning the corresponding necessity for suitable personal qualifications. It is at this point, now, that the new "Order" betrays a departure from the faith of the Evangelical Church, and a strong bias towards a doctrine which is essentially inimical to that faith. This doctrine is usually designated by the phrase *opus operatum*, the literal meaning of which is *a work worked*, or a *deed done;* that is, that there is such inherent absolute efficacy in the means of grace, that the mere outward attendance upon them, or formal participation in them, will work their effect upon the subject, without regard, or at least without much regard to personal fitness. According to this theory, then, a certain magical efficacy is ascribed to the means of grace, especially to the Holy Sacraments. *Taking sophistical advantage of the fact, (which no evangelical Christian denies), that the means of grace, and especially the Sacraments, do not derive their virtue from the pious thinking and feeling of the persons who use them, or have efficacy put into them by human subjects to whom they may be administered,* (an error which all evangelical theologians and Christians would repudiate*), this system inculcates the doctrine that they are objectively efficacious—that is, absolutely so, in themselves, to work the end of their institution, upon those who participate in them or receive them. Of the inconsistency of this doctrine with the Holy Scriptures, and of its pernicious moral effects, it is not necessary to speak. It is sufficient for our purpose to know that it is not the doctrine of our Church.

In proof, now, that the Revised Liturgy favors this error, is more or less pervaded by its bad spirit, and rests upon this theory of the absolute objective efficacy of the means of grace, and especially those which are inseparably connected with the office of the ministry, the following facts present themselves:

1. The chief authors and advocates of the new "Order" manifest extraordinary zeal against the prevalent evangelical doctrine upon this subject. They have long displayed great dissatisfaction with what they stigmatize as subjective Religion, that is, a religion which makes account of personal piety, of personal repentance, faith, love, peace and joy in the Holy Ghost. Of course, they dare not very openly denounce these "graces," but they mostly speak quite ungraciously of them, seem to hold them in comparative contempt. Because some fanatics or religious enthusiasts have run to extremes in this way, advantage is taken of the fact to bring all *such* personal piety into discredit. *Pietists* and *Puritans* are especially obnoxious to Dr. Nevin and his disciples, and on this account. All this, of course, is significant. The meaning is, that this way of thinking is supposed to detract from the objective efficacy of the Church and Church ordinances. And the strong and often exceedingly bitter dislike of this so-called subjective pietism, shown by Dr. Nevin and others of his mind, should be particularly significant for a Church which has had to bear reproach and calumny from the start on this same ground. Both blind Papists and bigoted ultra Lutherans (of the Hesshuss school) were accustomed to apply precisely such epithets as these to our Reformed fathers in the sixteenth century. Whether Dr. Nevin and his confederates borrowed the phrases from thoes foes of evangelical piety and Churchliness, I cannot say. But the resemblance is so close as to suggest such an origin. The bearing of the case is sufficiently obvious. What they

---

* It has often been impliedly or directly charged by Dr. Nevin and his more zealous disciples, that Protestant theologians teach this error, at least in substance. I deny the charge, and challenge Dr. Nevin to prove it, allowing him to appeal even to Dick or Dwight, or any theological writer of note or authority. Of course, he would not refer to such men as Parker or Emerson; for only Papists call every one a Protestant who does not kiss the Pope's toe.

denounce is *not* a subjectivism which denies a supernatural character to the means of grace, or that God uses them when He pleases for the conveyance of supernatural grace; for they know full well that those whom they reproach hold no such view. What they denounce, or mean to denounce, therefore, is that sort of subjectivism indicated above, which insists upon the *equal* necessity of personal qualifications or conditions, in order that the blessings promised through the means may be secured, a doctrine which has the entire Scripture for its foundation. And the theory on which the new "Order" rests, can only be understood or possess any such significance as is claimed for it, on the ground that it teaches a doctrine squarely opposed to that which its advocates denounce. But there is only one doctrine in that direction, and that is the *opus operatum* error.

2. Other facts which indicate the same thing are found in the distinctive peculiarities of the Sacramental services and other special offices. As illustrations, take the regenerative efficacy of Baptism taught in all the Baptismal forms; the propitiative efficacy of the Lord's Supper, considered in the sacrificial aspect which characterizes the service for that Sacrament; the power claimed for the Church in confirmation; and the extremely high, if not sacramental, virtue, claimed for ordination, in the service for the ordination of ministers. If anything can be found in Evangelical Protestant authorities to justify the ascription of *such* virtue or objective efficacy to the means of grace, it has yet to be produced. Certain it is, that any acknowledged standard of worship or doctrine in the Reformed Church will be searched in vain for arguments favoring that view. I do not say that it is unqualified *opus operatumism*. But I do affirm that if it is not, it is a marvel of close resemblance without sustaining blood relationship. And, furthermore, if the doctrine of the book on this point is not the error named, it is so very much like it that no one can be censured for mistaking the one for the other, or for supposing them to be twin sisters.

3. This judgment receives confirmation also, from the *Church theory* upon which the new "Order" is acknowledged to rest; and, finally, from the remarkable depreciating manner in which some of the leading advocates of the "Order" occasionally write or speak of that particular means of grace which seems more than any other to appeal to subjective co-operation for its due effect. It will be understood at once that *reference is had to the* WORD *written or preached*. For it has unhappily come to be a painfully distinguishing characteristic of this new "Order" school founded by Dr. Nevin and animated by his peculiar spirit, virtually to *lower* the authority and power of the *Gospel* by an unscriptural over-exaltation of the *sacraments*. Taking the system, therefore, at its own avowed repugnance to

the prevalent evangelical view of the relation of object and subject in the use of means of grace; and judging it from its self-chosen resemblance in form and speech to what is held by all evangelical Confessions to be a pernicious error, as well as from the company which it theologically prefers; we are justified in charging it with a strong bias, if not full committal to the *opus operatum* heresy. But if the facts in the case justify this charge, as I greatly fear they do, the new "Order" must, on this ground again, be declared irreconcilably antagonistic to the faith and cultus of the Reformed Church.

4. The last leading characteristic of the new "Order" by which it stands in hostility to our legitimate Reformed cultus, *is its exclusion of free prayer*. That this is done will not be denied by any ingenuous advocate of the system. The very theory of worship on which the whole "Order" rests, is necessarily intolerant of free prayer. It is true that Dr. Harbaugh and one or two others try to hush the complaints likely to arise upon a discovery of this part in the programme, and promises that the fetters shall not be suddenly imposed. The system will deal gently with the Church, and only by degrees enforce its principles. And then to justify this prospective withdrawal of our inherited Gospel liberty, Dr. Harbaugh by a slight historical mistake tried to prove that a certain French Protestant enthusiast, Labaddie, had *introduced* free prayer into the Reformed Church, and had been deposed for so doing. But Dr. Schaff set his erring pupil right at York in regard to this point, so that we shall probably have no more appeals to the case of Labaddie as a justification of the repudiation of free prayer by the new "Order" and its chief vindicators.

Dr. Nevin knew better than to make any pretence in favor of free prayer. After the wholesale condemnation of the practice in which he had indulged in 1862, and especially after having been reminded of that vehement tirade against the believer's great prerogative, as I took the liberty of doing in my former tract, it would hardly have done to deny the charge in any direct and positive way. And it is simply a fact which cannot be denied, in the face of the full and explicit exposition which the Committee has given of the theory of worship upon which the new "Order" is avowedly constructed, as well as in the face of the book itself. Where can free prayer come in, if the directions of the book are followed? There is no place for it in any of the services. This constitutes a very material difference between it and the Provisional Liturgy. Will any advocate of the system say, "you can substitute a free prayer as often as you please for one of the prescribed ones;" then we answer that this is begging the question. For that matter something else might be, and it is trusted will be substituted for the whole book. But the real point is, *how does the system view free prayer, and what does it propose to do with it?* And to these questions the answer must be that *the system regards free prayer with abhorence, and desires to have it wholly abolished from our Church.*

That this is utterly at variance with the genius and spirit of Reformed worship, will not be questioned by any one who cares for his reputation as a scholar. As shown on a previous page, the earliest Liturgy of the Church leaves room for free prayer. But even if no such specific provision for it had been made, even could we not show by documentary evidence that this was the fact, and the practice, we have what some of the advocates of the new "Order" seem at times to regard as superior to the written Word, we have the testimony of tradition in evidence of the fact. Free prayer has been so long authorized and practised, *in connection* with the occasional use of prescribed forms—for so long a time, that Dr. Harbaugh, in his great zeal to prove it a *modern* (puritanic?) innovation, over hastily seizes upon a phantom supposed to be discovered in the case of an erratic French *Brother* (Labaddie was Reformed, and probably more so than some who affect the name now, and under its cover seek to revolutionize the Church as poor L. is charged with having done). And having made this supposed discovery, it is employed to *demonstrate* that *free prayer* is a *modern innovation* upon the law of our Church, introduced *only two hundred and twenty-five or thirty years ago*, that is, about *fifty* or *sixty* years after the founding of our Church! The point must be quite apparent. We have two centuries and a quarter of Reformed practice certainly for free prayer, to a half a century, or three-score years *doubtfully* against it. And this by the reluctant acknowledgment of the enemies of free prayer!

Nor is this all. It is universally conceded—indeed, the fact is too patent to be denied, that the fathers of our Church aimed at establishing her cultus on the Apostolic basis. Now, free prayer was more common in the primitive Church than the use of prescribed forms. Consequently, the adoption of free prayer in connection with the occasional use of prescribed forms, was a natural and legitimate development of the genius and spirit of the Reformed Church. And why should she not develop "forward rather than backwards, and upward rather than outward?" (See extract from Dr. Nevin on p. 27 of this tract.)

As a further proof of the original recognition and practice of free prayer in the Reformed Church, it might be legitimately argued, that if the unvarying use of prescribed forms was, from the first, enforced, and was in harmony with the principles of our early cultus, it is not likely that those forms would ever have been partially supplanted by free prayer. It has not been so in the Anglican or Episcopal Church! And in the case of Continental Reformed Churches there was as much civil and ecclesiastical authority to effect the observance of prescribed forms, as in the case of the Anglican Church.

In every view of the matter, therefore, the recognition and practice of free prayer, in combination with the use of prescribed forms, must be regarded as a legitimate and distinctive characteristic of the Reformed cultus. This is a legacy which those who, by blessed experience, have learned to know its value, will be loath to surrender. It is a trust committed to the custody of our Church to which she will most assuredly not prove unfaithful. She will not permit her children to be deprived of a prerogative guaranteed by the Lord himself, rescued from the grasp of hierarchical and sacerdotal tyranny by our Reformed fathers, and to which they now have a birthright title. She will preserve and transmit to her spiritual posterity this precious privilege of free access to the throne of grace with such burdens of prayer as may from time to time oppress the heart. Suitable forms of prayer will not be discarded; a Liturgy to aid in the decorous observance of public worship, and to furnish appropriate services, especially for special occasions, will be provided. But no such prepared forms will be allowed to eradicate free prayer whenever the Holy Spirit, who is as really the Spirit of grace and supplication for the Church of the nineteenth century, as he was for the Church of the fourth, may prompt to a devout and believing use of the privilege. And the "Order of Worship," which aims at the abrogation of this precious Christian right, is an enemy to the spirit and genius, and a subverter of the legitimate cultus of the Reformed Church.

These, then, are the broad diversities, the irreconcilable antagonisms which exist essentially between the two systems of worship, brought now into open collision, through the attempt of Dr. Nevin and his associates to force the new Order of Worship upon the German Reformed Church. Should not good, unanswerable reasons be furnished by its advocates before they ask for or press its introduction? Should they not show by overwhelming arguments, that the past cultus of the Reformed Church, of all the Protestant Churches but one, (and that a qualified exception), is unscriptural, at variance with Apostolic and pure primitive practice, incompatible with the spirit of devout worship, and of far less moral power than the kind they have devised, and for which they seek adoption? But do they urge any such considerations, or sustain what they offer as argument or plea by any solid proof? Not at all. We look in vain for any other or better reasons for accepting this innovation of theirs upon our whole life and practice, than that it was so done in the third, fourth or fifth century, or that it is *based* upon the theology of the *Creed*, as that was interpreted in the centuries named. For I will not insult Dr. Nevin by supposing that the two or three appeals made to the

Old Testament, and the one made to the New (Hebr. 13: 10) were intended as true Scriptural authority for the special peculiarities of the new "Order."

Our Church is, consequently, asked and urged to repudiate a cultus which rests upon inspired authority, upon Apostolic principles and primitive practice,—a cultus carefully prepared by her fathers and founders, and adapted by them to her true genius and spirit; and in its stead to adopt one which its principal authors do not pretend is German Reformed, nor even constructed after an Apostolic pattern, but which *they* hold, in their own private judgment (other people must be cured in the employment of this dangerous weapon) to be vastly better, more beautiful, grand, impressive, and what not, than any produced since long before the Reformation! Had ever five men such presumption before? Does the history of the Church, replete as its pages are with narratives of strange things, furnish any approximate analogy to this case? A Church coolly asked and expected to let herself be quietly revolutionized in faith and practice, in doctrine and cultus, in soul and body, to be "transmogrified" from a true Evangelical Church of the Reformation, into a sort of semi Cyprianic and semi-Gregorian Church of the centuries during which, according to Dr. Nevin in 1844 (and the facts of ancient history have not changed since then), all sorts of Romish quackery had gained complete ascendency in the Church! (See back to p. 27).

This, then, is the true issue now before the German Reformed Church. It is not a question of *Liturgy* or *no* Liturgy. And when Dr. Nevin says it is, he must be consciously misrepresenting the case. I know well that he pretends to deny that the Agenda used in our Church were true Liturgies. But he knows that that is an assumption of his own, and not justified either by history or the prevalent judgment of the Church. The old Palatinate and similar directories for public worship were true Liturgies, and I venture to predict that in honorable remembrance, and even in the actual imitation of their essential principles, they will survive this attempt to resuscitate, with sundry modifications, the long since defunct and buried ritualism of the fourth and fifth centuries. For as the Apostles were greater than the Church fathers of the degenerate ages named, so a cultus patterned after the model of Apostolic worship should possess higher authority and be held in more sacred remembrance than one avowedly constructed in imitation of third and fourth century models.

Again. The issue is not, whether such material of the period named as may be in harmony with a true evangelical spirit, may be appropriated or not, in the preparation of a new cultus to be framed in accordance with Apostolic and Reformation principles. In this whole controversy no one has denied, that amidst the mass of superstitions which had accumulated during that period, precious Gospel gems of prayer might be found, and no one has objected to a judicious appropriation of them. So that Dr. Nevin again misrepresents those who oppose his extreme measures, when he says that they insisted upon an exclusive limitation of the work to Reformation Liturgies. But the point is, as Dr. Dorner intimates in one of the letters from Berlin appended to this tract, whether Reformation Liturgies shall be wholly ruled out and ignored, as is virtually done in the new Order of Worship. In my former tract I was especially explicit on this point, and made what some advocates of the innovations, even, regarded as very liberal propositions in the way of a fraternal compromise. So that the accusation of Dr. Nevin in regard to this matter is doubly unjust; and we are consequently no longer bound by the terms proposed in that compromise. But whilst the merits of some of the legacies of the centuries named are cheerfully acknowledged, and their title to a place in any new Liturgy is freely admitted, it is not believed wise or proper to allow them to usurp or even lessen the claims of Reformation works.

This, then, is the true state of the Liturgical question now before our Church. Let its merits be fairly weighed. No side issues on theological points alone should be allowed to divert the most earnest attention from the vast interests involved in the movement, considered in its ritualistic aspects. It is a question touching the preservation and perpetuity of our very life as a Church. The adoption of the new "Order" is necessarily the end of the Reformed Church of the sixteenth century. The three hundred years of her past life may not, indeed, be wholly lost. But she will become a Church of the past. Though falsely retaining the ancient name, her character, faith and practice will be as different from what it has been hitherto, as the Church of the Reformation was different from that of Rome. She will be a new sect, deceitfully clinging to an old and honored title, in order thereby the more successfully to conceal its true schismatic character, and the more effectually to accomplish its sectarian schemes.

Having thus designedly given special attention to those points involved in this controversy which relate to the cultus of our Church, and which present the practical question now to be settled, it will be the less necessary to spend much time in considering the remarkable theological development, to the exhibition of which Dr. Nevin devotes the second half of his "Vindication."

CHRISTOCENTRIC THEOLOGY.

By this newly-coined title has it pleased the author of the "Vindication of the Revised Liturgy, Historical and Theological," to designate the peculiar theology upon which that Liturgy is based, and by the spirit of which it is said to be pervaded and ruled. The novelty of this term, is in full keeping with the strange and foreign character of the peculiar cultus with which it is associated. That cultus, as has been seen, is an extreme innovation upon the legitimate Apostolic worship of the Reformed Church. It does not pretend to bear any essential relationship to any Reformed precedents; it is not justified at all by an appeal to Reformed practice. Why then should there not be an equally novel and alien theological system to match it? Such a system is avowedly delineated in the second part of the notable "Vindication."

When the theological objections to the Revised Liturgy, and even to some things in the Provisional Liturgy already, were first broached, it was done somewhat hesitatingly and hypothetically. It was felt to be a very serious thing to charge a book of which Professors in our Church Institutions, and especially in the Theological Seminary, were the chief authors, with containing doctrines at variance with the doctrinal standard of the Church. When some of those very expressions and phrases which now furnish ground of doctrinal accusations against the book, were challenged in the Committee, even before the publication of the Provisional Liturgy, one or another of those Professors labored to show that those challenged phrases did not mean what they were supposed by the objectors to mean, and tried to prove that they were in harmony with the doctrines of our Church, and the faith of our fathers. There was still a conscience at work on the subject which said: *you as Professors and ministers of the German Reformed Church, who are under a solemn oath to maintain and defend the particular doctrines of that Church, dare not introduce or advocate doctrines antagonistic to her accredited historical faith. Nay, you cannot consistently use the influence of your position, and of the respect entertained for you, in endeavoring to persuade the Church to exchange some fundamental articles of her faith for new and strange doctrines.*

That day, however, is past. All sensitive conscientiousness on this subject has yielded to zeal or ambition to be the founders of a new era in the Protestant Church. Timid intimations or hesitating charges of doctrinal error against the book, are met, not by an earnest attempt to defend it against those charges, but by a bold, defiant effort to show that the peculiar theology of the book is correct, whether Reformed or not Reformed. That it should be in harmony with our standard of faith, and with the doctrines ever maintained by our Church, is treated as a matter of little or no account. And this, indeed, seems to be a favorite notion of the leading advocates of the new ritualistic measures. Did not Dr. Harbaugh virtually assume this position in his inaugural address at Reading, the original copy of which was unfortunately lost. And has it not been reiterated more than once of late, over his signature, and that of others in the *G. Ref. Messenger?* It is now a prominent part of the policy of this school to ignore our denominational rule of faith, and have it so far set aside, that it, and the acknowledged authoritative interpretation of it, may no longer impede the progress of the "new measures." And why should they not aim at this? They have maligned and spurned our standard of worship* in the most indecorous manner. Why should they not at least *slight* or *repudiate* the doctrinal authority of the Heidelberg Catechism?

"Have we a pope?" they ask. That is, have we an authoritative expounder or exposition of doctrines? Must Mercersburg be bound by any such exposition? Of course the meaning of all this is plain, however contradictory of the theory of Churchliness of which that school sometimes can seem to make so much account. Dr. Nevin and his disciples wish to be hampered by no denominational system of faith. They claim the prerogative of making a system of their own, and they wish that to become binding. "No pope," therefore, in Dr. Harbaugh's sense, means no doctrinal standard by which to restrain the development of Mercersburg Christocentricities. Old Dr. Mason said somewhere, long before Dr. Nevin launched his anathemas against the "sect system," that whenever you hear a man denounce sects very violently, you may be sure he would like to start one himself. So it seems that this recently manifested Mercersburg zeal against a theological Pope, indicates too plainly to be mistaken, an aspiration of its own after autocratic power. One can hardly help saying to all this sort of pleading, and from such a source: "thy speech betrayeth thee."

But how "superlatively absurd" for a school which has affected such profound contempt of private judgment, and poured such burning maledictions upon it, now to ask that the private judgment and "subjective vagaries" of its leader's, should be made a standard of orthodoxy among us, a balance in which to try the faith not only of dissentient brethren, but of the fathers of the Church. Olevianus, Ursinus, all the earlier theological authorities, must be in error, rather than that Dr. Nevin's conceit should be condemned. Nay, the Catechism itself must be modified to suit the view of those new reformers!

No one can peruse the doctrinal pages of Dr. Nevin's tract, without getting the impression that, in the writer's estimation, the doctrinal standard of the Church is of no account, in comparison with the new Christocentric revelation he makes, and the profound theology which he teaches. He silently assumes that as "*denominational* theology is nothing to him," it is as little to the Church of which he is a nominal member. He takes

---

* If the Editor of the *Messenger* ventures to deny this, as he has most disingenuously denied some other facts, or allowed them to be denied without any of those Editorial scholias he seems so zealous to append to articles on the other side—then I challenge him to republish pp. 36, 37 and 62 of the "Liturgical Question," and the minority report to the Synod of Chambersburg, to which he seems to forget that his name is affixed.

it for granted, it would seem, that at sea himself, theologically and ecclesiastically, the Church also has torn loose from her ancient, sacred moorings, and is floating about in search of a harbor. And in all this he professedly speaks not for himself only but for others.

And is it possible that in these bold and revolutionary assumptions the leading advocates of the new "Order" are right? I cannot believe it. It is not true that the Church has tamely placed her faith as a lump of wax into the hands of three or four men, to be moulded and shaped to suit recently discovered Christocentric conceits. It is not true that the authors of the Revised Liturgy were commissioned and employed to use it as a means for insinuating strange, and, if our past creed has been true, most false and pernicious doctrines into the Church. The peculiarities of Mercersburg Theology and Philosophy may be good enough for those who like them, but I deny that they have ever been recognized as the doctrines of the Reformed Church, or that any Committee was ever authorized to substitute them for those doctrines.

No, we have a denominational standard of faith and doctrine, invested with as full authority now as ever. That standard, under the Holy Scriptures, is the Heidelberg Catechism, which is believed to contain the doctrines of the Holy Scriptures as held by the German Reformed Church. Dr. Nevin and all his associates are bound by it, as really and entirely as any minister or member of the Church. Nay, the Church herself is bound by it, and by her own organic life and law, cannot essentially change that doctrine, or even her Order of worship, without forfeiting her claim to the property she now holds. It will not avail, as the civil statutes in such cases now stand, to *pretend* to adhere outwardly to the Heidelberg Catechism, and yet really teach doctrines opposed to the obvious and traditional sense of that standard. A professor, or minister of our Church, may not teach Unitarianism, or Puseyism, or any other ism essentially and materially at variance with our standard, and yet shield himself beneath the Heidelberg Catechism, and so escape censure. Every such doctrinal standard has a definite historical sense, a sense fixed by traditional authority, and by that sense the teachers of the Church are bound. No attempted evasions will avail. And even though the judicial authorties of the Church should themselves so come under the power of the leaders of innovations as to change doctrines and customs to suit the views of those leaders, the Church should remember that the civil law will come to her aid against any such ecclesiastical usurpations, and shield her against being wrested from her true foundations by the power of a revolutionary majority.

Beyond all available contradiction, therefore, we have a fixed standard of doctrine, the true import of which can be definitely ascertained. And this Revised Liturgy must be tried by that standard before it can receive valid ecclesiastical endorsement. If it contains doctrines at variance with those of the Church it must be rejected. The Church even is not at liberty to retain a name which stands for a historical character and distinctive doctrines, and yet, fundamentally change both. We cannot become Baptists, or Episcopalians, in fact, and yet claim in form, to be German Reformed. We cannot adopt a Liturgy containing Unitarian, Swedenborgian, Puseyite, or Popish doctrines, and yet call it a German Reformed Liturgy. In regard to the case before us, therefore, it is evident that the point to be settled is, whether this new "Order" contains doctrines which are at variance with those of the German Reformed Church. If it is admitted that it does, or if it can be proven that it does, that must settle the point of its rejection.

All this seems clear enough. It is equally clear, therefore, that any valid doctrinal vindication of the Revised Liturgy should aim chiefly at showing that its reigning doctrinal spirit, as well as its special phraseology, was in full essential harmony with the standard faith of the German Reformed Church. And I feel persuaded that the general expectation of the more devoted friends of the new "Order" was, that Dr. Nevin would furnish a lucid, elaborate argument, strongly fortified by appeals to the Heidelberg Catechism, and to standard doctrinal authorities, to prove most incontrovertibly, that the doctrinal spirit, and particular utterance of his Liturgy was in complete harmony with the authorized confession of the German Reformed Church. How great must have been the disappointment at finding that the author of the defence scarcely deigns to make any appeal of this sort. He seems hardly to know that there is such a book as the Heidelberg Catechism, or that we have any certain evidence of what its authors regarded as the true sense of its language. In 1847, Dr. N. could, in his "History and Genius of the Heidelberg Catechism," write in language of high laudation of the superior excellence of that standard of our faith under the word of God. In 1851, he could furnish, in a preface to Dr. Williard's Ursinus, a glowing eulogy upon the chief author of the Catechism, and the author of the Commentary on the Catechism. Speaking of the value of the Commentary, he says in that preface, among other commendatory things: "No other, at all events, can have the same weight as an exposition of its true meaning." Why, then, are the Catechism, as well as the Commentary on it by Ursinus, so utterly ignored? Was Dr. Nevin so fully conscious of the essential incompatibility of his Revised Liturgy Theology with the Catechism and the Commentary, that he felt it to be most expedient not to place the two in very close comparison?

What, then, is this theology of the new "Order," which is heralded by its advocates as a sort of latest revelation dawning upon the Church; as the only "live theology" of the present day; as a system to which the old theology of the Reformed Church, and indeed of all Churches, should most cheerfully give place? Dr. Nevin declares himself so confident of its superiority, of its carrying with it overwhelming evidence in its favor, that he is sure that "the people only need a fair opportunity to judge its merits for themselves," to be induced to accept it. Let us, then, look in for a few moments upon this great masterpiece of modern genius.

At the very outset, however, of this inquiry, some perplexing difficulties meet us. This remarkable theology, by which the Revised Liturgy is said to be animated, is, *first of all, presented to us only in detached parts,* in broken sections. It claims, indeed, to be a system, and a very thoroughly organized system at that. And yet, strange to say, it has never yet assumed an organized form. How is this? For years we have been told that Dr. Nevin has had a manuscript system of Moral Philosophy, and manuscript Lectures on Theology so far prepared, that with a little labor they might be ready for the press. Why have these not been published long ago? I contend that if the philosophy and theology of this new school are what its unreserved disciples declare they are (and no men have more unblushingly trumpeted their own praises, and more nauseatingly boasted of their own superiority and vast erudition than the leaders of this school have trumpeted and commended theirs), if then this self-praise, however disgusting, is yet founded upon real superior merit, I contend that Dr. Nevin should long ago have favored the Church and the world with a full and complete deliverance of his doctrines. If the Christocentric theology comprehends the panacea for all the theological ills which now afflict a confessionally distracted Christendom; if it holds in its mighty grasp the key which opens the gates of a theological paradise for a universal Church, a Holy Catholic Church, now torn and mangled by its wretched wanderings through the thorny mazes of a "geocentric" theological desert; then it is the extreme of cruelty in Dr. Nevin to lock up this potent panacea in the "chambers of his own imagery," and to keep those gates bolted against a poor, struggling, fainting, Protestant Church (for be it noted, it is only Protestantism which is commonly supposed to be in so pitiable a plight). Surely there is something inexplicable or inexcusable in this Mercersburg theology as headed by Dr. Nevin, claiming to be the only live theology, the only profound theology, the only genuine orthodox theology, at least in the Protestant Church; and yet this wonderful theology is, after all, not a theology at all, but only a collection of theological essays on a few vexed questions, published now here, now there, without order, without connection, and sometimes with but little coherency! How will the great vindicators of the system reconcile all this with the lofty and loud pretensions of their system? And how can they ask the world's acceptance of a system not yet systematized—of an organic development not yet organically developed? Newton and Kepler, after the great Italian astronomer, fully and unreservedly proclaimed their discoveries. Each published his system in full. So with all truly great men, sure of their theories. Why has Dr. Nevin been so reserved, or at most so negative in the communication of his creed? Is he not yet quite sure of it? Has he not yet fully recovered his equipoise after the theological dizziness of 1850–55? With all his seeming intrepidity, does he still shrink from letting the Church know his real views upon all the important points involved in a true theological system? But if he is, what right has he to ask that others shall implicitly follow him in his Japhetic search for an ecclesiastical father or mother; and above all, what right has he to ask a whole Church to commit herself to his but partially developed and extremely unsettled Creed?

This is not the first time these questions have been asked, silently or openly. There are many brethren in the Church who, from a natural regard for preceptors and their Alma Mater, have struggled even against inward reluctance to adhere to Dr. Nevin and what seemed his theory. At the same time, however, they have often been perplexed by this very thing. If Mercersburg theology is what it claims to be, why does it not publish its entire system? A like question has been asked by good and earnest men of other Churches, *and in Europe*. My own belief has been, for seven years at least,—that is, ever since I saw the evidence of a determination to push these extreme ritualistic measures through,—that Dr. Nevin is afraid to publish his whole system; either because he would have to speak very doubtfully or ambiguously upon some important points, and thus lay himself open to ecclesiastical censure—or because to do so would involve him and his system in an open rupture with the Church.

Here, then, is a very grave difficulty in the way of any thorough attempt to judge of the merits of Dr. Nevin's theology as it is said to rule and pervade the Liturgy. We have no certain means of knowing what that theology is. Its author has, for reasons best known to himself, if those above premised are not the correct ones, thus far refused to publish it. Detached essays, or disconnected pronunciamentos issued on the field of ecclesiastical controversy,—and especially when these severally do not quite agree among themselves,—give but poor satisfaction. One is constantly told that they are mis-understood, or misrepresented. And so there is nothing definite and positive to lay hold of. This is remarkably the case in the present instance. No one, I am sure, could tell from the theological pages of this "Vindication," where Dr. Nevin stands, what he holds, in regard to some of the fundamental points of our evangelical faith. For all that we find here, Dr. Nevin might be as much of a Papist as Bossuet, or believe in purgatorial salvation as fully as Cardinal Wiseman. In vain do you look for any thing distinctively evangelical Protestant. Until, therefore, this system develops itself fully and consistently in all its parts, it has no right to complain of misrepresentation. Men must judge of the animal by the bones furnished, if the entire form is not before them. The bones of this Mercersburg system indicate its affinity with a known, well-known, species of ecclesiasticism. And until it proves, by a full exhibition of itself, that though some parts of the structure bear such a resemblance, the complete organism is a very different thing, it must endure the name of the species to which it seems to be most nearly related. To call a wolf a sheep does not change its nature; neither is every turtle a dove.

Great as this difficulty is, however, it is not the only one which confronts us, in any effort to ascertain what this wonderful theology is, which, as the soul of the Revised Liturgy, makes it so admirable a work. Another serious obstacle in our way is *the great diversity* of sentiment which is found between the different expounders of this new system. Dr. Nevin says this is a new thing in its essential features. Dr. Wolff blandly seeks to allay any anxieties or dissatisfaction which this confession may excite, and softly assures the people that it is not so new after all. When any one, taking the system at its own word, condemns it as an innovation upon the German Reformed Church, the editor of the *Messenger*, eager to seize every opportunity of proving the sincerity of his recent conversion to the new faith, takes up the condemnation as though it were an assault and insult upon the German Reformed Church in her corporate capacity. The Rev. Samuel Miller, of Pottsville, some years ago a minister of one of the German Methodistic sects, but now a minister in the German Reformed Church, and an ardent admirer of Dr. Nevin's system, is prompted by his zeal in the cause to write a book on "Mercersburg and Modern Theology Compared." This was naturally supposed to be a reliable exposition of the system, and somewhat authoritative. But just when we are congratulating ourselves on having at last gotten hold of something tangible, the *Mercersburg Review*, (revived,) edited by Dr. Harbaugh, frankly tells us that this affair of Mr. Miller's is not to be taken at all as a fair exponent of Mercersburgism. This is perplexing indeed. For Calvinism we have Calvin, and for Arminianism we have Arminius. But how shall we ascertain certainly and beyond a doubt what this Mercersburg theology is?

And yet this half-developed system—this theology which is, and yet again seems not to be—which, like some illegitimate birth, has half a dozen fathers, all claiming to be one and the same, and yet, in some cases, denying each other's true paternity,—this wonderful prodigy of these last days, which Mr. Miller of Pottsville attempts, as by authority, carefully to delineate, and whose delineation the Editor of the *Messenger* endorses, whilst the Editor of the *Review*, and, I think, one of the special contributors to the *Messenger*, delicately disown it,—this organism, a few only of whose bones and ligaments have been exhibited to view, and a little only of whose life has been revealed, and that little mostly of a terribly negative and *de*-structive character,—this piecemeal thing comes up intrepidly and asks a Church to adopt it soul and body, with all its known and unknown truths or errors, with all its obvious and hidden consequences! This system, confessing itself an innovation, and not denying that its adoption will be the abrogation of the legitimate confessional character of the Church, has the effrontery to demand ecclesiastical sanction and endorsement! And because the plea is presented and urged by the leader or leaders of a school, because Dr. Nevin favors and defends it, many seem ready to yield unquestioningly to the demand.

Under these circumstances the difficulty of ascertaining the true character of the but partially developed theology must be met, and we must make the best of such detached and disconnected revelations of its profound mysteries as have thus far been made. Following the plan of the "Vindication," so far as it may be suitable to our purpose, we shall pay attention *first* to what the author calls the *general scheme* of the theology of the new "Order," and then to the *doctrinal specialties* of the book.

Of the "*general scheme*" we cannot allow ourselves in this place to take quite as "broad" a "view" as Dr. Nevin proposes to himself. And this for three reasons: (1) We are not *latitudinarians*, either by taste or education. Without a blush, we confess ourselves to be so Churchly, and so much under the control of the "objective," that we find no pleasure in any theological or speculative view beyond the limits of the evangelical traditions of our fathers, that is, therefore, of the Word of God itself, from which they learned their faith. (2.) In the next place, we will not allow ourselves to be diverted from the consideration of the specially obnoxious doctrines of the new "Order." (3.) Finally, it will require but little space to show that in those general points in which the new theology differs from the evangelical faith of our Church, it is either of very doubtful value, or wholly unworthy of credence.

1. It will not fail to arrest the notice of the critical reader of the "Vindication," that the author quietly and speciously assumes some doctrines as peculiar to his system, which quite as really belong to every system of evangelical theology. This is done evidently for the purpose of deceiving and misleading those to whom he appeals. For it is simply impossible that, with all his extreme prejudices against evangelical Protestant theologians (and I do not believe that there is one whom he can endure), and

his aversion to the commonly cherished faith of evangelical Christians, he should really believe that they deny the Lord Jesus Christ, as he openly or impliedly charges them with denying Him. But if the infatuated author hoped to succeed by any such artifice, he presumed far too much upon the ignorance of our people. They are, indeed, for the most part, a single minded, unsophisticated people. Confiding, deferential to men in high positions, they may for a time be imposed upon. Those whom they trust as teachers may mislead them and cause them to err. But they are not ignorant. Neither are they indifferent to the interests of truth and the Church. And in this case, as in similar attempts made in other forms by servile imitators of their professor, it will be of little avail to represent all who do not endorse Dr. Nevin's notions, as anti-Christian heretics.

It is, then, *no peculiarity* of Nevinistic theology, that *God in Christ is its centre*, and that all Christian doctrines find their root in Him—in His person and in His life; and to claim it as such is simply a gross defamation of the entire theology of the Evangelical Church. And if the calumny came from a more creditable and authoritative source, it might deserve some extended refutation. As it is, nobody believes it, excepting those under the spell of the master's delusion, and it is harmless. Only as betraying the insolent anathematizing spirit of the false accuser of his brethren, is it calculated to excite our deep indignation. Dr. Nevin should know that Christ our Lord, incarnate for the salvation of men, was firmly held and faithfully taught in the German Reformed Church (other branches of our common evangelical Protestantism may, and can, defend themselves) long before his name was known in her borders. No one, therefore, will be likely to be deceived by the unfair but artful massing of all who reject his anti-Reformed and false conceits, with Ebionites, Gnostics, Socinians, Anabaptists, and metaphysical Calvinists.* There would be more reasons for charging his theory with the denial of the first article of the Creed, the doctrine of God the Father, than he can fairly give for accusing his opponents with a denial of the centrality of the doctrine concerning God in Christ. And it is noteworthy that whilst Dr. Nevin makes these bold assertions, he does not in a single case attempt to prove them. Here, again, he expects his mere domineering declaration to be accepted without a challenge. Why did he not furnish at least one illustration in proof of the accusation? The reason is obvious. He could not. When

---

* It may be noted here, as well as any where else, that so far as Calvin suits Dr. Nevin, or seems to suit him, he can boldly cite him as authority for the new doctrine. But true, legitimate Calvinism, the spirit of which pervades the Heidelberg Catechism as expounded by Ursinus, Dr. Nevin most cordially hates. I may add that Calvinism is the antipode of Puseyism and Popery.

those who differ from this new theology charge it with error, they support their charge by evidence derived from the writings of its vindicators. Dr. Nevin must do the same before he can convict the objects of his bitter animosity of the false doctrines he says they hold.

Much, therefore, of all he so vauntingly sets forth on many of the pages of this part of his tract, as though the credit of giving prominence to those Christological truths in these last days, were due to him, really amounts to nothing for his vindication. Our Church believed in all that is not strictly peculiar to his system, including the "objective and historical" in the Christocentric scheme, and even including the *Creed* long before Dr. Nevin was born, and before he favored the Church by subscribing to the Professor's oath contained in Art. 19 of our Church Constitution. The author of the "Vindication," therefore, has simply made his effort ridiculous by assuming the contrary, and indulging in such sweeping charges of gross heresy against each one in particular, and all in general, who refuse to bow to his Christocentric dogma.

He occupies his imaginary heliocentric position, like some theological autocrat, and dictates doctrines or anathemas to all the world. It is not simply the author of the "Criticism on the Revised Liturgy," nor the "clique" around him; not simply the "Professors at Tiffin" (all of them his former pupils), the victims of "ultra-montane jealousy" (sic), and the despised "Cyphers" from North Carolina, that become obnoxious to his censure He pronounces sentence against the entire Protestant world, at least in America, and regards all as lying in the bondage and night of error, who do not view things as he views them, or accept of *his particular* Creed. "Whoever refuses to come and stand where I stand," he seems to cry, "in this only true central position, must see things in a false light, and be involved 'in boundless error and confusion.'"

What "boundless" self-complacency! Shall it be most derided or condemned. And all this assumption, too, in one who quite forgot some most important points in the very "novel" astronomical illustration on p. 56. One is, that our *sun is not* the centre of the physical universe, and so Dr. Nevin's conception of the Person of Christ, and the purpose of the incarnation, may be false. Another is, the practical difficulty for an inhabitant of earth of *securing a position in the sun*. But a third, and the most fatal defect of the illustration is, that while it professes to place an observer in the best position for contemplating things, it fails to provide for his vision. A blind man would see nothing, though he stood in the sun; and a man with eyes would not see things aright from the most favorable position, *if he looked at them through a telescope with cracked, crooked, or colored lenses.* Dr. Nevin flatters himself that *he* at least, and those standing at his side, are in the only right position. That is exceedingly doubtful.

But that he and they are viewing them through distorting media, is too painfully certain. Let them look after their glass, as well as their position. Now, they think they see, and that they see aright. But so did some whom the true Son of Righteousness pronounced self-deceived and blind, notwithstanding their pretensions to clearer religious vision than their despised neighbors enjoyed. (See John ix. 39-41).

2. Correctly to ascertain the *characteristic peculiarities* of this self-styled Christocentric theology, those doctrines and sentiments which are common to genuine evangelical theology, must be deducted from the description of it given by its discoverer. Thus we must take from it the Christological features, in the proper sense of that term. It must be stripped of much of its arrogant usurpation of the *Creed*, as its own exclusive property. Its boastful assumption of being entitled to the sole credit of ascribing supernatural efficacy to the means of grace, the Word, the Sacraments, Prayer, must be considerably softened.

True churchliness, or faith in the Church as a truly Divine institution, or even an organism, a body, "the body of Christ," in the true Apostolic sense, the sense always held by the *holy* and *legitimate* Catholic Church heresy, must be deducted from the Christocentric scheme, as something peculiar to it. And so of all other articles of evangelical faith, which Dr. Nevin, in his vague, "broad" way of writing, *seems* to claim as belonging to his theology in an exclusive sense. But after all these deductions, what is left? Enough, alas, to furnish occasion for regret and alarm. Enough, also, to warn the Church against adopting a cultus which is now openly declared to be built on this false basis, and to be pervaded by the spirit of these novelties.

For the charge that our prevalent evangelical theology, and especially that of the Reformed Church, is heretical upon the doctrinal points above-named, proceeds wholly from the fact that in Dr. Nevin's scheme those doctrines are invested with a peculiar phase, stand under certain significant modifications. These phases or modifications constitute their party distinction. How far they involve serious departures from the acknowledged and *standard faith of the Reformed Church*, is the only point which concerns us now. Their abstract merits or faults, do not concern us in this tract. And if the author of the "Vindication" has for a moment supposed that he could mislead or confuse us by his "broad" sweep amidst seemingly vast, profound, or lofty theological speculations, so that in this way the real issue might be lost sight of, he was wholly mistaken. Whatever interest the opponents of his ritualistic and dogmatical innovations may find in aerial or subterranean excursions of this kind, or whatever aversion they may feel to the bold adventures of speculative curiosity into fields not open by Divine revelation, they remember that the important question now demanding adjustment, is, whether the doctrinal basis and distinctive doctrinal features of the Revised Liturgy are in accordance with evangelical Reformed standards of faith, or are contrary to them. We believe that what Dr. Nevin, speaking for his associates, declares to be the doctrinal basis of the new "Order," as well as the peculiar phase of the special doctrine named, can easily be shown to be in direct conflict with the acknowledged historical faith of our Church. To prove this will require no lengthened or labored argument.

Following Dr. Nevin's own order, the theology of the Revised Liturgy may be considered 1. As to its Christocentric character; 2. As to its relation to the Creed; and 3. In regard to its *objective* and *historical* pretensions.

First of all, then, what is this strange theory for which the author could find no suitable name in our extensive theological vocabulary, and which is presented to us under the somewhat mysterious and yet assumptive title of Christocentric? Its distinctive peculiarity may be discovered in the almost exclusive prominence which it gives to the *incarnation* of the Lord Jesus Christ, and "the mysterious constitution of His blessed Person." As the careful author of the "Vindication" throws out his views in the form of *questions*, rather than in any direct statements, we cannot quote his sentiments in a positive form. But taking the sum of these questions and general hints, there is no difficulty, with due care, in getting at the doctrine. It is, that the great purpose of the incarnation of the Son of God, was to furnish a substantial basis of a new organic order of life; so that our human nature, which is corrupt and depraved by virtue of its relation to the first Adam, may have a vivifying portion of the real personal life of Christ infused into it, and thus be regenerated, justified and saved. Hence the Lord Jesus Christ becomes as actual historical a basis of this literally infused divine human life, as Adam was the basis of the first or Adamic life of man. In the doctrine concerning the person and work of Christ, the chief thing, the only really essential factor, is His incarnation and the mysterious constitution of His person. All else pertaining to Him,—His humiliation, passion, death, burial, is but incidental and accessory. By virtue of this "mysterious constitution of His person,"—*not by virtue of His* atoning passion and death, He penetrates the Church with His own real, substantial personal life, so that it is but the continual reproduction and perpetual remanifestation of His incarnation; and this, it must be remembered, not in a dynamic spiritual way, but in a manner, which, while it is claimed to be supernatural, really lies within the sphere of the natural as much as any other operation of nature. For according to the Christocentric theory this real, substantial personal life of Christ, of the actual literal substance of His glorified nature, is as *really* transmitted through Baptism, consequently by the physical, or at most, psychico-physical act of the minister (for the theory denies that *the absence of intention* on the part of the minister would render the sacrament void), as the natural seed of human life is transmitted in human generation. Hence the life of the individual Christian, as of the whole body of Christians, or the Church, is in the only proper sense, according to this theory, a process and result of supernatural generation affected by such diffusion or conveyance of a portion of the actual, literal substance of the glorified humanity of the Lord Jesus Christ through a sacrament administered by a human agent as a medium of such conveyance.

Now, as said above, we have nothing to do in this place with the philosophical as well as theological absurdities which seem to us to be manifestly involved in this speculation. It claims, indeed, to rest upon a profound system of theological psychology of which Calvin and the other Reformers were unhappily ignorant. How utterly groundless all such claims are, may be fully shown some other time, and in some other form.* Meanwhile it will suffice to say, that as Dr. Nevin makes no appeal to any Protestant evangelical authorities in support of his theory, it is unnecessary to prove that none such could be found, unless, indeed, R. Wilberforce and his peculiar school should be claimed. (Those who have opportunity and leisure may refer to *Hagenbach*, Hist. of Doctrines I, 202–3; 380–81; II, 279–80, 454. *Ebrard*, K. u. Dogm.-Gesch. I. 99–115; 203–320; II. 241 &c.; III. 224 &c. The value of the author's appeal to the Apostle's Creed will be noticed below.

But contrast with this Christocentricity the true Scriptural Christology of the Heidelberg Catechism. Ask the Church as testifying through it, what is the chief doctrine concerning the Person and Work of the Lord Jesus Christ? · Ask her why He became incarnate; why God was thus manifested in the flesh? And at once you are told that the *incarnation* was in order to something else; that the mysterious theanthropic constitution of His wonderful Person, had reference not to any such speculative psychological scheme as is assumed in the Christocentric theory of Dr. Nevin and his Liturgy, but to quite another necessity. What this is, is affirmed in the answers to the 12th, 14th, 15th, 16th, 17th, and 18th questions. Let us take but the 16th and 17th:—

"Why must He be very man, and also perfectly righteous? Because the

---

* Hardly, however, in the *Mercersburg Review.* For I should have stated before, that a request made for the privilege of inserting the Liturgical and Theological portions of this reply to Dr. N. was first refused on the ground that the *Review* "could not be allowed to fight itself;" then partly granted, but under editorial *conditions*, to which no gentleman could submit. But yet Dr. N. was allowed to traduce Brethren in the part of his "Vind." published in the *Review.* So much for Mercersburg Theology Liberty.

justice of God requires that the same human nature which hath sinned, *should likewise make satisfaction* for sin: and one who is himself a sinner cannot satisfy for others."

"Why must He in one person be also very God? That He might by the power of His Godhead *sustain in His human nature the burden of God's wrath*, and might obtain for and restore unto us righteousness and life."

How " materially and essentially " different this representation of the purpose of the incarnation, of the necessity of it, of the end to be accomplished by it, from that of the Christocentric theory! So different indeed that the two conceptions are irreconcilable, not only formally but materially; not only in their explicit doctrines, but in what they necessarily involve. It is hardly possible, if indeed at all possible, to conceive of a point of harmony between the two. If human nature is redeemed and saved from its fallen and lost condition, not by the atonement of Christ, but by the incarnation of Christ,—if the former was simply an accessory consequence of the latter, merely necessary in some mysterious way to render it perfect and complete (and Dr. N's. disciples are prone to appeal to such misapprehended passages as Heb. ii. 10: " Make the Captain of salvation *perfect* through suffering ") then men are declared by the Christocentric theory to be saved, humanity to be delivered from the curse and power of depravity, and to be restored to adoption in the family of God, in a very different way from that taught in our standard, and proven true by the Word of God. For according to the evangelical doctrine, the Son of God assumed our human nature (sin excepted) that by union with it He might 1, enable it to endure the penalty of sin, and 2, give infinite, divine value to the penalty thus endured. But Dr. Nevin has discovered, or revived, and proclaims a very different doctrine. And now he asks that the German Reformed Church, by adopting his new Liturgy, shall substitute this new, and at the very best speculative and doubtful notion, for her old Scriptural doctrine concerning the true purpose and end of the incarnation! Will she do it? Will she permit herself to be shaken in her old Apostolic faith, by the hand of one who has thus ventured, under the "irresistible force" of a new idea in doctrine, as he was under the power of a similar fatality in regard to cultus, to disturb the "faith once delivered to the saints?" Mark, as before so I say now, that I do not hold Dr. Nevin responsible for doing this under the conviction that it is not true Scriptural doctrine which he seeks to inculcate and scatter abroad. But his thinking it truth does not make it cease to be error; and his holding the commonly received doctrine for error does not make it cease to be truth. I believe that the doctrine of our Catechism and Church is "the truth as it is in Jesus," and that Dr. Nevin has allowed himself to be betrayed by his own venturous speculations, and especially by his unhappily cherished dislike of evangelical Protestant theology, into a very pernicious, though possibly not fatal error. This error, it is gratifying to know, is not shared by all who are supposed to agree with ultra Mercersburg theology. Thus in the "Catechism for Sunday-schools, &c., by Dr. Schaff," in answer to the question, (p. 177) "Why did the eternal Son of God take up our human nature into fellowship with His divine person?" we are told: "In order that He might live, suffer, die, and rise again for us, and thus accomplish in our nature the redemption of man."

To prove that this has ever been the doctrine of the Reformed Church, by citations from theologians of acknowledged authority, would require us to copy scores of pages from the writings of the early fathers of our Church, as well as from numerous historians of the Reformation. But as Dr. Nevin does not at all pretend that he is teaching Reformed doctrine on this point, evidence in refutation of his views from Reformed authorities would be superfluous.

In the *second* place, then, *the claim which this Christocentric theory lays to being founded on the "Apostles' Creed" demands consideration.* Were one utterly unacquainted with the Christian Church, to read the " Vindication," or to hear Dr. Nevin's School speak as it does about the " Creed," he would certainly be led to believe that it was some precious treasure hidden or despised for ages, now first brought to light again and raised to its true position of honor and esteem in the Church. To those who know the facts in the case, all this blustering talk must seem not only ridiculous, but false. If thousands of us had not been taught the Creed in our childhood—if we had not heard it repeated time and again in our Church—if we had not known it to be taught faithfully and earnestly by hundreds of pastors in our Church, whom Dr. Nevin can unhesitatingly traduce, but whose hard labors he has never laid hold of,—we might possibly be deceived by such sweeping assertions as he makes. So far as these assertions are grossly detractive of other Churches, as the Lutheran and Episcopal, I leave them to answer for themselves.

But where so much is professedly made of the *Creed,* we naturally and justly expect that it will not be arbitrarily interpreted, according to private judgment or the fancies of some favorite theory. How great our disappointment, therefore, to find that instead of going to the Creed for a faith, this Christocentric theology goes to it *with a faith.* For nothing is more painfully manifest in all the appeals made to the Creed by Dr. Nevin and his School, that their partiality to it is mainly to be attributed to the fact that its articles are sufficiently general to allow of such a construction as any speculative theologian may put upon them. In this case a theory of Christianity and the Church is adopted—adopted on what are claimed to be profound philosophical grounds. This theory seeks in vain for justification in the current evangelical faith or theology; still less in the Scriptures. But there is the Creed! Is it not a remarkable coincidence, that its articles indicate that very system of organic development which Dr. Nevin and his School adopt? See the beautiful generic development! *First Christ* (so Dr. Nevin says—and I am not responsible for his assertions); then the Holy Spirit; then the Church, the continuous incarnation, &c. True, the Heidelberg Catechism, whilst greatly to be honored for honoring the Creed (though it does not take it alone, as Dr. Nevin says), gives no intimation of any such *organic* structure. But then the authors of the Catechism had not sat at Dr. Nevin's feet! And are we to interpret the Creed according to the Catechism, or not rather the *Catechism according to the Creed?* Do we not read such nonsense in Dr. Nevin's "Vindication"—and did he not give utterance to it at Dayton? And have not some incautious disciples, too heedlessly following their vaulting teacher, run into the same ditch?

Let me say to Dr. Nevin, that, simple-minded as we native German Reformed people are, we are not so dull as to be deceived by such gossamer sophistry as this. We understand very well that the choice he presents lays, *not as he would put it, between the Creed of the ancient Church, or no Creed, but between Dr. Nevin's Apostles' Creed, or that Symbol as our fathers understood it, in all essential points.* This is the true issue, and no confusion which the author of the "Vindication" attempts to produce, shall hide it from our view.

According to this system, then, the *Creed,* not as interpreted by the Evangelical Church, nor even as it may be Scripturally explained, *but the Creed as it is to be explained according to itself, or its own inner structure* must be our rule of faith, *and is the ruling spirit of the new "Order."* And yet this *Creed* did not complete this organic structure until more than *five hundred* years after Christ and His Apostles. Note the following significant facts in regard to the several Articles:

Art. I. The phrase *"maker of heaven and earth,"* was introduced nobody knows when, but as far as is known, *not before the seventh or eighth century.*

Art III. "What was conceived by the Holy Ghost, born of the Virgin Mary?" This did not receive its present form until after the Council of Constantinople, A. D. 381.

Art. IV. Underwent great changes in the course of ages, and especially by the *very late* addition of the clause: "*He descended into hell.*" *Pearson,* to whose work on the Creed we are chiefly indebted for all these facts, says of this part of Art. IV.: "It is certain, therefore, that the Article of the *descent into hell,* was not in the Roman or any of the Oriental Creeds."

The earliest date to which its use can be traced, is about *four hundred years* after Christ, and then in but a single Church, and not with any general acknowledgment.

Art. VI. This Article at first read: "He ascended into heaven and sitteth at the right hand of the Father." It did not, probably, receive its present form until some time during the 5th century or later.

Art. IX. This Article, so important to the Christocentric theory, both as to its form and position, has been unsettled in both respects. As to its form, it received *much addition* in the course of time, the latter part, "Communion of Saints," being *wholly* added, and the former part being augmented. For the article originally stood simply: "*I believe the holy Church*," the word "*Catholic*" not having been added until the fourth or fifth Century.

But what is still more noteworthy, the Article instead of holding its present place, immediately after those concerning Jesus Christ and that of the Holy Ghost WAS OFTEN PLACED LAST in the Creed.

Into what confusion this fact throws the theory of Dr. Nevin and his too docile disciples! How suddenly a house, however captivating in its outward splendor, but built on sandy assumptions, may be swept away by the flood of a few simple, undeniable facts.

Of the other clause in this Article, Pearson says: "*It beareth a something later date than any of the rest.*" It was "not in the Oriental or Roman Creed, nor in the African Creed expounded by St. Augustine," and so Pearson goes on enumerating where it was not to be found, until we are lost amidst the deepening gloom of successive centuries.

Art. X. Concerning the "forgiveness of sins," appears to have been always contained in the Creed, but as is implied in what was said above, *it often preceded* the Article concerning the Church, and *was not fixed relatively in its present place, until after the full development of ecclesiastical hierarchy and sacerdotalism and ritualism.*

Such is the foundation upon which the Christocentric ritualism is based! Not the *Creed*, remember; our Church has always held to the Creed; but that *Creed* interpreted *rigorously*, not by the light of the unchangeable "Word of God, which abideth forever," but by the law of its own *inner organism*. What organism? *That which it acquired or developed during the fourth, fifth, sixth, seventh, eighth hundred years after the time of Christ and His Apostles!* And yet this same Dr. Nevin told us a few years ago that the roots of all the abominations of Rome could be traced to the earliest of these centuries!

Fortunately for the cause of evangelical truth, this 4th and 5th century creed theory is not even specious enough to deceive the considerate mind. It is too obvious to escape detection, that Dr. Nevin, quite unconsciously, no doubt, is laboring under the delusion of his own fancy. Bewitched by his own seemingly profound philosophical scheme of faith, he has snatched at some imaginary analogy to it, or confirmation of it in the structure of the Creed. And the system seems so infatuated with its own conceit, that it really thinks it can carry a Church which for three centuries has held another faith, with it, though that faith rests " not in the wisdom of man, but in the power of God."

Here then we have a system whose advocates have been most loud in crying down private judgment, based in fact upon the exercise of private judgment in the most arbitrary way. A whole Church says—the Creed must be interpreted according to the analogy of faith in the Word of God. Dr. Nevin says: away with your stupid nonsense. Will you allow a modern Confessionalism to rule out the sense of the older Confessionalism? etc. (Vind. p. 75, etc.). Does the author of this sophistry suppose we are all silly children or fools, to be misled by such a begging of the question?

The point is not—shall the Confessionalism of the 5th Century be ruled by that of the 16th? And I cannot but think that he knows it is not. The point is, shall *we* be ruled by an arbitrary sense of the 5th Century Creed, put into it by Dr. Nevin, *or shall we be ruled by the Holy Scriptures?* Our fathers said: *By the Scriptures*. Shall Dr. Nevin be allowed to persuade their sons to deny their faith? The controversy is not between us who are opposing these encroachments, and those who are making them, but between these, as lead off by Dr. Nevin and the German Reformed Church. *He sets up his own private sense of the Creed as its only true sense;* he says it *must* be its sense, and denounces as Montanists, Gnostics, Muzzletonians, all who dare to differ from him. This sense, however, is wholly different from that which it bears in our Church standard, and which that standard supports by the Word of God. Thus the conflict by Dr. Nevin's own concession, is between him and the Church. We stand by the faith of the Church. Dr. Nevin thinks us very self-willed, very stubborn,—compares us (in imitation of his pupil, putting the cart before the horse, or whatever the proverb is) to the lonely but headstrong juryman, etc. We confess the crime, if crime it be. Dr. Nevin may remember it was said to his face in York, that he and his whole Mercersburg system were *less than nothing to us* (I speak for my brethren as well as myself) in comparison with our Church. And when the arrogance of this pretentious thing is duly considered, one may well indignantly ask, who is Dr. Nevin, or what is his theory, that he should dare to ask a Church like ours to modify her faith in accordance with his views?

He says, "twenty-five years ago the Creed had become almost a dead letter in our Reformed Zion." Never was an author more egregiously mistaken in his supposed facts. But this error may be committed like some others, because Mercersburg is regarded as the Church. And yet he flatters himself beyond all measure of truth, if he for a moment imagines that he is the father of the Creed in "OUR" Reformed Zion. He must think that we native members of the Reformed Church, whose fathers and ancestors found their spiritual home in her fold, are callous indeed, if he supposes that we can listen in quiet patience to such reproaches upon her earlier ministry and membership. Twenty-five years ago! That was in 1842; and that would be just a year or two after Dr. Nevin became a member and Professor in the Church! Ask the old men in the Church of which they heard first and oftenest—Dr. Nevin or the Creed.

It is plain enough then, what all this ado about the Creed means. Our Church is a Church of the Creed—has always been so in a true Gospel sense. But Dr. Nevin would take advantage of this attachment to an ancient and venerable symbol of the Church, and use it as a means of introducing a new and strange doctrine among us. Mark the logic! 1. Bring private judgment into full implicit obedience to the Church. 2. Make the existing doctrines of the Church bend to the organic significance of the Creed. 3. Determine that significance by the genius and spirit of the fifth century. 4. Let Dr. Nevin say what that spirit and genius are. With such a scheme no wonder that Dr. Nevin is greatly offended at a habit many persons have, *as he says*, of "following their own nose." He would think it far more decorous in them to follow his.

But following neither his nor ours, we prefer the experienced guidance of our Church, and her tried and true teachers, until their doctrines are proven erroneous, by far better evidence than is furnished by any arbitrary, unnatural, unphilosophical, and above all, unscriptural interpretation of the Apostle's Creed.

As a *third characteristic* of the theology which underlies the new "Order," we are told that it is "*objective and historical*." These qualities are assumed to be peculiarly distinctive of Dr. Nevin's system. It is very easy, as we have often seen, for the advocates of the innovations to arrogate things which do not properly belong to them, and then press their claims to consideration by derogating from others in a most fraudulent way. I claim that our genuine Reformed Theology is truly objective and historical, and that those characteristics of the innovating system which are called objective and historical, are really but mechanical, material, or magical.

It will not be necessary to repeat here what was said a few pages back on the relation of the objective and subjective. Let it be remembered that we hold, and have ever held, in accordance with the teaching of our Church as that harmonizes with the Word of God, that the means of grace have supernatural virtue and come to men invested with true objective power. We also hold that these means have served to maintain the true historical and spiritual organic continuity of the Church from age to age, and will do so to the end of time.

But what is the nature of this objective and historical character? And how is this real historical organic process maintained? Here it is that Dr. Nevin departs from the faith of evangelical Protestantism; and here, therefore, it is that we part from him.

Taking all he says, and all that has at different times been said by others of his mind, together, the "objective and historical" in this new (I mean of course new for the Reformed Church) system amounts to this: Christianity, or the Church, starting substantially, one might almost say materially, in the incarnation, is carried forward, developed, applied for the salvation of men, not by preaching to them the Gospel, not by their being thus convinced and converted, or led to repent and believe in the Lord Jesus Christ, but by having a vitalizing portion of the glorified humanity of Christ (Christ incarnate glorified) transmitted to them. This is done in the first place through Baptism, which, they say has been "ordained for the communication of such great grace." The life thus begotten, by an actual implanting in the soul of a literal portion of the glorified humanity of the Lord, is nourished, "objectively," is kept up and carried on "historically" by the conveyance of the literal life-force, an actual portion of the same glorified humanity to the soul in which it already exists, through the Lord's Supper. In natural human life, it is argued, the process is thus "objective," that is independent of any conscious personal co-operation of the subject. Thus the life of the first Adam is propagated "objectively," by an objective force, power, energy, in the constitution of the race, which operates through instruments indeed, (parents) but yet is a law, a potency above those instruments. This is claimed as an analogy of what holds in the supernatural sphere, in the process of the kingdom of grace. And it is by being thus objectively carried forward that it can become a historical or organic development.

Now we do not deny at all, but readily admit, that things in earth are made after heavenly patterns. But as the heavens are higher than the earth, so are heavenly things far exalted in their mode of existence and operation above all terrestrial copies or symbols. And Dr. Nevin errs egregiously not merely in assuming that his theory of the matter is the only correct one, but still more, we think, in adopting a theory which is so gross, carnal, material in its idea and constituents. Are then the "objective" powers of the kingdom of heaven bound down to such material instrumentalities as these? Is the Church produced, perpetuated from age to age by such communication through the Sacraments of the literal, substantial humanity of the Lord Jesus Christ? Is the life of the Lord Jesus

Christ in the soul only a blind force, an unconscious energy operating on the mind and heart of the subject, in a manner precisely analogous to that in which the law of our physical life works physically without any consentient co-operation or consciousness of the moral subjects in whom it is lodged? And is this life nourished and sustained by continually repeated communications in the same form and of the same kind; just as physical life is sustained by a process of unconscious inhalation and exhalation, respiration and absorption, digestion and circulation? The theory we are combatting lays claim, it is true, to being very profound, and philosophical. Indeed I am persuaded that it is so warmly embraced by its disciples, not because it comes with any true Church authority, for their arbitrary dealings with the Creed have been exposed, but because it seems to them so deep and so novel, or else because it seems to justify other peculiarities of their scheme. But is it really profound? Does it not rather seem, in the view in which it has now been presented, to be dark indeed, but not deep; to be speculative, but not sustained by the only source of true knowledge in regard to divine things.

And it is to be noted here, again, that no appeal is made either to the Holy Scriptures, or to any evangelical Confession, in proof of this phase of the objective and historical. Dr. Nevin finds it more convenient to fall back on *his Creed*—that is, on the *Apostles' Creed, as he says it* MUST be interpreted. Of course, it is easy for him to prove any thing, in this way, *to his own mind*. Others, however, may not be so easily convinced.

How strong the *contrast* in this case, also, between what Dr. Nevin pronounces the true import of the "objective and the historical," and the conception of these two factors or qualities of true theology or Christianity in the doctrinal standard of our Church! Here we have both, but in a really higher and deeper, because more Scriptural, manner. Here, too, we have the Church begotten and perpetuated by the communication of the life of the Lord Jesus Christ, who is our life; but this in a vastly higher, deeper, and more spiritual sense and form. It is not a power transmitted to the believer and working in him like a nixus, an instinct, wholly apart from his own consciousness and co-operation. The kingdom of grace is designed for moral, intelligent beings, and all its means and provisions, are strictly adapted to such: they are moral, rational means as really as supernatural. Dr. Nevin errs when he says that in its application the Divine act goes before the Divine Word. It was not so with the first great promise—with the entire history of the Incarnation, unless a forced figurative sense is put upon it. It is not so in any normal case of salvation recorded in the Scriptures. The Word is ever first, and then actual salvation. "Zaccheus, come down" precedes the "salvation in his house."

Peter preaches before the three thousand are brought to repentance and faith in Christ. The "Word is the seed" of regeneration, i. e., Christ Jesus received in a spiritual way through a spiritual moral medium. The "Word" is made the "life" of Christ to the soul apprehending Him *through* it. The "Word" is "*milk* for babes, and *meat* for strong men." Excepting from the controverted sixth chapter of St. John, no passages can be produced which teach that Christ as "the bread of life" is communicated primarily and chiefly through the holy Sacraments, half as plain and strong as those which declare that he is communicated through the Gospel. Dr. Nevin appealed to the Psalms in vindication of some of his ritualistic views. Suppose we should appeal to the same inspired authority for proof of the above statement! But why should any attempt be made to cite such proofs? The Old and New Testament are full of it. We read it in the parable of the sower and the seed; in the parable of the tares; in the Sermon on the Mount; in the avowed purpose of all the parables and teaching of the Lord; in the terms of the great Commission; in every chapter of the Acts of the Apostles; and find it scattered profusely through the remaining portions of the New Testament. The new life in Christ, they all say, is begotten by the Holy Ghost through the Word, proclaiming and conveying Him to the soul, or taking and grafting the inmost centre of man's moral spiritual life in Jesus Christ. As it is, primarily, man the living soul which needs redemption, and the body participates in redemption as a result of the psychical redemption, the great instrument through which the grace is received, is of a like nature. Even the Holy Sacraments are unmeaning except as the Word reveals their nature and design. This, therefore, is the divinely appointed *supernatural* means for disseminating ("the seed is the Word") the vitalizing, saving grace which is alone in Jesus Christ. And in this way, also, there is secured that presence of an "objective" power in divine form, through which the organic historical growth and advancement of the Christian Church, the spiritual body of Christ, is most effectively carried on.

This is the doctrine of the "objective, historical qualities" of the true Church, which underlies the Heidelberg Catechism. Dr. Nevin, after quoting (p. 86) what he calls the "soul-shaking!" answer concerning the necessity of regeneration in order to deliverance from natural depravity and condemnation, makes this astounding remark: "*How* this new birth by the Spirit is brought to pass, is not here of any account." Strange, indeed! The "*how*" is the very point at issue in this part of the controversy. And when it is remembered that the means and manner in which this is affected are mentioned, only a few questions further on, it is very significant that those questions should have escaped the author's attention. Thus in answer to question 20: "Are all men then as they perished in Adam, saved by Christ?" We are told: "*No, only those who are ingrafted into Him,* and receive all his benefits *by a true faith.*" And then immediately after this we are told that this true faith, by which we are "*ingrafted into Christ*" is wrought in the heart "*by the Holy Ghost, through the Gospel.*" Some say, however, that the Gospel here means, or at least includes the Sacrament. That it does not, is clearly proven by the answer to question 65, where the Gospel and the Sacrament are placed in antithesis to each other; and where the phrase "by the preaching of the Gospel" makes it still clearer that the *Word* is meant. Indeed the entire system set forth in our Catechism is based on this principle. The Catechism was taught to youth in the abbreviated form, or compendium. The complete Heidelberg Catechism, (*Catechesis Palatina,*) was not designed for youth, but for ripe Christians. (See *Ebrard*, K. u. Dogm. Gesch. iii, 215.) In the compend the first question asked is: "What is necessary for man to know in order to be saved?" (See Old Palat. Liturgy, translated, *Mercersburg Review,* 1850, pp. 266-7). But it ought to be superfluous to appeal to such evidence. And yet, in sppport of this new theology, appeals have been made to the Heidelberg Catechism, as furnishing evidence, that it assumed a theory of Christianity favorable to that theology, whilst the fact just stated in regard to the compendium always used in the instruction of youth, has been denied or ignored.

By these three characteristics, therefore, as claimed by Dr. Nevin to be distinctive of the ritualistic theology, it stands condemned before the standard of evangelical doctrines in the German Reformed Church. Our theology, our faith, is not Christocentric, in Dr. Nevin's sense; it does not spring from his version and interpretation of the Creed; it is not "objective and historical" in his view of those qualities. On all these important and fundamental points he and the Church differ materially and essentially. And they differ thus, because the Church derives its faith from the Word of God, whilst he makes fifth century theology his rule of faith, and does so by his own confession.

On liturgical as well as theological grounds, therefore, we must refuse to adopt the Revised Liturgy as the Liturgy of the Church. Unless we are willing radically and fundamentally to change our faith, as well as our worship, we must reject the ritualistic Cultus which Dr. Nevin and his associates are endeavoring by all the means at their command to introduce into the German Reformed Church.

DR. NEVIN ON THE OFFENSIVE.

Under a seeming sense of having failed in his sophistical attempt to exhibit the theology of the new order in an acceptable light, and so as to convince his impartial readers, the author of the "Vindication," by a sudden manoeuvre, adroitly turns from a defensive position to one of offence. Weary of striving to parry the hard blows of fact, documentary evidence, "stupid" details, he concludes to try an assault. With some of the hard names he applies to the luckless *Brethren* who differ from him, most persons were probably unacquainted. Let it suffice to say, that they are terrible indeed. It is bad enough to be a Montanist, and a Gnostic, but to be called a Muggletonian, and that by so august a judge as the Rev. Dr. John W. Nevin, former Professor of Theology in the German Reformed Church, and who "stands now where he stood then!"

But let it pass. If the unhappy author of those overwhelming epithets thought he could harm those at whom he threw, on whom he poured them, by such stuff, his credulity must excite compassion. And if he supposed for a moment, that, by calling *us unliturgical*, who used Liturgical forms long before the swathing bands of ritualistic drapery were wound around his loins; if he thought by charging us with denying or having no actual faith in the Incarnation, because we discard his half ubiquitarian and half-pantheistic Christocentric conceits; or if he supposed by accusing us of denying sacramental grace, because we reject his baptismal regeneration and sacrificial-altar notions; I say, if by levelling such indictments at us, he expected to disturb our peace, destroy our name, or so excite us as to make us forget his errors in trying to defend ourselves, never was a man more mistaken. The artifice does not succeed.

There is but one point in this portion of his tract which I will notice. That is the outrageous misrepresentation of what Professor Rust said at Synod in connection with the subject of infant Baptism. Dr. Nevin pronounces it rank Pelagianism. He knows this is not true. He knows that Professor Rust did not deny original sin, any more than Ursinus does when he says: "BAPTISM DOES NOT MAKE OUR CHILDREN CHRISTIANS, THEY ARE SUCH BEFORE BAPTISM." Professor Rust was opposing the unscriptural doctrine of that Revised Liturgy which Dr. Nevin does not pretend is German Reformed, viz., *that the children of believers are as much under the power of the devil as the children of unbelievers.*

This doctrine stands intimately related with Romish exorcism in Baptism; and in opposing that error he made the remarks which have been so grossly perverted. When I think of the bad design of this perversion, and consider that Dr. Nevin must have known that he was grossly misrepresenting a brother, in order to screen himself from the sharp edge of the sword of truth, I feel tempted to apply to him two Latin words which he once cast at one who differed from him, and against whom he was ashamed to use such language in plain English. This is all I have to say of the author's offensive strategy.

SPECIAL POINTS.

As this tract has already extended beyond the limits originally set for it, I will not follow Dr. Nevin in what he says with regard to the special points of objection raised against the Revised Liturgy. Indeed, he does not attempt at all to deny the charge, that the Revised Liturgy rests upon a theology and a conception of the Church, which make the ministry a priesthood; which ties the forgiveness of sins to the declaration of pardon by the minister;* which teaches Baptismal regeneration, and that the Holy Supper is a kind of sacrifice offered on a propitiatory altar unto the Lord. (No wonder, now, that Dr. Nevin hates the 80th Question of our Catechism). Should it be deemed necessary, however, these points may be taken up at some future time. It will suffice, meanwhile, to remind the reader that they are all involved in the three characteristics of the Christocentric theology, and therefore fall with them. For if it is virtually admitted that the Revised Liturgy is open to the serious doctrinal objections which were urged against it in my first tract, why should it be necessary to repeat the proof of those objections here?

CONCLUSION.

1. By the explicit concessions, then, of the advocates of the new Order, as well as by what is manifestly involved in that work, it is made evident that the Church is called upon to decide the following vital points:

a. Shall we maintain our distinctive form of Liturgical worship, or shall we adopt one which would destroy our denominational identity; subject us again to a yoke of ritualism, essentially like that cast off by our Reformed fathers; barter our free and yet duly restrained liturgical character for rigidly imposed ritualistic formalities; and sunder the bonds of spiritual fellowship with our nearest ecclesiastical kindred.

b. Shall we cleave to the true Apostolic faith, delivered to us by our fathers, in that incomparable standard, the Heidelberg Catechism,—to the doctrine of the Incarnation of our Lord Jesus Christ therein set forth,—to the doctrine that regeneration is wrought by the Holy Ghost through the Word of the Gospel,—to the doctrine of the universal common

---

* Lest this should be thought an extreme statement, I will give the doctrine held and taught in the carefully written language of one of the leading abettors of the innovation. "A SINNER MAY BE PENITENT FOR HIS SINS, BUT UNTIL HE HAS RECEIVED BAPTISM AS GOD'S ACT OF REMISSION TO HIM, HE HAS NO TRUE ASSURANCE OF REMISSION. AND WHEN AFTER BAPTISM HE SINS THROUGH INFIRMITY, HE CANNOT BE SURE OF PARDON TILL HIS ABSOLUTION IS SPOKEN, SIGNED AND SEALED BY CHRIST, BY THE MEANS OF A DIVINE ACT THROUGH THE CHURCH."

Do any ask: is it possible that this is the doctrine taught those who are being trained for the ministry in the Reformed Church? I answer that it is. O how blessedly different from this is the doctrine set forth in the Answer to the 56th Question of our Catechism.

priesthood of all Christ's people, in opposition to a specific sacerdotal caste in the ministry,—to the doctrine of a true mystical personal union of the believer with the Lord Jesus Christ, in a higher, more spiritual and potential form than the semi-physical, carnal-psychological view which Dr. Nevin teaches,—to the doctrine of the Holy Sacrament as signs and seals of grace already possessed, and so far invested with *sacramental* grace, in opposition to that theory of this new Order which makes every thing to be effected by the sacrament in a magical or mechanical way,—to the doctrine that the penitent believer in Jesus may feel certainly assured that his sins *are* pardoned by the Lord, in opposition to the doctrine now taught by the advocates of the new Order that " when after Baptism he sins through infirmity, he can not be sure of pardon till his absolution is *spoken, signed* and *sealed*, by means of a *divine act through the Church*," thus making repentance or penance a sacrament, and putting the peace of the contrite, broken-hearted sinner in the power of the priest.

Shall we then cleave to our old evangelical faith which is tried and true, or shall we be tempted to exchange it for a system for which no better ground is furnished than a fanciful, speculative construction and interpretation of the Creed somewhat in accordance with its fifth or sixth century sense?

Only let the Church duly realize these facts, be convinced that our very life as a Church, in all the important characteristics of that life, is at stake, and I am persuaded that this extreme ritualistic innovation will be repelled.

2. This controversy has been forced upon the Church by those who are striving to introduce the innovations. They were intrusted with an important work. Great liberty was granted in its execution. A Liturgy prepared under the liberal instruction given would have done its authors honor, and have served to promote the best interests of the Church. But under the unhappy influence of a theory of worship and doctrine acknowledged to be at variance with the faith and practice of the Church, they allowed themselves to transcend or falsely construe their instructions. The result is the Revised Liturgy, or new "Order of Worship." This they are seeking by the use of all the means in their power to have adopted by the Church. Its adoption, as clearly shown, would involve the most fatal consequences. And must we sit still, and see the evil progressing, without interposing our protest, without raising decided opposition? A man concludes to renovate his house. It is a goodly mansion, reared many generations back by his honored ancestors. But in the course of time it has grown somewhat gray and faded, and needs refreshing. The owner employs an architect—tells him what he wishes, but especially provides that the general plan and foundations of the structure be not disturbed. The

architect begins his work; after a little, proposes some modification in the plan of renovation, but agrees that if they do not suit, they need not be accepted. The work goes on accordingly; and, after some time, is finished. It is found, however, that the modifications have not been fairly followed; that the alterations are of the most radical kind; that from the foundation up the whole old homestead has been changed. Many of the household complain, object, and beg that the building be preserved in its original plan. Then comes the conflict. The architect raves and denounces. Had he not told them what he was going to do? Had they not known what he was about? And now, after all his toil and trouble, will they dare to throw the work on his hands?

What is to be done? Either we must lose our home, or contend for its preservation. Can we, should we be reproached for engaging, and engaging earnestly in this struggle? We believe the Church had no idea of the extent and bearings of the innovations proposed, nay that by far the greater part of the Church even now has no clear conception of their nature, and of the consequences of their adoption. And shall we be blamed for speaking out? I say again, what I may have in substance said before, that for my part, the Church of my fathers as they gave her to me; the Church in which under God I was born and brought up, is more, beyond all computation more to me, than Dr. Nevin and all his theories, highly as I may have regarded him in other days. And I can say, even now, after all the unjust and indecorous calumny with which he has tried to overload me, that I have no personal controversy with him, excepting as he is using his influence to rob me and my brethren of my Church. For if the German Reformed Church is once shaped and modelled after the pattern of this new "Order" she ceases to be the German Reformed Church, however tenaciously she may still cleave to the name.

The fault of this controversy, therefore, rests not upon those who are contending for their ecclesiastical inheritance, but upon those who are seeking to deprive us of that inheritance. And this very fact gives the former an immense advantage in this conflict. They are struggling to preserve the Church; the others are seeking to subvert her practice and her principles.

Many sad fruits of this ritualistic innovation have been already produced.

The theory and principles which underlie and pervade it, have caused many of our ministers to leave the Church. Most of these have gone either to the Romish Church or have become high-church Episcopalians. It is of no avail for Drs. Harbaugh or Nevin to try to turn these things into ridicule. Every honest, intelligent advocate of the theory involved in the new "Order," will confess that such defections are a legitimate effect of the theory. Mr. Stewart of Burkettsville may, as they say, be of small account. They did not say so years ago. And it is simply disingenuous and deceitful in any of them to deny that the natural tendency of their scheme is in the same direction in which Mr. Stewart went. Two most estimable brethren, who, I supposed, would be among the last to be so far carried away from a firm evangelical faith, have said in my own hearing: *either this new Order system, or Rome!*

Another, who was once sorely entangled by the theory he had been taught at Mercersburg, but who seems to have escaped the meshes, told me: Dr. Harbaugh need not call this charge, and the fears felt in regard to the tendency of these things "humbug," "spooks in the garret," etc. It is not true. There is more reality in the complaint than many suppose. It was no humbug in the case of poor Snively; it was no humbug with me in ——; it is even now no humbug with ——, and ——, and ——, whom I know to be unsettled and disturbed in their minds in regard to some fundamental points of Evangelical Protestant faith and practice.

More than a year and a half ago, consequently more than a year before Mr. Stewart's apostacy, a prominent minister of our Church had a conversation with him on the whole subject. He was in sore difficulties on account of having introduced the Liturgy (Provisional in its extreme forms), and expressed great regret that he had done so, or allowed himself to be ensnared by the system. In not very elegant terms, but yet in a style which seems to be authorized by his former Professor, he said: "If I could kick the miserable thing to where I would never see it again, I would do so."

But not only is this extreme movement an occasion of harm in this way. It causes dissensions and grief in congregations, and at this time there are scores of members of our Church who are sincerely attached to her, who are driven for the time to the shelter of other Churches by the offensiveness of these ritualistic measures, forced upon the congregations without their consent. More are, for the sake of peace, enduring with silent grief these mournful departures from the mode in which our fathers worshipped God.

Are we prepared, then, as a Church, to endure these unavoidable results? I know that all the defections are not in one direction. The new measures are a wedge which splits in many pieces, and cause the parts thus sundered to fly indiscriminately on every side. And the worst has not yet come, if the innovations are allowed further sway.

If, then, Dr. Nevin and his chief disciples, think they have a new revelation, have discovered a faith and cultus better than that of our fathers, let them go like upright, brave men, and build a house for themselves on that basis. Why seek so to remodel an existing Church so as to make a wholly new thing of her. When John Winebrenner supposed he found a more excellent way than that of our fathers, he left us, and started a sect of his own. We condemn his schismatic notions; but if he would not give them up, it certainly was commendable in him to try to carry them out in his own way. Why, then, if this theory has a new creed, does it not venture boldly forth with its creed as a basis? Who knows but it might become the honored foundation of that great Church of the future in which all the "disjecta membra" of both Protestantism and Popery should find their unity and strength. Why should it seek to make a new sect of an old Church, and under cover of an ancient, honored name, cover its revolutionary character, and strive to accomplish its really schismatic scheme?

4. As we love the Church of our Fathers, therefore, and desire to have her true Apostolic faith and practice handed down to her posterity, let us stand up firmly and unfalteringly against these ritualistic innovations. We are not the only Church disturbed by this evil spirit. On every side of us we hear the clangor of a similar conflict. To brethren of other evangelical denominations we owe it to be strong and unyielding in this contest. The oldest daughter of the Reformed family must not be the first to surrender her virtue to the enticements of this old seducer. Seeing how manfully the true-hearted portion of the Episcopal Church, with the learned, undaunted, venerable Bishop McIlvaine at their head, are struggling against the encroachments of a similar evil—and how, in other branches of the true Protestant family, they are fighting manfully for the faith of their ancestors,—let us give proof both of our ability to distinguish the merits of truth from the meretricious attractions of error, and of our being worthy of the inheritance of truth bequeathed to us, by cleaving to the Church as our fathers gave it to us.

And why should we not? The friends of that Church are the friends of genuine Apostolic truth and worship. But who are they that look with approbation upon Dr. Nevin's unhappy scheme? The Presbyterian Church, of whose very close affinity with ours he spoke so warmly in his inaugural address at Mercersburg, disowns him. The Dutch Church, of whose tender consanguinity with ours, he descanted so lovingly at one of the Triennial Conventions, discards his vain anti-Protestant conceits. Even the great theologian of Germany, Dr. Dorner, writes regretfully of this Mercersburg defection from the genuine evangelical faith. And Dr. Nevin himself, with a dark, gloomy consciousness of having proven recreant to the faith of his fathers, and of all his former brethren, seeks comfort in holding them up to derision and contempt. He has a harsh anathema for every one of them—and, in turn, is sorely reproached by all *but one!* And shall we suffer his scheme so far to prevail that our beloved Church shall become as marked an Ishmaelite among other evangelical Churches, as he has made himself, and is making inconsiderate followers, among evangelical theologians?

That Dr. Nevin will ever return to the evangelical ground he has forsaken, I think there is no room to hope. But why should he be allowed to draw a whole Church after him?

We do not oppose progress and development in our Church life. That progress, however, should not be revolutionary, destructive? There are many reasons why, for the sake of evangelical Christianity, we should earnestly strive to maintain and improve our distinctive denominational life. But this may and should be done in harmony with our true genius and character, and not in violent subversion of them.

I close with words which expressed the sentiments of Dr. Nevin as he once thought and felt, and which, though he would now discard them, express as important a truth as when they were first uttered:—

"*If the original distinctive life of the Churches of the Reformation be not the object to be reached after in the efforts that are made to build up the interests of German Christianity in this country, it were better to say so openly and plainly.* * * * *Why keep up the walls of denominational partition in such a case, with no distinctive spiritual being to uphold or protect?*"

"*Let this system prevail and rule with permanent sway, and the result of the religious movement which is now in progress will be something widely different from what it would have been under other auspices. The old regular organizations, if they continue to exist at all, will not be the same Churches. Their entire complexion and history, in time to come, will be shaped by the new course of things.*" (Anxious Bench, pp. 10, 19.)

Considerations like these moved us to oppose what were called Methodistic New Measures in 1843 to 1847. Those same considerations constrain us to resist the encroachments of the *High Church ritualistic new measures* now.

For three centuries the Reformed Church has, with slight exceptions, maintained her distinctive life, and endeavored to work out her proper mission. The Lord has prospered her labors, and rewarded her zeal. Shall she now be allured by a new Gospel, which *is* not, even, a Gospel, proclaimed by one who sneers at devout usages taught us by our fathers, and brands as heresy, doctrines which those fathers derived from the Word of God, and so faithfully handed down to us, to abandon our sacred inheritance, and embrace his innovations? Never, no never! It cannot be that the Church of our fathers has been preserved to this day, to be now subverted by the Christocentric cultus or theo'ogy of the author of the "Vindication."

10

SUPPLEMENTARY ARTICLES.

In accordance with what seems a just and reasonable request, the following three papers are appended to this tract.

The first is a reply of the Rev. G. W. Welker, of North Carolina, to a most uncalled-for aspersion of the delegates of his Classis by Dr. Nevin. It needs no words of mine to commend it to careful consideration. The editor of the *Messenger* refused to admit it into the columns of that *general church paper*. It seems his rules forbid the admission of personalities—that is, when they bear against the leading advocates of the innovations. This, therefore, was the only medium of self-defence for the Brethren whom the author of the "Vindication" had so unkindly stigmatized.

The second is a letter from a member of our Church now completing his studies in Berlin. It is especially interesting for the opinion it reports, by authority, of the Rev. Dr. Dorner, the eminent theologian of the Berlin University. Dr. Dorner has sometimes been claimed as an endorser of Dr. Nevin's views. This letter will correct that mistake. It will be noticed that whilst he is favorable to the German Reformed idea of a Liturgy, he does not endorse "responses," and *insists upon maintaining free prayer*. The brother who received this letter requested the editor of the *Messenger* to insert it, but for prudential reasons he declined to do so. It too strongly confirms the reasons urged against the innovations.

The third is a letter from another member of our Church, also completing his theological studies in the Berlin University. It speaks so clearly and earnestly for itself that it needs no comment.

Both these letters are from gentlemen who enjoyed the very best opportunities for becoming fully acquainted with the subtleties of modern Mercersburg theology. We only ask for these documents a calm and candid perusal.

I.

[For the German Reformed Messenger.]

DR. NEVIN *vs.* THE CLASSIS OF NORTH CAROLINA AND HER DELEGATES.

A valued friend has just sent me a copy of Dr. Nevin's "Vindication." The attack on the Classis of North Carolina and her Delegates to the late Synods invited my attention. It should not have been a surprise, and yet it was altogether unexpected. I do not propose to write a vindication of this unfortunate Classis, "*Historical, Theological,*" or otherwise, for it is only quackery that usually needs either puffing or Vindication. It is not so certain but that the *results* of the Liturgical movement and the Mercersburg theology to the Church will be her most effectual vindication. Indeed, it seems that a part of the Church already feels that her protest against these novelties was *timely* and just. Besides this, it is possible that the Classis will speak for herself at her next meeting. Neither is it proposed to review the "Vindication," for that would be presumption entirely insufferable in a *cipher*. The attack is found on page 47, in these words, viz:— "Two of these colleagues (of Dr. Bomberger) besides were the delegates from the Classis of North Carolina, which has been in a state of ecclesiastical secession from the Synod ever since the present Liturgical movement commenced, and whose representatives therefore allowed themselves, with very bad grace certainly, to be brought North at this time for the purpose of meddling with it in any such factious way. Aside from these ciphers the clerical vote on that side stood next to nothing." In this three points are made: 1. That the Classis of North Carolina, owing to her previous bad conduct, had no business to be in the Synod at *this* time. 2. That her delegates showed themselves factious by their conduct in Synod, and meddled in matters when good manners forbid. 3. That they were brought *North* by others to be used as tools in the warfare on his bantling of a Liturgy.

I shall not copy the example of Dr. Nevin, nor quote his own epithets as applicable to the character of these charges. I trust to be preserved from his spirit, while it is shown how great wrong he has done this Classis, her delegates, and the whole German Reformed Church. However wrong the *action* of the Classis in respect of the Liturgy and the Mercersburg theology (and no infallibility has ever been claimed) may have been, and whatever rights that conduct may have forfeited, her appearance in the Synod was not of her seeking. She was there on the reiterated invitation of Synod, from whose roll her name had never been erased, and that year after year elected of her ministers as members of the Board of Domestic Missions. Almost every Synod made efforts to secure the return of her delegates. The Synod of 1857 appointed commissioners, of whom one visited the Classes, to seek a reunion of the severed Classes. The Synod of 1858 passed the following resolve, without a dissentient voice, viz: "Resolved, That this Synod is *gratified* at the presence of the Commissioners from the Classis of North Carolina, and *cordially* invites the Classis, through them, to resume its *former* relation to Synod." When the great rebellion was over the Synod of 1865, in a letter addressed to the Classis, expressive of its affection and wishes, by the President of Synod, says: "While therefore we sincerely regret that adverse circumstances have prevented you from sending delegates to meet with the brethren in Synod assembled regularly during the last four years, we now express the hope that, with God's blessing, you may, etc.,—and *hereafter* send delegates to mingle with us in our Synods." On such invitations, so full and without reserve, thus repeatedly and pressingly made, it was, that Classis, with great and *anxious* deliberation, determined to appoint delegates to the Synods of 1866, and thus "resume her *former* relations to Synod." There never had been any *conditions* even hinted at. Not any guarantee was demanded. It was an unconditional reconstruction. We resumed our *former* relations to Synod. We were placed on a perfect equality with every other Classis, as it respects rights and privileges in the Synods. Her delegates had the right to participate in the discussion of all matters, and to vote on *every* question. To this, no doubt, the *Church North* welcomed her. Or was all this persistent demand for re-union only a sham? Were all those greetings at York and Dayton only a mockery? Was it not a cordial welcome of the Classis to her former relation? Dr. Nevin implies that she was expected very penitently and *gracefully* to sit by and wonder and admire, but be silent. Doubtless the Synods of Frederick and Lewisburg gave honest expression to the desire of the Church. And the letters of the sainted Father Helfenstein and of Drs. Porter, Zacharias and Fisher, intended no reserve in their hearty invitation to return. At York and Dayton, excepting Dr. Nevin and a *very* few spirits as intolerant as himself, never was so kind and loving welcome given personally to the delegates of a Classis as those of North Carolina Classis received, as well by those who admire the new Liturgy and hold the Mercersburg theology as by others. It is not credible that Dr. Nevin speaks the mind of the Church, and he has no doubt grievously wronged her spirit, and cast an unjust imputation on her candor and honesty.

What was the conduct of the delegates of the Classis of North Carolina? In what were they factious? In what were they guilty of meddlesome impertinence? Were they guilty of any act at York or Dayton not warranted by their age or service in the Church, or as the representatives of a Classis that was in the full enjoyment of all her rights, in virtue of having resumed *former* relations? The appeal may be safely made to *all* the members of those Synods in proof. Did they officiously obtrude themselves or their views—if ciphers are permitted to have views in a German Reformed Synod? No! their crime was voting with "Dr. Bomberger and his company." Doubtless this was done, but quietly and honestly as they hold the truth. Synod was fully aware of the views of Classis when urged to resume her *former* relations. But they are the "ciphers" in this "miserable faction." But even ciphers may fill a *place*—for them, too, there is an office, and if they fill it well they have done all that *good* ciphers can do, be it at the *right* or left of the *significant* figures. It is claimed for them that they fairly represented the views of their Classis as well as their own. It was their right and their duty to vote as they did, for the rules of Synod *required* them to vote. This is their offence—no more! They made no speeches—ciphers should not; they abused no one for differing from themselves. They, I suppose, treated all men courteously; made no effort to pervert justice or the truth. But then, they were wanting in not instinctively discovering the transcendent merits of the new Order of Worship. They did not gracefully choose an orbit about the central sun of Mercersburg theology. What crimes! How well merited the assault on them. It is true such dolts are not able to grasp the profound questions involved in this controversy—they had not sat at the feet of Drs. Angelic and Seraphic, and been taught the beauties of the new Liturgy, or the depths of the theology of Mercersburg. Would not this have been reason for sparing the harmless creatures such a castigation? They unto whom little is given, of them the *just* one requires but little. They do humbly own that they are not able to harmonize the *doctrines* of the New Liturgy with the teachings of the Heidelberg Catechism, or to discover the superiority of its *order* of worship over that received of the fathers.

This is not all the crime of the silly representatives of this Classis. They allowed themselves to be made the tools of that "miserable faction" who oppose what they consider the insidious errors of Dr. Nevin, and which pervade the new Liturgy. When the delegates were chosen, there was no thought had of this controversy. They purposed to go to Synod, because Classis had resolved by them to resume her former relations. There never was any hesitation about their going, unless it were from the inability of Classis to meet the expense growing out of their attendance. It is true, they were written to, but never a word was written to the writer of this about the Liturgy question in this connection. The invitations were alike for its friends and those who oppose its adoption. Ciphers as they are, it is not characteristic of them to be the tools of others, or that bribery or aught else could affect their conduct. If this imputation be true, they are utterly unfit for the ministry that they would thus have disgraced; and Synod should exclude so corrupt a Classis. It is to be hoped, however, that it is the lonely preëminence of Dr. Nevin to attempt to revive prejudice against the Classis by the allusion to the past—and to insinuate corruption and bribery.

These are the facts. They place Dr. Nevin before the Church as a false ACCUSER of the brethren. Why should the attack be made? It was not needful to the argument. Neither the Classis nor its delegates had in any way assailed him, or been wanting in respect toward him. Can it be that his ambition is so insatiable that this Mordecai at the King's gate so stirs the heart within him that it destroys his peace? Can it be that this "Secession" Classis, with its ciphers, refusing to bow to his dictations, so vexed his soul, that it thus boiled over with redundant bitterness? or had the events of the two Synods—the well-directed thrusts from the "miserable faction"—so surcharged his soul with rancour, that the preceding forty-six pages of the "Vindication" had failed to afford him space on which to discharge it, and that the dregs were poured out on the hapless Classis of North Carolina? She can bear it. Her members have had very significant training from the same manner of spirits during the war, and their past experience enables them to bear the cruel contempt of Dr. Nevin. But it is not the Spirit of the Master, and it may yet appear that these despised men are owned of Him who says,—"Inasmuch as ye did it unto one of these, the *least* of my disciples, ye did it unto me."

There is yet one other fact in this connection that demands notice. On page three of this "Vindication" is the request of twenty-one Elders for its preparation. These, doubtless, are worthy men—Christian gentlemen. Personally we have knowledge of but two or three of them. Does Dr. Nevin also wrong them in this unprovoked attack upon their brethren, or was it for such purpose they invoked his pen? We hope—we believe not, and yet it is under the cover of, and in compliance with, their request, that these gratuitous wrongs are done to the Classis of North Carolina and her representatives. Why should these brethren involve a pen so potent for abuse upon us? Surely their partizan spirit did not so prejudice them. We do admit the idea. Their confidence has been abused, and they are needlessly and recklessly made responsible for what their souls abhor. It is not to be credited that these Elders, representing twelve or thirteen Classes, would consent to wound a sister Classis, now crushed to the ground with great sorrow and suffering, or that they are a party to these great wrongs until they avow it.

It cannot be forgotten that the author of this "Vindication" is the controlling mind and pervading spirit of the Liturgy it seeks to vindicate. As we read its pages we were struck with the stream of undiluted gall that coursed through them. His opponents only deal in "*wholesale* slander of the vilest sort"—"*wholesale* misrepresentation"—"*wholesale* falsification," etc. Their productions are "sheer nonsense," "botched stuff," "blind unreserving prejudice," etc. They are "a miserable faction," "ciphers," etc. There is no desire to detract one iota from his reputation, nor would we, if we could, abate the admiration of his friends; but we must be allowed in all frankness to say that the *abuse* of these pages is more effective than their *logic*, and that his opponents are more likely to be driven from the field by bitter denunciation, and by the aspersion with wicked motives than by invincible argument. It is a matter of regret that one occupying his position cannot but use a style that is more violent than chaste, and often borders on the vulgar and ferocious. Whoever may dare to dissent from his views, cannot be better than a fool, a slanderer, a rationalist, or a puritan. Put forth what plea you may, all we would reply is, that out of the abundance of the heart the mouth speaketh. Our great pattern was *gentle*. The greatness of Dr. N. and that of Christ do not appear under the same form. He may be great on the "*Christocentric*," but perhaps it were well to bestow a little effort on the *Christlike*. But this is the Spirit that moulded and animated the Liturgy! If such a spirit lurks beneath their forms—if it breathed its life into them, then may all unite to pray fervently—from such a spirit good Lord deliver the Church. It must go far to destroy respect for the Book, to read such a "Vindication." As a work of art it may be surpassing,—the claims of a Church-like spirit cannot be so well made out. When we take up the book, our devotional frame is gone the moment the remembrance of the flow of Synod and the turbid stream of vindictive abuse that rushes through this "Vindication" forces itself unbidden on our thoughts. We ask ourselves, can a fountain thus send forth at the same time both bitter and sweet waters? Indeed the author has not yet entered into the spirit of the German Reformed Church. In his emigration from his ancestral church he brought with him that one great blemish of the Covenanter—*intolerance*. Perhaps it had been better for the church of his choice if he had brought with him rather that simple, grand and Scriptural Creed he now reviles, and left behind him this excrescence on a noble faith. To those North and South, East and West, who, with the Classis of North Carolina, are rudely and rancourously assailed in this "Vindication," I would say: "With malice toward none, with charity for all, with firmness in the right as God gives us to see the right, let us strive on to finish the work we are in." So to act toward those that revile, ridicule and acrimoniously assail us, that let the result be what it may, we shall have no regrets—that our *enemies* can point to no line or word that dying we should wish to blot. Life is too short, our work too grand, the day of the Lord too near, to allow us to waste, in attempts at vindictive triumph, the few sands that remain Let us not forget that not only for idle words and wicked deeds, but for bitter and wrongful words we shall be brought into judgment, and also that he who says to his brother thou fool, shall be in danger, etc. CIPHER.

II.

Berlin, March 20th, 1867.

DEAR BROTHER,

Am much obliged to you for sending me a copy of the Revised Liturgy, together with Dr. Nevin and Dr. Bomberger's Pamphlets, and those numbers of the *Messenger* which contain the discussions at the General Synod. You know I have always been in favor of a Liturgy, and I have looked forward with the deepest interest to the final decision of our Church on the Liturgical question. It was not to be expected, therefore, that we should remain indifferent with regard to this late liturgical movement. The new Liturgy, strongly recommended on the one hand, and with no less earnestness rejected on the other, challenged all for approval or disapproval. We, too, felt it our duty to decide, whether we ought to be for it or against it; to pretend to hold a neutral ground, or to have no opinion on a question of such vital importance to the church, is impossible for any Christian be he ever so humble. There was, however, but little hope for me to come to a proper understanding of the whole matter. The subject is sufficiently deep and broad for the best theologians of the present day. Yet I could not rest satisfied with the mere consciousness of this fact. Serious charges had been made against the Revised Liturgy; against some of its doctrine, and, at the same time, against some of the most prominent men of our church. Whether these charges had any foundation in the Liturgy itself, or in what had been said in defence of it, I thought I could best learn by giving the Liturgy, with all the writings relative to it, together with a copy of "Mercersburg Theology" into the hands of Professor Dorner, a man who is known to be neither onesided Lutheran or Reformed, but strictly Evangelic, and who, in our own church, is regarded as the greatest theologian of Germany at the present day. About three or four weeks ago I handed him the different articles, and yesterday I went to him, to see if he had formed any opinion on the subject, and whether he would communicate his views to me. I will here report to you the few plain statements he made, as nearly in his own words as I can: "I look upon Dr. Nevin as a pious and able man; his doctrine of the Lord's Supper, as set forth in his 'Mystical Presence,' is the pure Calvinistic doctrine; he is right in his zeal for a Liturgy, over against free worship, for though I believe the so-called revivals have done much good, and are not to be condemned; yet they are liable to degeneration (*ausarten*), and there must be order in the congregation. It is true also that in the use of a Liturgy the congregation is more free in its worship than when it is made to depend upon the free prayer of the minister. The people can better pray with the minister when they know beforehand what is coming. Not all ministers can pray well. But after all, *free prayer must have a place*. Moreover, Dr. Nevin was right, when, for the preparation of a Liturgy, he went back to the Church of the third and fourth centuries, and studied their Liturgies. Some of the old Greek liturgies of those times, although not pure in doctrine, contain most beautiful prayers, for instance those of Chrysostomos, and there ought to be room to depart in some points at least from the old Palatinate Liturgies. But it was not right for Dr. Nevin to go back to the ancient Church, in such a way as to set aside the Church of the Reformation. There is a Romanizing tendency underlying his thinking; he seems to see truth only in the old Church; the material principle of Protestantism, Justification by Faith, is to a great extent set aside (*tritt sehr in den Hintergrund*.) He has not, however, understood the ancient Church. It cannot be shown that she had Dr. Nevin's view of the ministry. This view of the ministry belongs to the Anglican Church. The Liturgy makes ordination a sacrament, which is not in harmony with Protestant doctrine. "Mercersburg Theology" is not clear; it is hard to see what its exact views are; it is, however, not what it claims to be, namely, German Evangelical Theology. German Theology is not its basis. I do not know to what German Theologian Dr. Nevin would appeal for his views. He speaks of Ullmann; but his views are not those of Ullmann; he has not understood Ullmann. The doctrine of the Person of Christ, as laid down in "Mercersburg Theology," is not in harmony with my views; indeed I have been charged with holding such a view; but I have refuted the charge in the second edition of my work on the Person of Christ. Dr. Nevin will hardly appeal to me in support of his views after he has read my late work: "Geschichte der Protestantishen Theology, 1867."

This, then, is the opinion of Professor Dorner on the "Liturgy," on "Mercersburg Theology," and on Dr. Nevin's thinking in general. It may surprise you, as it did me, yet would it not be well to make these things known to the Church at large. I think it would give a fresh impulse to all for a more thorough investigation of the whole subject, than has hitherto been made. It is very probable, too, that before long, you will see something from Professor Dorner himself on this question.

III.

Berlin, March 28, 1867.

DEAR FRIEND:—* * * * * * * * * * * * * * * A more weighty reason for my writing just now, may be found in our mutual relation to the Church in the great conflict which is now going on in her bosom; for as it was a source of great comfort and encouragement to us to hear on which side you stand, so it may possibly be to some degree strengthening to you to know that, though far removed from the scene of conflict, we are, with heart and soul, with you and with all those who like you are standing up against the tide of innovation which is rolling in upon the Church and threatening to sweep away everything before it. At such a time it is important that the friends of the truth should know each other's views, and take counsel together for their own mutual strengthening and consolation. I say this not from any sense of my own importance in the matter, for, unhappily, I feel myself as yet insufficient for the work and responsibility involved in coming forth in public defence of the most vital doctrines of the Church against error in high places; yet, because I am aware that some are accustomed to think and speak of us who are here, as belonging exclusively to their party (the Mercersburg school), I think it important to make it known as far as possible to all whom it may concern, and especially my friends, *that such is not the case!* For however little our opinion may be worth, however slight an influence it may exert, be it but the small dust of the balance, it is nevertheless a matter of conscience with us to have that little cast into the right side of the scale. Hence, although we lay no claim to learnedness much less *authority*, yet for *this* reason if for no other, we may, in this momentous crisis, venture to express our opinion to our friends, viz., that we may be comforted together *in* and for the defence of that Gospel which *has made us free.* We would give our mite towards strengthening *you* who *on* the broad principle of evangelical truth, in the spirit of Christian love, and free from dogmatic quibblings, are giving your labor and your substance for the building up of the blessed Redeemer's kingdom, and whom we consider to be one of *the pillars of the Church*, in a truer sense *than those* theologians are, who, in love with their own notions, theories and speculations, are consciously or unconsciously to themselves, distracting the Church and leading it from the right way, the plain path of Scripture.

I have been compelled, against my will and prejudices, to change to a great extent my views in regard to Mercersburg Theology, and consequently the new Liturgy too,—I say *compelled*, because it was not without a struggle that I could be brought to give up that which from *natural* preference and *education*, I had so long ardently admired and firmly held for truth, and on the other hand to adopt views which are in principle and of necessity different from and in some *points* in direct opposition to those I formerly entertained. This, according to the Rev. T. G. Appel's late exposition (in the *German Reformed Messenger*), would have to be pronounced heresy and schism. But it occurs to me that the symbols of the German Reformed Church are the law according to which it must be judged and decided whether a member of the Church is guilty of heresy or not, *not* the theology of the *Mercersburg school*. The conception "Mercersburg Theology" is too narrow to answer to the idea of the German Reformed Church, and it implies no small degree of presumption for it to make such claims. It is scarcely known here, except among theologians, that such a theology exists. It would seem, therefore, as if it had no right to arraign members of the German Reformed Church, on the charge of heresy, because, forsooth, they may not believe in Mercersburg Theology, or may even go so far as to speak against it. But however this may be, in our earnest endeavors to find the truth, we have felt ourselves constrained to change our position with reference to some of the cardinal doctrines of the Mercersburg school theology. Should this turn out to be heresy, we are ready to abide the consequences unless it can be shown that we are in error. Of course it is not possible within the narrow limits of a letter to give you a full and satisfactory account of our views and thinking, on such wide and important subjects; yet I must endeavor briefly to say something. I have been brought to see things as I now do, by means of the clearer, stronger light which, from the minds of the learned and pious men of *this Protestant land*, beams in upon the field of theology, and enables one to perceive more fully the *extent* of the science as a whole, as well as more correctly to estimate the character of its particular branches, schools, etc. Having, as we hope through the lectures of such distinguished theologians as Dr. Dorner and others, gotten a somewhat wider and clearer view of the whole subject, in particular of the relation and difference between Roman Catholicism and Protestantism, we think we are better able to understand and appreciate our Mercersburg Theology, than we could ever have been had we remained entirely within its sphere. The thinking of men in the sphere of Christianity, whether clear or *dark*, is not to be received as absolutely true at once, but must be closely examined—must be tried by the Symbols of the Church, and above all by the infallible Word of God. To speak in the most general way, I have been brought to believe, indeed am most firmly convinced, that our Mercersburg Theology is seeking something which *does not*, and in the nature of the case *cannot* exist, viz., a middle position between Roman Catholicism and Protestantism. This I believe to be its aim, its most general and distinguishing characteristics, consequently, although it claims to be something "*new*," "*an advance upon any thing that has preceded it*," "the latest development," "the only *live* theology," etc., etc., it is in reality the renewal and fuller "development" of the same old Romanizing tendencies and errors which have before appeared at different times in the Anglican Church, especially in Puseyism and Irvingism. The most general distinction between Roman Catholicism and Protestantism is this: Catholicism places *between the individual believers and Christ, a consecrated order* (consisting of Pope, Bishops, Priests, etc., *essentially different from all other Christians in that they possess extraordinary gifts, powers*, etc. ($\chi\alpha\rho\iota\sigma\mu\alpha\tau\alpha$), *and upon this order in various ways the individual is made to depend for salvation, because only through it and through faith in its mediation is it possible for him to come to Christ!* Protestantism on the contrary admits of *no such priestly intervention in any sense*. According to its principle the individual stands in **an** immediate personal relation to Christ, and is justified through faith in Him.

Just here, it seems to me, is the fundamental radical error of Mercersburg Theology, an error which, if persisted in, must, of logical necessity, carry its followers over to Rome, viz.: *it wants to have a consecrated order—the Apostolic succession and the Priesthood.* Men may persuade themselves that there is no harm in this, may try to explain it away or deny it, but it is true, nevertheless, that the idea of such a consecrated order involves a *third sacrament,* is an interference with the direct personal relation of the believer to Christ, and an attack upon the very *life principle* of Protestantism. The idea of a priesthood involves at least three things: 1. Something which out of common Christians, makes priests, *i. e.,* an anointing or communication of peculiar and specific supernatural gifts or powers ($\chi\alpha\varsigma\iota o\nu\alpha\chi\rho\alpha$), or, in other words, a *sacrament.* 2. A *sacrifice* to be offered before God, or *mediating intercession* to be made with Him by the priest in behalf of needy men. 3. *Persons* who are themselves in need of a priest to intercede for them with Christ. It is easy to see from this, not only that *the Evangelical Church has no need of* ANY *mortal priesthood,* but *that it is in conflict with what she holds to be the teaching of the Holy Scriptures.* She can have no such sacrament, because the Lord has instituted no such sacrament. She needs no sacrifice beyond the *one great sacrifice* OFFERED ONCE FOR ALL. She teaches that all true believers are priests, which of itself, does away with a *special order* of priests. We have one Great High Priest who has passed into the heavens, and who has made us all kings and priests unto God, and to whom we offer ourselves as living sacrifices of *thanksgiving in love, and we need no other priest.*

Mercersburg Theology lays much stress on an "objective Church" and an "objective Christianity." Indeed, it goes so far in this direction as to make but small account of the *inward experience of the Christian,* the Holy Spirit witnessing with our spirits that we are the children of God, which is, after all, the most direct and convincing evidence we have. But it is to be feared that its objectivity, like that of the Roman Church, is, notwithstanding, *subjective;* for that which owes its existence to the *thinking* and *invention of man,* and has not its ground in the Divine Word, is, however objective it may claim to be, in the end purely subjective. Such an objective Christianity we have in the Roman Church: let us not incline too much that way, but rather seek that objective Christianity which is of the Lord, which is in perfect harmony with His written Word, and which, moreover, *becomes at the same time subjective.* Could we all find this I am inclined to believe we would not dispute so much about matters of minor importance.

Mercersburg Theology is not clear on many points. For instance, as to its idea of the Church. At one time it says "the Church is an organization," etc. Very vague: so is a tree. Again: "our Church" (meaning the German Reformed Church) "is the *Church* of the Creed." Have you ever found out what they mean by this expression "Church of the Creed?" I wish they would, once for all, tell plainly what it may signify. On this point they are all the time soaring among the clouds; will they not, for once, descend to the regions of *common* comprehension? I can see that we are *a Church* of the Creed in the sense that other churches are who profess the same faith in the use of the same Creed, but as to what further is meant I am all in the dark.

These *objections against Mercersburg Theology apply with equal force to the new Liturgy,* because the principle I have before mentioned underlies it. It is the legitimate, though I believe not the last nor the worst fruit of that system of thinking; and, however excellent it may be in some respects, yet, *on account of its prin-*

ciple, the Church, if it will remain *Reformed and true* to the written Word and to its own symbols, *must reject both it and the doctrines which underlie it.*

It is true this error has become wide-spread in the Church. Yea, it even claims that it is itself the doctrine of the Church; but this need not surprise you, knowing that the schools have, for so long a time, been in the hands of the defenders and propagators of this doctrine. I know from experience how a student is accustomed to feel and think after he has passed through a College and Seminary where the cardinal aim of all religious instruction was, to make the *subject sound in Mercersburg Theology*. But let us be of good cheer. Though the error is so wide-spread that it seems there is but one man left who has courage to raise his voice in defence of the truth, yet I firmly believe the day is near at hand when the *Protestant consciousness* of our *people* will be aroused, and when the now slumbering Church will awake and hurl from her troubled bosom this foul incubus.

Yours in the Lord.

Marienstrasse 29, 3tu Etage Rechts.

www.ingramcontent.com/pod-product-compliance
Lightning Source LLC
Chambersburg PA
CBHW030317170426
43202CB00009B/1039